Clara Buitrago Valencia

Missionaries: Migrants or Expatriates?

Guatemalan Pentecostal Leaders in Los Angeles

INTER-AMERICAN STUDIES
Cultures – Societies – History

ESTUDIOS INTERAMERICANOS
Culturas – Sociedades – Historia

Volume 30

Clara Buitrago Valencia

Missionaries: Migrants or Expatriates?

Guatemalan Pentecostal Leaders in Los Angeles

Wissenschaftlicher Verlag Trier

Copublished by

UNO University of New Orleans Press

Missionaries: Migrants or Expatriates?
Guatemalan Pentecostal Leaders in Los Angeles /
Clara Buitrago Valencia. –
(Inter-American Studies | Estudios Interamericanos; 30)
Trier: WVT Wissenschaftlicher Verlag Trier, 2021
ISBN 978-3-86821-818-3
Zugl.: Diss., Bielelefeld, Univ., 2019
New Orleans, LA: University of New Orleans Press, 2021
ISBN 978-1-60801-210-7

SPONSORED BY THE

Federal Ministry of Education and Research

The project, on which this book is based, has been funded by the German Federal Ministry of Education and Research (Bundesministerium für Bildung und Forschung, BMBF). The responsibility for the content of this publication lies with the author.

Cover Image: "Guatemalan Independent Pentecostal churches in Los Angeles"
© Clara Buitrago Valencia

Cover Design: Brigitta Disseldorf

Library of Congress Cataloging-in-Publication Data
Names: Buitrago Valencia, Clara, author.
Title: Missionaries : migrants or expatriates? : Guatemalan Pentecostal leaders in Los Angeles / Clara Buitrago Valencia.
Description: Trier : Wissenschatflicher Verlag ; New Orleans, LA : University of New Orleans Press, [2021] | Series: Inter-American studies : cultures, societies, history = Estudios interamericanos : culturas, sociedades, historia ; volume 30 | Includes bibliographical references.
Identifiers: LCCN 2020044528 | ISBN 9781608012107 (paperback)
Subjects: LCSH: Hispanic American Pentecostals--California--Los Angeles. | Pentecostals--Guatemala. | Guatemalans--California--Los Angeles--Religion. | Pentecostal churches--California--Los Angeles. | Pentecostal churches--Guatemala. | Missionaries--California--Los Angeles. | Missionaries--Guatemala. | Immigrants--California--Los Angeles.
Classification: LCC BR1644.5.U6 B85 2021 | DDC 289.9/4089687281079494--dc23
LC record available at https://lccn.loc.gov/2020044528

Publisher: WVT Wissenschaftlicher Verlag Trier, Postfach 4005, D-54230 Trier,
Bergstraße 27, D-54295 Trier, Tel. 0049 651 41503, Fax 41504, www.wvttrier.de, wvt@wvttrier.de

Copublisher: University of New Orleans Press, 2000 Lakeshore Drive, Earl K. Long Library,
Room 221, New Orleans, LA 70148, United States, 504-280-7457, unopress.org

Acknowledgments

This book and the interview material used within this text were collected during the fieldwork in Guatemala and Los Angeles, which were funded by the Center for Interamerican Studies (CIAS) at Bielefeld University through the project "The Americas as Space of Entanglements." I thank Professor Heinrich Schäfer for his support, trust, and inspiration during his supervision. My thanks also go to Professor Olaf Kaltmeier and Professor Wilfried Raussert for their support and advice, and I thank Professor Thomas Faist, who agreed to be my second supervisor on short notice. Huge thanks go to Robert and my mother, for their loving support during all these years. Last but not least, I thank all the participants of our study: It has been both a pleasure and an honor to benefit from their experiences as independent Pentecostal leaders.

Table of Contents

1. Introduction

> ... about 25 years ago, in 1989, I went to Los Angeles for the first time, because of the special invitation of a preacher ... There, we went to some missionary conferences, where ... a lot of impetus was given to missionary work, and in fact that is what remained in my heart: those teachings of missionary work. And it is also where in my heart has been born the idea of opening churches in different places, in other countries ...

These are the words of Pastor Alvaro Sánchez[1] when he referred to his first trip to Los Angeles in 1989. Alvaro Sánchez is the president of an independent Pentecostal church, with congregations not only in Guatemala City, but also in Los Angeles, CA, North Carolina, El Salvador, Costa Rica, and Mexico. In this missionary effort, Alvaro Sánchez is not alone. Many men and women of Guatemalan origin, who participate actively as leaders of independent Pentecostal churches, dedicate an important part of their time to evangelizing in the context of the Interamerican social space established between Guatemala and the metropolitan area of Los Angeles, CA. They are an example of the new modalities of religious expansion in times of transnational migration.

This dissertation focuses on the universe of these religious agents, considering the general context of social conflict, change, and inequality that Guatemalans have to face in Los Angeles. The study explores the trajectory of Guatemalan independent Pentecostal leaders who evangelize in Los Angeles, considering how they understand their work, their religious beliefs, and the interaction between their religious praxis and the social, economic, and cultural dynamics in which they are involved. To accomplish this task, after a detailed description of the social, economic, and cultural dynamics as well as the reconstruction of the religious field of Los Angeles, biographical narratives of Guatemalan independent Pentecostal leaders are analyzed using the Habitus Analysis approach.

---

1 The names of interviewees and congregations that have participated in this study have been modified. In addition, the information regarding their age, place of birth, and the residence of the congregations are presented in general terms and without detail for the purpose of maintaining their anonymity.

1.1. Pentecostalism in Guatemala

Pentecostalism is a movement within Protestant Christianity that originated in the United States in the early twentieth century. Different authors (Dayton 2004, Droogers 1998) define Pentecostalism as a religious movement that finds its doctrinal foundation in the passages of the New Testament, which speak of the descent of the Holy Spirit upon the followers of Jesus Christ, as described in the second chapter of the Book of Acts. While practices vary, Pentecostal worship services often involve experiences that believers consider "gifts of the Holy Spirit," such as divine healing, speaking in tongues, receiving direct revelations from God, and exorcism.

This religious movement made its appearance on Guatemalan soil in 1934, when the American denominations *Church of God* and *Assemblies of God* sent missionaries to El Quiche and Totonicapán (Garrard-Burnett 1998, 37). However, it was not until the 1960s that Pentecostalism experienced years of rapid and steady growth (Garrard-Burnett 1998). According to the 2014 Pew study "Religion in Latin America: Widespread Change in a Historically Catholic Region" for most of the twentieth century, from 1900 through the 1960s, at least 90% of the Guatemalan population was Catholic. Today, at the beginning of the twenty-first century, Protestantism[2] has gained massive influence with many Guatemalans having joined evangelical Protestant churches. Roughly four-in-ten Guatemalan adults (40%) describe themselves as Protestant, making it a significant religious movement in this country (Pew 2014). At the same time, "*evangélicos*"—as Protestants in the region are often called—include many Christians who belong to Pentecostal churches.

According to this Pew study, across all Guatemala, nearly three-quarters of Protestants (72%) identify themselves as Pentecostal Christians, either because they belong to a Pentecostal denomination or because they personally identify themselves as Pentecostal regardless of their denomination.

---

2 Protestants in Latin America, like Protestants elsewhere, belong to a diverse group of denominations and independent churches. But unlike in the United States, where the labels "born again" and "evangelical" set certain Protestants apart, in Latin America "Protestant" and "evangelical" are often used interchangeably. In this dissertation, "Protestant" is broadly used to refer to members of historical Protestant churches (e.g., Baptists, Seventh-day Adventists, Methodists, Lutherans or Presbyterians), members of Pentecostal churches, and members of other Protestant churches.

This astonishing growth of Pentecostalism in Guatemala is usually linked in the literature to the occurrence of three consecutive events: (1) During the 1960s, the concentration of evangelical missionaries of US origin, who carried out door to door evangelism and extensively used mass means of communication, namely radio, led to a considerable increase in the number of believers (Garrard-Burnett 1998). (2) During the 1970s, national Pentecostal churches, which are economically and structurally independent of all foreign missions and have a national—Guatemalan—pastorate, emerged. These splits within organizations of foreign missions were presented and justified in many cases as a "revival" led by the Holy Spirit, causing not only an increase in the number of national Pentecostal churches, but also the "pentecostalization" of a significant number of Protestant denominations once "nationalized" (Garrard-Burnett 1998). (3) Parallel to the configuration of national Pentecostal congregations, a branch of Pentecostalism, called "Neopentecostalism," concerned with the idea of "divine healing," also emerged. In this kind of Pentecostalism, exorcism and prosperity are central elements as well as the presence of energetic, charismatic leaders exhorting huge gatherings and providing continuous worship services in public buildings such as cinemas and auditoriums (O'Neil 2010).

The increasing popularity of Pentecostalism coincided with the decline of the Guatemalan economy, a profound political crisis, and clashes between revolutionary movements and military forces that led to an escalation of violence in Guatemala since 1970 (Hamilton and Stoltz Chinchilla 2001). At the same time, a change in migratory flows ceased to have an interregional character, becoming international when Guatemalan migrants began to go to the United States. Based on data provided by the United States Immigration and Naturalization Service, Jonas and Rodríguez (2014) point out that since 1980 the number of Guatemalans residing in the United States has grown steadily until reaching more than 1.2 million in 2010.

Since the 1980s, migration from Guatemala to the United States has been seen as a way to survive in a context of political and economic crisis, violence, and armed conflict. However, for many Pentecostal believers, the possibility of traveling abroad has an added connotation: Traveling involves carrying out evangelization efforts.

As Droogers (2001) indicates, in Pentecostal teaching there is a constant reference to the mission that each believer has in the extension of the kingdom of God, that is, in the conversion of others. Hence, many Pentecostals feel that it is their obligation to go to other places, regardless of national boundaries, and gather new converts. Therefore, it is not surprising that since the 1980s Guatemalan Pentecostal believers have begun to develop active ministries beyond the borders of Guatemala, especially in those places with a considerable number of migrants from Latin American countries, as is the case in the United States.

The parallel realities of migration, economic changes, and the development of global patterns of transportation have contributed to the growth of Latina/o[3] Pentecostalism and have facilitated the spread and cross-fertilization of Pentecostalism across political boundaries. Nevertheless, while the importance of Pentecostal church movements in Guatemala is already the subject of numerous studies, the role of Guatemalan Pentecostal movements in the transformation of the religious landscape in the United States is considerably under-researched. One of the aims of this dissertation is to provide some insights in this regard.

1.2. Inter-American Mobility and New Pentecostal Missionary Flows: Evangelizing from the South to the North

The Guatemalan Pentecostal missionary efforts mentioned above are part of a larger religious phenomenon within Christianity: the emergence of new and unusual missionary flows. In the context of this dissertation, "mis-

3 Two terms are designated to refer to the population with a Latin American and Caribbean origin or ancestors: Hispanic and Latino. Both terms have similar backgrounds, but they also present differences. I have chosen to principally use the term Latino because most the people I talked with in Los Angeles refer to themselves as "Latina/o." But I will also occasionally use Hispanic as fully synonymous with Latino, particularly when the sources I am citing use that term. Because Latino is a Spanish term, it has gender. Spanish commonly uses the masculine to refer to both males and females but assumes that the feminine can refer only to females. Because Spanish is my mother tongue and one of the languages in which I publish, I hope that eventually we will be able to find grammatically acceptable ways to break out of the *machistas* tendencies of this language. But until this happens, I want to name the problem and seek ways to address it. Therefore, I attempt to address this issue by using Latina/o whenever I refer to both female and male.

sion" or "missionary work" is seen as what churches and Christian communities are commissioned to do in a broad sense, encompassing activities such as preaching both inside and outside one's own circles, recruitment of new members, worship, education, social services, political advocacy, and many other aspects (Währisch-Oblau 2012, 225-226). "Evangelism" is understood in a narrower sense and illustrates any activity aimed at recruiting active church members who adhere to the belief system and the ethical rules of the recruiting community. In this sense, evangelism is an aspect of a "mission," which carries greater or lesser importance, depending on the theological school. For evangelicals and Pentecostals, evangelism is the most important mission, relegating any other church work to lesser significance (Währisch-Oblau 2012, 225-226).

From a historical perspective, Christian missionary efforts have gone from the north—mainly Europe and the United States—to the south—Latin America, Africa, and even Asia. The missionary flows coming from the south, however, are transforming the Christian missionary universe since they bring new forms of transnational religious complexity, in which significant flows of migrants coming from the south are bringing their own interpretation of Christianity and Pentecostalism to the United States and Europe. As a result of these processes, one of the most striking contemporary developments in the religious field in the United States is the rapid growth of evangelical Protestantism, particularly Pentecostalism, among the Latin American population residing in this country.

Although the majority of this population still identify as Catholics, this percentage has decreased in recent years, from 67% in 2006 to 59% in 2013, according to the 2014 Pew Study "The Shifting Religious Identity of Latinos in the United States." This study also mentioned that almost a quarter (22%) of the same population identify as Protestants, roughly the same as in Latin America (19%). Among the Latina/o population in the United States, fewer than three-quarters of Protestants (71%) describe themselves as Pentecostal by church denomination, self-identification, or both. These figures make Latin Pentecostalism the fastest-growing religious movement in the United States (Pew 2014).

In addition, according to Espinoza (2004), it is possible to say that there are more than 10,000 non-Catholic Latina/o Christian congregations in the United States (most of them headed by Latino/a ministers), but only 1,441 (14%) of these are mainstream Protestant churches. This means that more than 8,500 are Pentecostal congregations. Considering all these aspects, it is possible to say that the Americas[4] have undergone a process of profound religious reconfiguration during the twentieth century. This also means that immigrants, rather than de-Christianizing religion in the United States, have in fact "de-Europeanized" U.S. Christianity (Fenggang and Ebaugh 2001, 271).

The overwhelming majority of these churches are independent ministries, which, while clearly charismatic in character, usually call themselves "nondenominational" and have members from diverse national backgrounds. According to pastors and leaders, these churches are not meant to be "migrant" churches where migrants can find a "home away from home" and preserve their culture and piety of origin. Rather, they are presented as missionary endeavors with a clear evangelistic calling toward the whole of U.S. society. Sunday sermons admonish believers to reach out to non-Christians, regardless of their ethnic and national background.

Most churches regularly organize evangelistic events like street preaching, gospel concerts and what they call "evangelistic campaigns." Despite their stated goal of evangelizing or reviving "the United States," members of most Latino-led churches have a Latin American origin, although they are not mono-ethnic but rather composed of a mixture of different Latin American nationalities and ethnicities (Martínez 2011). Some larger churches have been successful in evangelizing other migrants, but

4 There are a number of ways in which the term "The Americas" is being deployed in recent academic discourse. First, it refers to the geographic region of South, Central, North America, and the Caribbean. Second, it refers to people of Latin American or Caribbean descent who are historically connected and speak either Spanish, Portuguese, or English and live in any of these aforementioned regions. And third, it refers to those groups of people who share a common history and cultural ancestry. These three definitions tend to understand the Americas as a "container space," that is, as a recipient that contains specific cultural, economic, political, and social elements that distinguish these spaces through discrete borders from other container spaces. In the research group within which this dissertation project takes place, we also refer to "The Americas," but in the light of the recent debate on spaces, we prefer to go beyond territorial concepts. Therefore, we propose the use of the concept of the Americas as a space of entanglement. For us, the Americas can be seen as imagined spaces of interactions, articulated around relations of power-space-knowledge, in which geopolitical strategies of institutional actors, economic interests, media, social movements, and daily life experiences are taken into consideration.

generally Latino-led churches have not been able to recruit and keep large numbers of U.S. citizens without a Latino background. Nevertheless, like Pentecostal and Charismatic churches in general, Latino-led churches are strongly evangelistic in character (A. Anderson 2007).

1.2.1. Missionaries from the South to the North: Expatriates or Migrants?

As noted before, these missionaries' efforts are an example of the new modalities of religious expansion in times of transnational migration. The question that arises is: How can be defined the agents, who go from one country to another with the idea of carrying out a religious mission? In the dominant North Atlantic discourse, two terms serve to categorize people involved in such endeavors. One is "immigrant" and the other is "expatriate."

According to Währisch-Oblau, the term "expatriate" is connected with power and abundant economic, social and cultural resources. Expatriates "go to a foreign country (usually from the North to other parts of the world) with a sense of purpose, to do a certain job, or to live out an ideal. They move freely and can go back home if they chose to do so" (2012, 137). Moreover, they are employed by international companies or organizations. In contrast, the term "migrants" or "immigrants" connotes people in movement due to contingency as "refugees, asylum seekers or economic migrants fleeing from poverty and deprivation, and once they have arrived, they cannot go back" (Währisch-Oblau 2012, 137). They are seen as victims rather than agents.

When one speaks of missionaries coming from countries like the United States, they are designated as "expatriates." Due to their mission to evangelize and engage in international humanitarian work, religious communities from the United States heavily engage in expatriation. But what about Pentecostal believers who come from countries like Guatemala, with hardly any institutional support but a great motivation to expand the gospel, who face serious structural limitations in their countries of origin, in their displacements and establishment in other countries? Are they expatriates or simple immigrants? To answer this question, a detailed literature review of the studies dealing with the expansion of Latin American or Latino Pentecostalism in the United States was carried out.

There are not so many studies regarding Pentecostal missionaries coming from the south to work in the north. Most of the literature focuses on the relationship between Pentecostalism and migration. In this line of research, there are two main approaches (see Chapter 2). The first approach, which can be called "the incorporation approach," has focused on the role that Pentecostalism plays in the adaptation of people with a Latin American origin in U.S. society. The literature following this approach points to the centrality of Pentecostal organizations as sources of social and economic support in the settlement experience of newcomer immigrant groups (León 1998; Vasquez 1999; Lorentzen and Mira 2005; Maduro 2007). Authors pursuing this approach also consider that the agents expanding Latino Pentecostalism are migrants. Although this literature offers significant insights in order to understand the relation between migration and Pentecostalism, these studies also have some limitations. A crucial one is that they tend to analyze factors that are external to the religious praxis and nothing is actually said about the nature of that religious praxis.

The second approach is the "religion on the move approach," which follows developments in the studies of globalization and transnationalism, pointing out that circulation and linkages are basic characteristics of religious life. Migration and the development of transnational relations have facilitated the spread and cross-fertilizations of Pentecostal missionary efforts across political boundaries. Thus, religious beliefs, practices, and organizations allow people to stay closely connected to their homeland, and to be members of a shared culture, tradition, and faith. Pentecostal believers and their organizations act as both agents and subjects of power in their transnational relationships with the North, rather than as marginal players reacting to forces of globalization that are beyond their control (Menjivar 1999; Vasquez and Marquardt 2003; Martínez 2013; Danielson 2015). According to this approach, the agents responsible for the expansion of Latino Pentecostalism are expatriates.

Authors using this approach have offered striking insights into the conceptualization of religious life, connecting people and faith throughout the world. They have also helped to redefine the understanding of global and transnational processes. However, as with the first approach to Pentecostalism and Latino migration, this approach also has some limitations. First, it is mainly focused on the effect of external factors on the growth of Pentecostalism around the world, disregarding the study of Pentecostalism itself. As in the first approach, authors are mainly interested in what religious praxis does, not in what religious praxis is. Second, their units of analysis are organizations and they have largely left aside the study of individual participants or religious leaders. While immigration is at the heart of the studies on Latino Pentecostalism in the United States, none of these studies have really analyzed the role of Pentecostal leaders, how they see themselves and the world, and the way they understand their missionary work.

This study, which is to some extent aligned with the "religion on the move approach" and is based on six months of empirical research in the transnational social space articulated between Guatemala and Los Angeles, is precisely set out to counter these two limitations. First, to inquire into the contents of the Guatemalan independent Pentecostal praxis in Los Angeles, this research aims to answer the following questions: Considering the general context of social conflict, change, and inequality that Guatemalans in Los Angeles have to face, what are the beliefs and practices of Guatemalan independent Pentecostal leaders, which religious identities and strategies emerge from them, and what is the relation between their religious praxis and the social, economic, and cultural dynamics in which they are involved? In order to answer these questions, the dissertation follows the Habitus Analysis approach, which allows the study to capture external factors, thus integrating the specific contents of Pentecostal belief and practice.

With this approach, we turn the people themselves into the key variable in order to analyze the complex flows of missionary praxis. For the purpose of better understanding how time, change, and habitus interact, we enrich the Habitus Analysis through a close look at the biographical narratives of seven Guatemalan independent Pentecostal leaders, placing them within their social space and showing the different practical logics in which they live. Although biographical methods do not offer sufficient data to make definitive statements about the overall nature of Guatemalan Pentecostal leadership in Los Angeles, this research does provide a fresh perspective for considering the self-presentation of Guatemalan Pentecostal independent leaders considering the social and economic context they face. Guatemalan Pentecostal leaders were chosen following the logic of theoretical sampling. This implies selecting participants based on specific theoretical characteristics, in this case, linked to the definition of "missionary from the South." Once established a trusting relationship with the appropriate interviewees, I asked them for new people to interview following the indications of the snowball sampling technique.

1.3. Guatemalan Independent Pentecostal Leaders in the Interamerican Social Space Established Between Guatemala and Los Angeles: A Praxeological Approach

This dissertation follows a praxeological approach in its theoretical and methodological frameworks. The Habitus Analysis approach follows several theoretical ideas derived from Pierre Bourdieu's (1980) relational sociology. The study of religious phenomena following Bourdieu's praxeological approach entails a fundamental rethinking of what "religion" is and of what it means to be "religious."

Bourdieu conceptualizes *praxis* as the relation of mutual interdependency between agent and structure, dispositions and positions under the condition of change in time. This particular analytical perspective implies a conception of religion as human praxis, in which one is concerned about what people do with religious practices, and what they make of themselves and their worlds as followers of these religious practices. Religion is praxis —mental and material praxis, operating through signs and material elements. It involves beliefs and practices as much as it involves the social conditions and struggles in which people live.

This approach makes it possible to attach special analytical importance to religious beliefs and practices and, at the same time, to understand them from the point of view of their multiple relationships with the social life of the participants, their relations with other religious agents, and their positions in society's power relations. In this sense, a religious praxis is never a preexisting, external and unreachable realm in relation to human activity, but rather a multifaceted, vibrant reality in constant interaction with its environment, continuously exposed to both internal and external resources, limitations, tendencies, and pressures (Maduro 1996).

Besides, religious phenomena have an intrinsically double reality as any other social phenomenon. One side of a religious praxis is what people believe; the other side is the power and capability to act in relation to the social opportunities and constraints in which agents are situated (Schäfer et al. 2016a, 153). The question that arises is: How can this double reality be captured in the case of religious phenomena? Following the Habitus Analysis approach (Schäfer et al. 2016a, 153), one way to combine cognitive and material aspects in a significant form is by looking at experiences of contingency and the interpretations that social agents give to them.

Any human being reacts to such experiences by interpreting them, ascribing meaning to them. Religious agents interpret social experience in the same operational mode as non-religious agents do: They ascribe meaning to it. The difference resides only in the fact that religious agents employ different semantic contents. It is precisely in these moments of contingency when a religious praxis gains significance. As religious agents, individuals and organizations interpret experience by means of a promise of "salvation," referring to a transcendent entity (Schäfer et al. 2016a, 154). Invoking "salvation," they imagine a transcendent reality or entity, which can produce different social effects, from legitimizing domination and generating social cohesion to revolution and desires for radical social change (Schäfer et al. 2016a, 154).

From a praxeological perspective, it is precisely the relation between "earthly" experiences and "otherworldly" interpretations that creates religious identities, strategies, and, finally, the praxis itself. The reference to transcendence made by religious agents is, therefore, the crucial element from which one can reconstruct the structures of meaning, and thus the forming of religious identities and strategies (Schäfer et al. 2016a, 156).

Religious beliefs and practices do not rely simply on the semantic content of a given religious movement. Religious praxis, instead, hinges on agent-specific social positions within the social structure and the ascription of religious meaning to them (Schäfer et al. 2016a, 156). The meaning of religious beliefs and practices is, therefore, closely linked to the social context. Every religious praxis is intertwined with the social opportunities and constraints in which agents are situated. Religious agents resort to particular contents in response to particular events and circumstances, developing different understandings of the relation between transcendent forces and society or history and, of course, different strategies in social conflicts and competition. In consequence, religious identities and strategies can provide an alternative and sometimes more effective ways of coping with challenges.

Biographical narratives of Guatemalan independent Pentecostal leaders working in Los Angeles are analyzed in order to capture Guatemalan independent Pentecostal leaders' beliefs and practices including their relationship to the general context of social conflict, change, and inequality that Guatemalans have to face in Los Angeles, in a moment in which the global expansion of Pentecostalism coincides with migratory flows of thousands of Latin Americans caused by the expulsion or marginalization from ongoing processes of economic globalization.

After a close description of the challenging social contexts of departure and arrival of Guatemalans from 1970 to 2014 in addition to the reconstruction of the impact of Latino Pentecostalism in the religious field of Los Angeles in the 2010s, the dissertation analyzes the biographical narratives of Guatemalan independent Pentecostal leaders, asking for the experiences related by the interviewees and the meaning they ascribe to them. The search for references to transcendent entities and their meaning are particularly significant since they allow the researcher to capture the dispositions or mental maps according to which the leaders assess and act on the social space in which they are located and delineate their identities and strategies. Their biographical narratives serve to elucidate their agency, trajectories, and their strategies in the migratory context.

In order to systematically analyze the biographical narratives, the research relies on the *praxeological square*, which was also developed by Heinrich Schäfer (2005; 2009; 2015) within the Habitus Analysis approach. The *Praxeological Square* can be defined as a discourse analysis method oriented to grasp insider's accounts on experience and its interpretation, and it is designed to structure the underlying practical logic according to very general formal categories. In this method, slightly structured interviews are considered the basic sources of the accounts since they evoke utterances of four different kinds: negative and positive experiences together with the interpretation of these experiences.

1.4. Structure of the Dissertation

This dissertation inquires into the biographical narratives of Guatemalan independent Pentecostal leaders, who are evangelizing beyond the national borders of their country and who work actively in congregations in Los Angeles, focusing on their identities and their strategies. Chapter 2 begins by examining and discussing the literature for the study of pentecostalism in the Americas, distinguishing between two approaches: the above-mentioned "incorporation" and "religion on the move" approaches. The chapter deals with each approach, highlights their achievements and limitations, and finishes by mentioning the advantages of following a praxeological approach for the study of religious phenomena.

Chapter 3 presents the theoretical and methodological frameworks of the dissertation. It presents some considerations regarding Bourdieu's social praxeology, discussing the implications of such an approach for the study of religious phenomena. This theoretical discussion serves to delineate the theoretical and methodological propositions of the "Habitus Analysis," which is the framework of this dissertation.

Chapter 4 describes the demographical, economic, political, and religious context of Los Angeles in the 2010s, which has been the result of several long-term trends. After this contextualization, a brief historical description of the changing migratory flows of Guatemalans to Los Angeles from 1970 until 2010 is presented, using some biographical remarks of the interviewed individuals.

Chapter 5 reconstructs the religious field in Los Angeles in 2014, delimiting the scene of Latino Pentecostalism in this metropolitan area. The chapter displays the religious affiliations among Latinos, with particular regard to Central Americans in Los Angeles. Then, it explores the dimensions of "achievement of eminence" and "authenticity," which are the critical dimensions for the study of the religious field according to the Habitus Analysis approach. The logic of the field-model will profile the positions of different groups of agents in the context of religious competition in Los Angeles. Finally, the chapter indicates the position of the Guatemalan independent Pentecostal leaders studied in Los Angeles's religious field, distinguishing between "leaders by divine consecration" and "leaders by professional consecration."

Chapter 6 analyzes the biographical narratives of seven Guatemalan independent Pentecostal leaders working in Los Angeles, using the Habitus Analysis approach. This chapter presents some methodological considerations regarding Habitus Analysis and its praxeological square. It also shows the overall results of the analysis of the biographical narratives using this approach, displaying the thematic areas of the four positions of the praxeological square, which are *negative experience*, *negative interpretation*, *positive experience*, and *positive interpretation*. The examination of these categories maintains the distinction between "leaders by divine consecration" and "leaders by professional consecration" and also provides reasons for the most important result of the analysis of the biographical narratives, namely the significant majority of positive experiences and interpretations in comparison with negative experiences and interpretations. Presenting themselves as missionaries, the Guatemalan leaders interviewed retain a strong sense of agency: they are not victims, but people whom God called upon to achieve his aim of worldwide evangelism.

Chapter 7 inquires specifically into the references to a "transcendent entity." In the case of Guatemalan independent Pentecostal leaders, the transcendent entity is usually *God* and sometimes the *Holy Spirit.* The chapter begins dealing with the accounts to the semantic field *God's call*, which was the most often referenced symbolic operator regarding God. Then, other symbolic operators associated with God are analyzed, showing that there is some diversity among the beliefs of Pentecostal leaders once considered within the social position of the interviewees. Three religious habitus formations were found: God as restorer, God's love, and Spiritual warfare.

Chapter 8, the final chapter, presents the conclusions of the study, relating them to previous research, showing the paradoxical character of being a Pentecostal missionary from the South to the North. On the one hand, it provides cognitive and emotional resources to fully give sense to a life on the move, retaining a strong sense of agency. On the other hand, however, being a Pentecostal missionary in Los Angeles serves to reproduce the patterns of domination over the self and the body that have been central in the marginalization of Latina/os in the Americas.

2. Literature Review: Delimiting Pentecostalism and Outlining Studies Dealing with Latino Pentecostalism and Migration in the United States

The Guatemalan Pentecostal missionary efforts mentioned above are part of a larger religious phenomenon within Christianity: the emergence of unusual missionary flows. Historically, Christian missionary efforts have mainly gone from the North—Europe, the United States and Canada—to the South—Latin America, Africa, and even Asia. Nowadays, Pentecostal missionary flows go instead from the South to the North. In this chapter, I will present the literature that analyzes these Pentecostal reverse missionary flows. First, in the next section, I will define Pentecostalism.

2.1. Delimiting Pentecostalism

In the introduction, the term "Pentecostalism" was used without providing any definition. This section aims to offer a conceptualization of Pentecostalism, which is anything but easy since this extremely multifaceted movement seems to have neither a common dogmatic basis nor a universal institutional framework. Numerous authors from several fields, among them theology, religion, sociology, and anthropology, have tried to offer a definition of this religious movement that emerged at the beginning of the twentieth century. Some of them opted to follow essentialist categories, others pointed out Pentecostalism's historical and synchronous connections, and others decided to provide a catalog of markers that might conform a kind of always changing Pentecostal identity.

One of the first authors conceptualizing Pentecostalism is Donald Dayton (2004). In his groundbreaking book *Theological Roots of Pentecostalism*, he presented a definition of Pentecostal dogmatism. Dayton notes that Pentecostalism is much more than "speaking in other tongues" (15) and mentions four elements (21-22)—salvation, healing, baptism of the Holy Spirit, and the second coming of Christ—, which are in his view the roots of the Pentecostal theology. As he points out, they are not the exclusive patrimony of Pentecostals, nor have they been invented by them, but the way they there are incorporated in both faith and practice is exclusively of Pentecostalism. Beyond context-specific nuances or peculiar emphases, these four elements together are a common denominator of Pentecostal praxis. This definition of Pentecostalism, while precise, has the problem that it is limited to North American white "classical" Pentecostalism; the contemporary history of Pentecostalism in other world regions such as Latin America, Africa, or Asia are not present in Dayton's inquiry as Walter Hollenweger (1997) has adequately argued.

Following an elaborate theological model, Walter Hollenweger (1997) exposes how Pentecostalism emerges from black oral religion, Catholicism, the Holiness Movement, political criticism, and ecumenism. Using the Azusa Street Revival[5] as a paradigm, Hollenweger presents Pentecostalism as a border-crossing movement characterized by an oral liturgy, a narrative theology, maximal lay participation, acceptance of dreams and visions, and a deeper understanding of the unity of body and soul. Hollenweger's contribution has also served to highlight Pentecostalism's globalized nature as well as its particular way of living and practicing faith and theology. For him, Pentecostal praxis is oral rather than written, narrative rather than systematic, experiential rather than doctrinal. Although Hollen-

---

5 The Azusa Street Revival was a revival meeting that took place in Los Angeles, CA, in April, 1906. The revival had its origins in Kansas. A preacher, Charles Parham, began a Bible school in Topeka, Kansas, teaching that speaking in tongues was the evidence of being baptized in the Holy Spirit (Espinosa 2014, 26). One of his students was an African-American preacher named William Joseph Seymour. In 1906, Seymour was invited to preach at a church in Los Angeles. There, he presented Parham's doctrine regarding speaking in tongues as evidence of the Holy Spirit. Disagreeing with his message, the leaders of the church banned him from preaching. However, Seymour started to hold Bible studies in the home of one of the members of the congregation (Espinoza 2014, 33). Shortly after, numerous members of the group began to speak in tongues for the first time. As the news about what was happening disseminated, larger crowds formed. They were not only composed of African Americans but also Latinos and Whites, which was an exception at a time when the norm was segregated church services. The group ended up renting a building at 312 Azusa Street in downtown Los Angeles. Seymour also began a rescue mission in the same building (Espinoza 2014, 34-35). The meetings were loud and boisterous. There were reports of healing and speaking in tongues along with shouting and spontaneous preaching by those who felt led by the Spirit to speak. The leaders were sure that this was evidence of revival (Espinoza 2014, 35). Therefore, Azusa Street Revival is considered the catalyst of the worldwide growth of Pentecostalism and the Charismatic movement.

weger's conceptualization captures important elements of Pentecostal praxis, his analytical construction offers an all-encompassing picture difficult to be implemented as a defining tool.

In an attempt to provide better analytic tools to delimit "Pentecostalism," Michael Bergunder (2007) argues that the provision of an essential definition of Pentecostalism is impossible and argues for a diachronous and synchronous connections approach. According to Bergunder (2007, 65), the label of "Pentecostal" can only be given to a church or a movement upon the fulfillment of one of the following two premises: 1. Evidence of a historical connection to the "vast and vague international network" surrounding the Azusa Street Revival of 1906, or, 2. Evidence of a synchronous interrelation with other groups, churches, or individuals, which similarly can be traced back to the beginnings of the movement. According to these criteria, it might be possible, in theory, to delimit "Pentecostalism" and to decide once and for all whether a certain church or ministry can or cannot be labeled as "Pentecostal." But in practice, the issue remains problematic.

In a critical response to Michael Bergunder, Allan Anderson (2004, 13) notes that it is difficult, if not outright impossible, to establish such connections to the first stage of Pentecostalism for all "third-world" Pentecostal movements and churches. Though the criteria are clear, they are not always operationalized in practice. This is especially true in the case of independent churches, particularly in a migratory context as it is the case of this study, where historical connections are often impossible to verify.

Considering the multifaceted variety within the Pentecostal movement and the significant growth of Pentecostal independent churches in the world, particularly in the global South, Anderson suggests that the term "Pentecostal" is pertinent "for describing globally all churches and movements that emphasize the working of the gifts of the Spirit." More precisely, quoting Robert M. Anderson (1979, 4), Pentecostalism should be seen "as a movement concerned primarily with the experience of the working of the Holy Spirit and the practice of spiritual gifts." Despite the belief in the direct intervention of the Holy Spirit as a defining feature of Pentecostal praxis, the definition provided by Anderson continues to be very broad and need to be further specified.

Some specifications can be found in the work of André Droogers (2001, 41-61), who provides three common characteristics of Pentecostalism from an anthropological perspective. The first of these common characteristics is the central place given to the presence of the Holy Spirit, which is argued to be experienced in the gifts of healing, speaking in tongues, and prophecy, having the human body as their locus. The second common characteristic is the role that a conversion experience plays in the life of the believer. Conversion is seen as "a dramatic personal event, by far the most important of their lives" (45). This experience leads one into the church as an alternative community. The last common characteristic is a dualist worldview which means that after the conversion the believer tends to see the world as divided into two parts: "the part of God and his believers" and the one of "the devil and his followers" (46). In addition, this worldview tends to generate a kind of "narrative compulsion" since they are invited to share the "experience of the Holy Spirit" to others (46).

Michael Bergunder also points out some features of a distinguishing Pentecostal identity. According to him, Pentecostalism has "something to do with a certain spiritual praxis (intuitive, experiential Spirit-centered devotion; oral liturgy; firm Biblical orientation; narrative theology and testimonies; strong lay participation; healing, and so on)" (2007, 64). Bergunder also notes that this praxis is subjected to constant change and it is dependent on mutual affirmation.

David Martin (1990) also proposes some characteristics that, in his view, all Pentecostal followers share. According to him, Pentecostals are focused on conversion, the work of "miracles" and the influences of demons and they reject the corruptions of "the world." The case studies cited refer mainly to lifestyle changes among Pentecostal believers. For instance, his findings show that Pentecostals avoided the fiesta system and secular entertainment, especially drinking, and thereby saved money (Martin 1990, 211). Martin also notes that Pentecostalism in Latin America (especially since 1960) has been a grassroots movement and that Pentecostals mostly have had a lower level of education (Martin 1990, 227-228). According to him, Pentecostalism offers its believers equality of participation, equal access to gifts of the spirit, a new sense of selfhood and the capacity to choose, opportunities for developing personal skills of expression, and opportunities for leadership. Martin claims that in the long run, those positive aspects of Pentecostalism may be relevant to modest advancement and may make Pentecostals more disposed to capitalistic forms of development (Martin 1990, 230-232).

André Corten (1999), a political scientist, adopts a discourse-theoretical approach to study the construction of different categories of the poor, claiming the importance of the "emotion of the poor" in Pentecostal praxis. According to him, Pentecostalism allows its followers to freely experience emotions, which serve to prove their immediacy to God and the Bible without needing any theological training; thus, emotions form the basis of the religious discourse, enacted and exteriorized in glossolalia, singing, free speech, and gestures. In relation to praise, he mentions that it is an illocutive "original" or "primary" utterance which is neither true nor false, but "unacceptable" within the political discourse. Finally, with respect to organizational tendencies, he notes that Pentecostals tend to be organized as a "sect," functioning as what could term the "anti-politics of the poor" (1999, 126) (though this may change as a more formal church develops). Regarding this last point, Corten's markers of Pentecostalism are somewhat problematic since the lower-class position of Pentecostal believers is referred to as a generalized characteristic. Yet, a more refined typology would include not just churches that specifically address the poorest people in society, but also churches that seek to attract people from middle and even upper classes.

In this respect, Heinrich Schäfer presents a richer typology regarding the composition and expansion of Pentecostalism in Guatemala during the 1980s. According to him, Guatemalan society during this period was deeply divided into a rich, white upper class and a very poor, mostly indigenous lower class. This social division deepened during the counter-insurgency war in the late 1970s and 80s. The rural population was strongly affected by massacres, napalm bombings, the concentration of indigenous civilians in strategic hamlets, torture, and many other measures of this kind. In the capital, on the other hand, military and secret service violence were considerably lower, so the urban middle class was relatively spared from the direct terror of the first phase of the war, although the psychological effects of insecurity and violence largely remained (Schäfer 1992). At that time, he identified two types of Pentecostal believers: the Neopentecostals, who belong mainly to the modernizing urban upper-middle and even upper classes, and the Classical Pentecostals, who belong mostly to the traditional lower class living in the countryside and in urban slums. Both movements in the early 1980s operated with an almost identical inventory of religious signs and symbols—the traditional Pentecostal ones (Schäfer 1992). To researchers at that time, these movements seemed to be one and the same, so that nobody noted a substantial difference (Martin 1990; Stoll 1990). By contrast, and following Pierre Bourdieu's conceptualizations,

Schäfer developed a praxeological approach, called Habitus Analysis, demonstrating that in fact two very different practical logics guided Pentecostal work in Guatemala (Schäfer 1992).

According to him, Pentecostals of lower socioeconomic background—referred to as "Classical Pentecostals"—especially in rural areas, are the main victims of the war. For them, the problem was not only the insecurity but also the pressure of economic need, the impossibility of working their land, of feeding their family, and of sending their children to school, and, finally, the lack of any way to express their own preferences through social or political mobilization. The corresponding grievances deriving from this situation express a feeling of having lost any prospect of future betterment in this life (Schäfer 1992). To answer such a demanding situation, classical Pentecostalism developed an apocalyptic religious response. According to it, the agents should counter their perception of the situation with the hope of the immediate return of Christ. Christ is supposed to return in the present time and "rapture" the true Church out of the world's suffering and into heaven. In contrast to a situation without a future, faith offers the perspective of a heavenly future. The religious identity of these believers derives from this millenarian scheme. They see themselves as the true Church in preparation for the rapture. From this position, the explanation for their lack of perspectives on this earth becomes evident: During the apocalyptic end times, everything necessarily changes from bad to worse. The reason for the loss of all opportunities is interpreted as a logical consequence of living in the end of times and therefore being the victims of a divinely necessary progression from bad to worse conditions. Social action is not only seen as impossible (as the more general predispositions of the rural lower class might also suggest), but also as counter-productive (Schäfer 1992). Accordingly, on the level of experience, Schäfer presents a religious community that faces an extensive loss of opportunities for survival. In this situation, they opt for the following strategy: a clear break with political and social action and a withdrawal into the community of believers—exactly the strategy that, under repression and misery, facilitates their survival and strengthens their self-esteem through in-group solidarity. To sum up, people cope with this hopeless situation through this belief in being raptured into heaven. As Christians in preparation for this event, they refrain from any social or political mobilization and concentrate—*de facto*—on solidarity among their religious kin. Hence, a strategy of withdrawal from a hopeless situation into a manageable community of mutual support and solidarity was developed.

Pentecostals in the modernizing upper-middle class—referred to as "Neopentecostals"—also faced deteriorating social conditions during the late 1970s and the insurgency of the early 1980s. They suffered from economic decline and increasing public violence, two parallel processes that put their dominant political role in Guatemalan society deeply at risk. For instance, they were no longer able to pay debts resulting from the purchase of real estate; they suffered personal setbacks such as alcoholism and bulimia as a consequence of stress; they endured corrupt politicians; they felt an existential void or else they simply felt that there must be something better in life. Applying his methodology, Schäfer (1992) shows that these grievances reflect a sense of a generalized threat to middle-class power, including control over one's own body. Neopentecostal religiosity answers these demands charismatically, focusing on the power of the Holy Spirit, which followers can embody in the church by attending, praying, speaking in tongues, and realizing ecstatic practices. This embodiment of power counters the experienced loss of control in their lives, and it leads to their self-description as empowered individuals. It is not the church as a community but rather the individual embodiment of divine power that shapes this religious style (Schäfer 1992). From the position of empowered individuals, the believers ascribe the reason for the crisis to the action of demons. Satan and his demons control social agents that compete somehow with (upper-)middle-class interests, such as unionists, guerrillas, indigenous people, some politicians, and so forth. Further, Satan afflicts an individual by taking control of his or her life. Thus, alcohol or drug abuse, bulimia, and other problems are definitely caused by demons as well. Accordingly, the strategy is an active one, based on a war against Satan and his demons. In contrast to the Classical Pentecostals of the same period, the Neopentecostal religious praxis orbits around power. It is not directed toward a heavenly future, but it rather proclaims an all-mighty God through the so-called Prosperity Gospel (Schäfer 1992).

To sum up, upper-middle-class citizens feel that an overall crisis in society challenges their control over their own economic, political, and personal lives. They cope with this situation by holding a firm belief in empowerment through the Holy Spirit in order to be able to fight the demons, which have caused the loss of control in the first place. As this social class still has (in contrast to the lower class) real opportunities to act in society, religious mobilization serves to concentrate their power and to sharpen their strategies to cope with these threats. Thus, in contrast to the former example, they largely implemented a strategy of dominion (Schäfer 1992).

Taking as guides the parameters presented by the authors mentioned above, in order to conceptualize Pentecostal praxis, I have opted to focus on the practice exhibited by Pentecostal agents during the worship services that I could observe during my fieldwork in the churches studied both in Guatemala and Los Angeles, following Bourdieu's suggestion that it is the inquiry into the practice carried out by the actors themselves, where the researcher can find the material to elaborate good definitions of a social phenomenon. Based on my participant observation in worship services, certain practices have shown themselves as suggestive of a Pentecostal praxis. They include the following: Oral liturgy; absence of liturgical clothing/vestments; gestures movement, dance, and openly shown strong emotions, especially during praise and worships times, but also at other times during the worship service; communal prayer times during which everybody may pray aloud at the same time (sometimes, in some congregations, this included speaking in tongues); sharing testimonies within the worship service; congregational participation in the sermon through calls, shouts, songs, and gestures; prayers for healing and deliverance (possibly with laying-on of hands, falling down of the person prayed for, and other manifestations); strong lay participation in leading the worship, preaching sermons, and conducting prayers; evangelistic altar calls or a call to rededicate one's life to Christ.

It is also important to note that these practices partly constitute expressions of certain discourses which circulate globally within the Pentecostal movement, both through mass media and through the varied and international personal contacts that this network provides. The appropriation and adaptation of such discourses into the cultural and spiritual frameworks of each particular Guatemalan independent Pentecostal church serve as a true example of what we could term a "glocalized" movement (Corten and Marshall-Fratani 2001) in which individuals can combine both global and local forms of religious praxis.

Alongside the observation in the churches, data collected through the interviews also allows the identification of some topics that Pentecostals themselves and outside observers alike consider as Pentecostal identity markers. These, sometimes overlapping, topics include:

- Constructing a biography which sets an experience, usually the conversion experience, as the starting point of one's Christian life;
- Recounting one's life as a moral tale: moving from sin and wickedness in the past into holiness today;
- Formulation of a spiritual narrative (often quite unsystematic) in which mundane experiences are interpreted as positive events in one's life (e.g. physical healing, a visa for stay in the United States, financial prosperity), as God's answer to faithful prayers, and in which, conversely, negative events are interpreted as satanic attacks, possibly due to a lack of faith or insufficient prayer. In these narratives, some interviewees allude to the "power of God through the Spirit," mentioning how through the power of the Holy Spirit, one can confront the "powers of darkness", etc.;
- An interpretation of dreams, visions, auditions, inner urges, intuitions, etc. as God speaking through the Holy Spirit;
- A literal, Biblicist, reading of the Bible that treats individual verses (often without any contextualization) as speaking directly to the reader, providing guidance and answers to concrete questions;
- The claim that the Bible can be understood without any theological training, simply through the guidance of God or the Holy Spirit;
- An understanding of salvation that is tied to a "decision for Christ" based upon one's free will, and a consequent baptism by immersion, rendering infant baptism invalid.

These two inventories of practices and topics do not mean that a Pentecostal praxis is limited to these features. Pentecostalism is a movement without clear borders, and practices and semantic fields will be defined in distinct ways by different people in diverse contexts and are constantly being negotiated and renegotiated. In addition, the inventory of practices and semantic fields has to be located in specific social conditions to establish the practical logics at work.

2.2. Studies on the Relation Between Latino Pentecostalism and Migration in the United States

Having established a definition of Pentecostalism, in the following pages I will deal with the literature focused on Latino Pentecostalism in the United States. As mentioned before, current Pentecostal missionary flows are allowing changes in the direction of missionary flows, which are now going from the South to the North. These significant changes in the religious field have generated a growing academic interest in the study of Latin American Pentecostalism in the United States, turning the study of religion and migration again into a crucial sociological research field.

Since the mid-1990s there has been a veritable explosion in the literature on this topic, as "sociologists who study religion have hectored immigration specialists to pay attention to religion" (Stepick 2006, 11). Although the sociological inquiry into a religious praxis developed beyond the boundaries of the country of origin of its believers has been closed connected to the study of migration since the beginnings of the twentieth Century, when European immigrants arrived in the United States, the interest in the role that religion played in the immigration context largely disappeared in more recent migration flows.

Most analyses of the immigration patterns derived by the 1965 Immigration and Naturalization Act were focused on other outstanding issues, particularly the ever-increasing diversity brought to American soil by the new immigration wave. Due to the increased racial and ethnic heterogeneity of these new immigrants—especially in comparison to earlier immigrants—scholars became increasingly focused on issues related to the sociodemographic background of immigrants, their involvement in the labor force, the effects of legality and immigration policy on immigrants' lives, as well as on family dynamics, social networks, and gender relations among these immigrants. These issues are vantage points from which to estimate immigrants' progress and incorporation; however, they do not diminish the importance of religion for immigrants. Several contemporary studies have demonstrated that religious praxis has remained central in immigrant life, particularly in the beginning of the twenty-first century when immigrants with a Latin-American origin started transforming Christianity in the United States.

The focus of this chapter is primarily on studies regarding Pentecostalism and Latino migration in the United States, although it also includes some research on Pentecostalism and immigration around the world. This does not mean that an exhaustive summary will be given of what has been written about Latino Pentecostalism in the United States: My primary purpose is to discuss the different approaches to this topic that can be derived from the literature. After a detailed review of all the relevant studies since 1995, it is possible to distinguish two dominant approaches in the study of

Pentecostalism and Latino migration: the "incorporation approach" and the "religion on the move approach."

2.2.1. The "Incorporation Approach"

The first approach, which can be called the "incorporation approach," has been focused on the role of Pentecostalism in the integration in U.S. society of people with a Latin American origin, focusing especially on how Pentecostal affiliation and participation help immigrants to confront the challenges they face in a new land. Studies within the "incorporation approach" have followed the tradition of the historical accounts of immigration and religion in the United States, which describe and analyze the remarkable place that the church has played in the lives of immigrants. Religious organizations in receiving areas act, according to this view, as vehicles through which immigrants endure the traumas and hardships of immigration and, at the same time, maintain their cultural heritage and reaffirm their ethnic identities (Hagan 2008), developing an intricate welfare system to serve the needs of the newcomers.

In former studies of European immigration to the United States, for instance, Oscar Handlin (2002) and Will Herberg (1955) have pointed out the psychosocial benefits of religious membership for newcomers. Participation in ethnic churches provided solace and refuge from the trauma of the migration experience since immigrants could pray in their native languages and practice cultural rituals in the comfortable company of family and friends. According to Handlin (2002), ethnic churches played an essential role in the incorporation of the newcomers since immigrants became Americans by first becoming ethnic Americans.

Hence, accounts of contemporary immigration continue to point to the centrality of Pentecostal churches as sources of social and economic support in the settlement of various newcomer immigrant groups. The steady growth in the last decades of the Latino Pentecostal population in the United States has made this line of research particularly relevant. The rapid conversion to Pentecostalism by many Catholics has generated all sorts of questions concerning Latinos religious patterns, affiliations, and shifting identities. In this view, Pentecostal churches, scattered throughout the country's landscape, provide an array of spiritual and material services to facilitate immigrant settlement and integration (León 1998; Vasquez 1999; Lorentzen and Mira 2005; Maduro 2007). These are no small matters considering that the number of people with a Latin-American origin in the United States, many of whom identify themselves as Pentecostals, has steadily increased since the 1965.

According to these authors, upon arrival, newcomers rely on Pentecostal organizations for services that include housing referrals, job opportunities, and language training, as well as for knowledge that facilitates civic and political participation. For instance, Otto Maduro (2007) describes some aspects and dynamics characteristic of Pentecostal Latin American churches in the United States based on a study in Newark (New Jersey), which in his view are crucial in attracting, retaining, and supporting an increasing number of immigrants. According to him, these aspects—the language of the cult; the leadership; the music (instruments, rhythms and melodies); the worship space itself (located usually in the midst of humble slums); the body (even the exploited, tired, sweaty, smelly and modestly clothed body of immigrants on the return from a long and hard day's work); the spontaneous expression of a broad spectrum of emotion and the belief in divine healing stimulated by the Pentecostal tradition—serve immigrants to see themselves as an absolutely important person chosen, called, pushed, blessed and protected by God, a person with a sacred mission that must be carried out daily for the rest of his or her life. Hence, Pentecostal churches often act informally as information and relationship agencies; they are often the only ones which function as such freely, permanently, voluntarily, in the language of the immigrant people and served by other immigrants who see and feel their respectful, selfless, and spontaneous service as a sacred obligation assumed with pleasure. In these churches, according to Maduro (2007, 107) newcomers find all sorts of guidance and assistance in finding housing, employment, transportation, education, as well as medical, psychological, and legal assistance. For those who arrive without economic means, language skills, contacts, expertise or employment, all things necessary to survive the shock of everyday life in a hostile and foreign environment, the information received and relationships developed in the church are, truly, their salvation.

At the same time, these places of worship, which are often erected or transformed by immigrants, also facilitate the development of relationships and trust with co-ethnics as well as a venue for expressing ethnic identities, thereby creating more religious and cultural diversity across America's religious geography. In this sense, Luis León (1998) in his article "Born Again in East LA: The Congregation as Border Space" examines the ways that members of *Alcance Victoria*, a Chicano Pentecostal church located on the east side of Los Angeles, negotiate and rework their identities in the context of often overwhelmingly adverse social conditions, developing a religious understanding of time and place, self, and society. According to him, the participation in this Pentecostal congregation provides a fresh and expansive locus from which to invent an evolving Chicano cultural form, one that combines Mexican, American, and Christian evangelical elements into a fresh identity. Based on a critical review of the previous academic work about the expansion of Pentecostalism in Latin America, he points out that this literature falls into two interpretative categories, *Marxist social determinism* and *rational-choice humanism*, and it certainly offers elements to interpret Chicano Pentecostalism in Los Angeles. The *Marxist social determinism* approach, represented by the work of Anderson (1979) and Lalive d'Epinay (1969), claims that Pentecostalism offers a mechanism for social disengagement by channeling people's repressed energies and social dissatisfaction into spiritual obsession and eschatological hope that preclude critical political thought and revolutionary practice. *Rational-choice humanism*, represented by Stoll and Garrard-Burnett (1993), considers that the Latino religious "consumer" is endowed with all the necessary information and freedom to choose, based on reason, the religious adscription that best fits his or her particular needs. According to Leon (1998, 192), neither of these binary paradigms fully explain the complex phenomenon of Mexican American or Chicano Pentecostalism. Nonetheless, both are to a certain extent illuminating. Certainly, there are escapist elements in Pentecostalism, just as there are modes of free election and empowerment. According to him, Alcance Victoria at once enables the reproduction of both modes of empowerment and modes of docility or domination. Through Alcance Victoria, those without much economic success, the disinherited, come to embrace the myth of the America dream: their lives matter; they are special, chosen, with a divine commission that comes directly from God himself. By stressing individual election and achievement, the discursive community of Alcance Victoria confers self-worth, ultimate meaning, purpose, and a way to make sense of a harsh world. In this way, Alcance Victoria is an empowerment phenomenon. However, León argues that the choices of many of these believers have been so deeply determined by their social conditions that the ability to imagine choices is in itself limited. Therefore, Alcance Victoria enables people to work happily and productively within their social limitations, but its members for the most part are not individuals endowed with privilege and the ability to make rational choices; instead, most of them are people who are often faced with exploitative and degrading choices (192).

In this line, Manuel Vasquez (1999) in his article "Pentecostalism, Collective Identity and Transnationalism Among Salvadorians and Peruvians in the U.S." explores the role that Pentecostal ideas, practices, and forms of organizations play in the construction of community and collective identity among Salvadoran and Peruvian Pentecostals in the United States, particularly Peruvians in Paterson (New Jersey) and Salvadorans in Washington D.C., exploring the ways in which Peruvian and Salvadoran Pentecostals turn to their religious resources to redeploy their *latinidad* in response to the multiethnic and multicultural milieu of their receiving localities. In this study, which follows Donald Dayton's Pentecostalism definition and makes a critical use of the results provided by the literature on Latin American Pentecostalism, particularly the influential works of David Martin and Jean-Pierre Bastian, Vasquez argues that Pentecostalism offers a variety of survival strategies for Latino groups suffering the impact of increasing poverty, community disintegration, welfare reform, opposition to affirmative action, and anti-immigrant policies. These strategies range from the micro—re-articulating the self (threatened by drugs and domestic violence) and repairing broken families—to the macro—maintaining communities, building collective identity, preserving cultural patterns, and providing a certain degree of empowerment for women. According to him, strategies within Pentecostalism are deployed as a function of factors such as the immigrant's social class, level of education, length of stay, or place of residence. For instance, as Vasquez (1999, 630) explains following the case of Peruvians, some of the Pentecostals of Latin American origin and a relatively high socioeconomic status in their countries of origin find in Pentecostalism a way to hold in check the downward mobility pressures produced by the process of migration and even to regain some of the lost status. Therefore, they tend to define their collective identity as membership in a "multinational" community of the saved, a community that cuts across narrow notions of national identity. In fact, national identity is for them synonymous with the archaic, "corrupt" Catholicism of feasts and processions that the believers have left behind. It would seem, then, that by eroding their national identity, Pentecostalism is facilitating assimilation to the melting pot, in line with Martin's (1990) argument about the role of Pentecostalism in rejecting the old hierarchical world of Hispanic Catholicism and introducing the "Anglo" values of freedom of conscience and action. Nevertheless, this does not mean that they substitute their *latinidad* for an Anglo-Saxon identity. Rather they now become members of a pan-Latino collective that includes all Latin American nationalities. Pentecostalism, then, is not fostering a process of Anglicization among Latin American immigrants. Instead, it leads to the re-affirmation of Hispanic roots and the formation of a pan-Latino identity as a defensive maneuver (as Bastian (1993) had argued for Latin American Pentecostals) against the discrimination they suffer.

In contrast, as the case of the Salvadorians studied by Vasquez shows, for other Pentecostals with a Latin American origin who came in large numbers to the United States from the same rural areas escaping war, Pentecostalism means the reconstitution of the closely-knit rural community that they have left behind, a kind of refuge or buffer zone against the evil outside world. As first-generation immigrants, Pentecostalism offers them a sense of community, of being personally recognized and welcomed, of connecting in a more permanent and warmer way with other human beings, of being treated as equals, of not being despised and marginalized in the church because one is illiterate, allowing the re-ordering and re-inscription of their national identity and cultural roots in an alien milieu (Vasquez 1999, 631-632).

The role of Pentecostal organizations in the incorporation of new migrants has also been explored from an anthropologist perspective. An especially relevant work following this approach is that of Lorentzen and Mira (2005). They analyze the role of a Pentecostal, working-class, Spanish-speaking church with a high percentage of new migrants in the San Francisco Bay Area with a particular focus on the articulation of the gender relations. Following the studies that deal with the "feminization of machismo" (Brusco 1995, 63-69) or male "domestication" that takes place in some Pentecostal groups, particularly in Latin America, these authors argue that the Pentecostal church they study not only offers support for the preservation of families, social life, and communities, as well as networks for assistance in daily life preoccupations such as finding an apartment, a job, and child care, but also influences gender roles and relations. The women at that church receive social support from the church community, including child care. Many who are married emphasize how responsible their husbands are. And, through testimonies, prayers, praise, speaking, and occasional preaching, their voices are frequently heard. For all of this, they felt grateful to the church community. In addition, husbands after conversion are less likely to be unfaithful, to drugs or alcohol abuse, or to physically assault their wives. All of these problems are addressed in the church preaching. Men are also encouraged to get more involved in the nurturing of their children, and, indeed, one sees men taking care of children, pushing strollers, and taking on such "female" tasks as cooking for church events. Members seem more willing to cross gender lines, at least in terms of task assignment. Similarly, because of financial constraints that require both men and women to work outside the home to survive, the church often acts as a surrogate family, providing for child care. This means that although gender roles have not been dismantled, the church provides opportunities for new arrangements.

Although this literature offers significant insights in order to understand the relation between migration and Pentecostalism, they also have some limitations. First, they tend to analyze factors that are external to the religious praxis. The specific contents of Pentecostal praxis—beliefs and practices—are hardly taken into account. While they show that Pentecostal churches are indeed sources of social and economic support for a variety of newcomer immigrant groups, facilitating the incorporation in the U.S. society, nothing is actually said about the contents of that religious praxis.

Religious praxis—in this case, Latino Pentecostalism—seems only significant for its contribution to the adaptation of people with a Latin American origin in the U.S. society, not as a phenomenon of intrinsic importance as such. In other terms, studies in this approach are interested in what religious praxis does, not what religious praxis is. Another limitation of this approach is that authors differentiate between the society of origin and the host society, conceptualizing each as a container, forgetting that there are actually multiple relations between them.

There are, by contrast, numerous authors claiming that in the contemporary world religious praxis is more than just a vehicle for incorporation and identity reaffirmation. As sociologist Peggy Levitt (2001; 2007; 2013) has pointed out, religion also enables people to stay closely connected to their homeland and to be members of a shared culture, tradition, and faith. This point of view is the cornerstone of the second approach to the study of Pentecostalism and Latino migration: the "religion on the move" approach.

2.2.2. The "Religion on the Move" Approach

This approach has emerged in parallel to the studies on globalization, in which scholars that are interested in religion seek to understand the challenges and opportunities posed by the increasing trends of globalization and particularly transnationalization. Scholars in this approach remark that Pentecostalism has been one of the major success stories of the past several decades of cultural globalization (Robbins 2009). They argue that this version of Christianity focused on the availability of the gifts of the Holy Spirit to all contemporary believers has rapidly spread around the world (Droogers 2001). Besides, they note that Pentecostalism's rapid growth in Latin America, Africa, Asia, and Oceania has turned it into the fastest growing branch of Christianity and a dominant transforming force of Christian demographics. Partly as a consequence of this growth, most Christians now live in the Southern Hemisphere rather than in Europe or North America, the birthplaces of both Christianity and, particularly, Protestantism and Pentecostalism (Robbins 2009; Miller 2013).

Moreover, these authors argue that the relationship between religion and globalization has been controversial since the economic interpretations of globalization have impaired the correct understanding of the relation between religion and globalization (Vasquez and Marquardt 2003; Csordas 2009; Hüwelmeier and Krause 2010). According to them, globalization has often been understood exclusively in economic terms as an ineluctable and monolithic process that, for better or worse, determines every aspect of social life. Csordas (2009) specifies that under this paradigm the relationship between religion and globalization is conceptualized as one between two separate analytic domains. One is the domain of economic globalization, encompassing international organizations, neoliberal economic theory, and the growing importance of the Internet. The other is the sphere of religious praxis, which can be considered as a reaction to globalized economic discourse. As stated by Vasquez and Marquardt (2003), religious convictions and practices appear in the writings of globalization theorists as an antimodernist "fundamentalist" movement that seeks to assert local identity and tradition against the social pathologies generated by global neoliberalism.

Works advancing this view include Comaroff and Comaroff (2001) on the expansion of African Christianity as a form of rationalized and privatized spirituality that individuals purchase as a commodity in a "religion market." There is no question that religion and global capitalism are connected. Nonetheless, the connection is far more complicated than the one presented by these authors. Csordas (2009) considers that it is much more productive to understand globalization as a multidimensional process. In this process, religion, popular culture, politics, and economics coexist simultaneously and are intimately intertwined, as they are in the lives of agents responsible for bringing about globalization. Hence, he stands up for the globalization of religion rather than the dichotomy between religion and globalization.

Within these new conceptualizations, some research regarding mobility also emerged. In this sense, Csordas (2009) has claimed that the globalization of religion is linked to the idea of travel or mobility both in geographical and cultural spaces. He considers that traveling religions rely on portable practices and transposable messages. Hence, in the "religion on the move" approach, circulation and linkages are considered as basic characteristics of religious praxis. It is argued that religious praxis cannot be "understood as a stable set of beliefs and practices rooted in a particular bounded time and space, but as a contingent clustering of diverse elements that come together within to-be-determined space riddled by power and interest" (Levitt 2013, 160). For these authors, religious assemblages made up of individuals objects, technology, and ideas travel at different rates and rhythms, across various levels and scopes of the social fields in which they are embedded.

In parallel to these developments, scholars of the "religion on the move" approach concerned about the growth of Pentecostalism also claim that the current transformation in Christianity is not, as it was in its earliest phase of globalization, the result of the power of a Church that was the dominant world institution of its time. The current wave of Christian globalization and transnationalization is rather driven by the rapid and dramatic spread of Pentecostal or charismatic evangelization by movements, ministries, fellowships, or independent leaders taking advantage of all the newly available travel and communication technologies (Csordas 2009).

According to them, Pentecostal missionary efforts were previously conducted by North American missionaries, who have been generally successful in regions undergoing rapid transformation and subject to extreme economic stratification (Jenkins 2002, 2); however, in recent times a real change has taken place. The very success of the original Pentecostal missions has generated new flows of missionary efforts from the South to the North. A large number of Latin American migrants to the North came precisely from those areas that were the targets of North American missionaries. Many of these migrants carried with them their understanding of Christianity from the South to the North (Miller 2013). This recent rise of "Pentecostal reverse missionary movements" has been the object of growing academic literature. In these studies, Pentecostal missionary flows are portrayed as a new form of religious praxis that draws on a global identity, mass-mediated popular culture as well as on transnational and migrants' networks (Corten and Marshall-Fratani 2001; Droogers 2001; Vasquez and Marquardt 2003; Robbins 2004; Csordas 2009; Levitt 2007).

Within this approach, some authors focused on the study of Pentecostalism and Latin American migration to the United States have analyzed transnational Latino congregations and ministries (Menjivar 1999; Vasquez and Marquardt 2003; Martínez 2013; Danielson 2015). In these studies, Pentecostal organizations are described as both agents and subjects of power in their transnational relationships with the North, rather than as marginal players reacting to forces of globalization that are beyond their control. Nowadays, migration and the development of transnational relations have facilitated the spread and cross-fertilizations of Pentecostal missionary efforts across political boundaries.

In this sense, Cecilia Menjivar (1999, 608-609) has analyzed how religious institutions located in Washington, D.C. and its vicinity shape Salvadoran immigrants' links to their communities of origin, focusing on the Catholic and evangelical churches' organizational structures. By comparing four churches, two Catholic and two Pentecostal, she shows that though the churches in her study are eminently transnational in their broader objectives and they take advantage of the twin processes of multiculturalism at the local level and transnationalism globally, their local institutional responses to these processes vary according to their organizational structures and doctrines. Catholic churches as formally organized entities with a "communitarian" emphasis tend to encourage policies that forge multicultural models based on a pan-ethnic identity as "Latino" in line with non-religious and more politically rooted efforts, trying to become more accessible and relevant to parishioners. While doing so, they relegate the membership's ethnic and national interests to a second plane, discouraging any expression of those interests within the spaces that the church provides. In contrast, Pentecostal churches tend to emphasize the individual's personal relationship to God and a grassroots perspective, which make them malleable organizations that not only accommodate easily to the challenges of transnationalism, but at the same time benefit from such trends to expand their mission. The goal of universalizing their church, shared by both the religious leaders and the members of the congregation themselves, contributes to create institutional social spaces for immigrants to sustain relations with their communities of origin. However, the responses to globalization and transnational processes are not identical in Pentecostal churches. Variables such as ethnic homogeneity/heterogeneity play a significant role. Pentecostal churches with a homogeneous ethnic composition tend to focus their transnational interests and objectives to one place—the place of origin of their adherents—rather than to all corners of the world. Ethnically heterogeneous Pentecostal churches, on the contrary, do not make direct efforts to forge links with one specific place of origin, but instead try to create links to all the members' homelands. In this way, by forging such links, they achieve their universalist objective of "spreading the Word" to as many places as possible. In addition, these churches tend to unite their membership under one umbrella, forging unity. According to Menjivar (1999, 609), "they do not foster a pan-ethnic Latino identity, but rather a new 'Christian' identity, not based on nationality but on the church's beliefs and principles."

Vasquez and Marquardt (2003), in turn, compare and contrast the ways in which gangs and Pentecostal churches help young Salvadorans to respond to dislocations resulting from war, migration, and economic change. According to them, gangs provide vulnerable and dislocated Salvadorans youths with discourses, practices, and forms of organization that enable the reterritorialization of their lives and the reassertion of locality against global forces that have disintegrated their communities and families. At the same time, gangs offer a context in which loyalty and collective identity are central, allowing reaffirmation of the self in an intimate setting. Nevertheless, the localizing and re-ordering resources provided by gangs are conflictive since they operate through the forging of a defensive identity which reverses the rules of the democratic game and fosters social violence manifested by criminal activity and drug addiction. Under the same structural conditions of war, migration, and economic change, Pentecostalism has emerged as an alternative space where the synthesis between self and community can take place. Although Pentecostals are often locked with gangs in a battle for young souls, the two groups share striking similarities in relation to their practices and the unintended consequences of their actions (Vasquez and Marquardt 2003, 120). Both Pentecostal churches and gangs operate through transnational networks leading to a reinscription of locality through the creation of a closely connected community and a strong sense of individual identity. To illustrate how Pentecostal churches provide alternative ways for young Salvadorans to negotiate dislocation and multiple marginality, Vasquez and Marquardt (2003, 134) point out some relevant characteristics of Pentecostalism that make a radical difference in the way Salvadoran gangs function. First, Pentecostal churches operate transnationally due to a mixture of theological and sociological variables. In Pentecostalism, conversion marks a radical transformation, an experience of being born again in Jesus Christ, who redeems the sinner. Actually, gang members, who reject all societal conventions and choose criminality and drug addiction, are among the greatest sinners. Hence, churches that reach out to gang members can prove how the Spirit of God works through them. In addition, as gangs are transnational organizations, churches must follow their potential converts, tracking them across national borders. This is not especially difficult, as most Pentecostal churches are transnational themselves, and, as such, can mobilize their networks of local contacts to deal with the challenges posed by transnational migration. Finally, a genre of evangelical Christian literature called "spiritual warfare" has become very important in the Pentecostal scene, especially regarding the conversion of former gang members. By presenting a repertoire of war-like remedies against the devilish spirits that cause such sins as homosexuality, drug addiction, lust, incest, rape, and murder, the discourse of "spiritual warfare" makes ex-gang members experience an identification with the church as "their new home" or "their new family." The articulation of a family and a place called home is accompanied by the emergence of a new, cleansed sinless self.

Following Droogers's definition of Pentecostalism as a "paradoxical" religion that involves rupture as well as continuity, individualism as well as communitarism, otherworldly eschatology as well as worldly pragmatism, Vasquez and Marquardt (2003, 142) conclude that similar paradoxes take place in the work carried out by transnational Pentecostal churches with gang members in El Salvador and the United States. On the one hand, Pentecostal churches offer resources to "domesticate" the new converts. By reducing the effects of multiple marginalities, Pentecostalism might help to rebuild the Salvadoran fabric of sociality. On the other hand, the same churches, with their language of spiritual warfare, inculcate a habitus of exclusionary difference that has potentially negative consequences for a sending society that is struggling to strengthen the values of solidarity, tolerance, and reciprocity and for migrants seeking full participation in the public sphere in the United States. Thus, Pentecostalism facilitates the articulation of oppositional identities and alternative public spheres, making it possible for Latino migrants to assert agency and locality in the face of powerful reterritorializing forces. However, oppositional identities and alternative public spheres are conflictive and contradictory, sometimes even reproducing exclusionary logics.

Another important study on transnational Latino congregations and ministries is Martínez (2013) on how immigrant-based Latino Pentecostal churches in Southern California minister in transnational networks and how such networks are changing these churches' understanding of their mission, focusing on the transnational network-based ministry of five Pentecostal churches. According to Martínez (2013, 205), Latino Pentecostal churches are leaving behind traditional ways of doing Protestant missions and are using instead models that neither require a great deal of money nor much formal education. These models make ample use of familial and social networks and involve the transnational migrants themselves in mission efforts. From their perspective, international borders are a nuisance, but they do not define a mission. Since Latino Pentecostal churches do not see their ministry in terms of a geographically located parish, they do not see a fundamental difference between their local networks and their international ones. Therefore, they have no problems crossing international borders in their missionary projects. They do missionary work in much the same way that they send remittances to their families and friends. These networks are "permeable, expanding, and fluid" and so become an effective way to experiment with missionary projects, particularly with short-term, concise ones (Martínez 2013, 218). According to Martínez, there are positive outcomes derived from these new missionary models. Since these missions are articulated between informal and personal networks, they are able to avoid many problems of dependency common among Protestant mission projects in Latin America. A local congregation or project is expected to assume from the beginning a certain economic responsibility. In addition, these transnational projects seem to be able to improve the links between the local churches; they do not seem to be perceived as threats to the existing churches. The leaders have limited missionary expertise and, therefore, they have not always reflected on the impact they achieve. But because they have long-term relationships with the local population, some of the potentially negative impact seems to be absorbed in the process of working together. According to Martínez (2013, 219), even though traditional Protestant missionary work will continue, much of the growth of these churches will happen through the work of the migrants described in his study.

While Martínez (2013) offers a view of Latino Pentecostal congregations grounded in the United States whose membership is mainly composed of migrants with a Latin American origin and the transnational patterns they implement in their missionary work, Robert A. Danielson (2015) examines the growth and expansion in the United States and Canada of one of the largest Pentecostal churches in El Salvador, focusing on key elements of transmigrant churches in the current globalized world. Danielson begins the article defining transmigrant churches as groups in which people with a migratory background gather for religious and social reasons while maintaining the language and customs of their home country. At the same time, they keep transnational connections, often looking to the home country for religious leadership, teaching, or financial support. For this type of transnationalism, some scholars have argued that it requires the movement of people back to the country of origin, but according to Danielson (2015, 112) in light of the undocumented situation of many immigrants from Latin America in the United States, a transnational field can be formed only through gifts, telecommunications, and particularly remittances. The story of the development of "Elim" Pentecostal church in El Salvador is a case in point. It is a religious organization that has been following the "cell church model" since 1985, after the approach pioneered by the Korean Pentecostal pastor David Yonggi Cho (114). Based on this "cell structure model," every new convert to Elim is initiated into a 26-week discipleship program that starts with theological training and spiritual formation, but quickly moves into leadership training as well, since every Elim member is viewed as a potential cell leader. According to Danielson (2015, 116), due to this focus on the cell growth model, which empowers lay leadership, its strong spiritual foundation in Pentecostal theology and the tremendous flow of Salvadorans out of their country as immigrants and refugees, Elim has become a transnational immigrant church without any organized mission plan. Hence, several internal key factors have made Elim succeed as a transnational immigrant church. First, Elim trains all its members to be potential leaders. Second, it has created a strong organization that allows gifted leaders to emerge within the church. Third, Elim holds a Pentecostal theology that emphasizes the priesthood of all believers and the gifts of the

Holy Spirit, which allows people with limited educational opportunities, but with natural leadership abilities, to succeed. Fourth, the cell system requires little in the way of financial resources to start and maintain a church.

As we can see, social scientists studying Latino Pentecostalism within the "religion on the move" approach have offered remarkable insights into the conceptualization of religious praxis, connecting people and faith throughout the world. They have also helped to redefine the understanding of global and transnational processes. However, as with the first approach to Pentecostalism and Latino migration, their studies have some limitations. First, the authors have mainly paid attention to the growth of Pentecostalism around the world, relying on external factors rather than on Pentecostalism itself. As in the first approach, authors are mainly interested in what religious praxis does, not in what religious praxis is. Second, they have been focused on organizations and have largely left aside the study of individual participants or religious leaders. While immigration is at the heart of the studies on Latino Pentecostalism in the United States, none of these studies have really analyzed the role of Pentecostal leaders, how they see themselves and the world, and the way they understand their missionary work.

These are, then, the gaps that this dissertation seeks to address: the analysis of the religious praxis itself and the role as religious leaders that individual agents play in the spreading of Pentecostalism from the South to the North. This dissertation analyzes the biographical narratives of seven Guatemalan independent Pentecostal leaders, placing them within their social space—relations and structures—and showing the different practical logics according to which they live. In doing so, the dissertation follows a praxeological approach, which allows the capture of external factors, integrating the specific contents of Pentecostal belief and practice.

The present research study follows an empirical research question: Considering the general context of social conflict, change, and inequality that Guatemalans in Los Angeles have to face, what is the relation between, on the one hand, the social positions of Pentecostal agents and, on the other hand, their religious identities and strategies? In the next chapter, a description of my study, highlighting the praxeological approach I follow, will be presented.

3. Description of the Research

3.1. Theoretical Framework

Religions can be analyzed from multiple perspectives and understood in many ways. They could be seen, for instance, as juxtaposed, discrete, static organizations, each one of them with its own bureaucracy, belief system, moral code, and liturgical rules. Similarly, religion can be seen as a function of the "social system" or of the product of the abstract, utility-maximizing individual. I suggest instead, along the lines of Pierre Bourdieu and Heinrich Schäfer (2005; 2009; 2015), that religions should be understood as examples of social praxis. According to this perspective, any study of "religion" should focus on the subjective (practical sense) and objective (fields, social space) conditions of production of practices and discourses since religious life cannot be separated from the material circumstance in which specific instances of religious behavior and imagination arise and to which they respond.

Hence, the theoretical and methodological frameworks of this dissertation follow a praxeological approach. This praxeological approach is called "Habitus Analysis" and has been developed by Heinrich Schäfer and his team at the Center for the Interdisciplinary Research on Religion and Society (CIRRUS) at Bielefeld University[6].

The Habitus Analysis approach follows several theoretical ideas derived from Pierre Bourdieu's (1977) relational sociology, based on concepts such as *habitus – practical sense – practical logic – field – social space. Habitus* points to dispositions, schemes of perception, judgment, and action; *practical sense* expresses a social sensitivity that constitutes the world as meaningful by spontaneously anticipating its immanent tendencies; *practical logic* refers to the diffuse logic of the lines of action engendered by the habitus, which defines the ordinary relation to the world; while *field* refers to social positions and to stakes, capital, and power involved in these positions, and *social space* refers to styles, economic production, education, and dominance. Following these conceptualizations, according to Bourdieu, *praxis* can be defined as the relation of mutual interdependency between agent and structure, dispositions and positions under the condition of change in time.

---

6 The author of the dissertation is also a member of CIRRUS.

Following the Habitus Analysis approach, religious praxis is understood for the purposes of this dissertation as a product of the operation of affective, cognitive, and bodily dispositions that guide the perception, judgment, and action of social agents (Bourdieu 1980).

These dispositions are the result of conditions and processes of individual and collective socialization and, as such, they structure the way agents perceive and act upon society. In this sense, religious convictions and practices refers to the social conditions of existence: as products, as symbolic transformers, and as practical operators (Schäfer et al. 2016a, 49). This approach makes it possible to attach special analytical importance to religious beliefs and practices and, at the same time, to understand them from the point of view of their multiple relationships with the social life of the participants, their relations with other religious agents, and their positions in society's power relations.

Relying on these theoretical premises, in the following section I will present some considerations regarding Bourdieu's social praxeology, discussing the implications of such an approach for the study of religious phenomena. This theoretical discussion serves to delineate the theoretical and methodological propositions of the "Habitus Analysis" approach.

3.1.1. Praxeological Approach to the Study of Religion

A central aim of Bourdieu's sociology is to overcome the epistemological antinomy between objectivism and subjectivism. In doing so, he proposes an approach called *social praxeology*, which weaves together "structural" and "subjective" elements, relating the worldviews of agents with objective social structures (Bourdieu and Wacquant 1992, 7). Bourdieu's social praxeology starts by pointing out that the social world has a "double life" (Bourdieu 1990). It exists twice: in the "objectivity of the first order" characterized by the distribution of material resources and the means of appropriation of socially scarce goods and values; and in the "objectivity of the second order," in the form of systems of classification, the mental and bodily schemata that function as symbolic templates for the practical activities—conduct, thoughts, feelings, and judgment—of social agents (Bourdieu and Wacquant 1992, 7). For Bourdieu, objectivism and subjectivism are not antinomies, but rather complementary points of view.

According to Bourdieu and Wacquant (1992, 7), to capture the "objectivity of the first order," one has to return to the strength of the objectivist or structuralist point of view. The objectivist or "social physics" approach—represented by Durkheim in *Suicide* (1968), by Saussurean linguistics in *Course in general linguistics* (1966), and by Lévi-Straussian structuralism in *Structural Anthropology* (1963)—states that social science aims to establish objective regularities (structures, laws, systems of relations, etc.). Nevertheless, there are some caveats in an objectivistic approach that should be avoided.

Lacking a principle of generation of the regularities, objectivistic approaches tend to reify the structures they construct by treating them as autonomous entities endowed with the ability to "act" as historical agents. In doing so, they forget individual consciences and wills (Bourdieu and Wacquant 1992, 8). For Bourdieu, a materialist science of society must recognize that the consciousness and interpretations of agents are essential components of the reality of the social world. Individuals have a practical knowledge of the world and invest this practical knowledge in their ordinary activity.

To deal with the "objectivity of the second order," subjectivist or constructivist approaches—represented by Sartre (1956) in *Being and Nothingness*, by ethnomethodology and by rational choice—offer significant elements since they allege that the social world can be conceived as the emergent product of the decisions, actions, and cognitions of conscious, alert individuals to whom the world is given as immediately familiar and meaningful. These approaches are also somewhat problematic. Understanding social structures as the mere aggregate of individual strategies and acts of classification does not allow to see the objective configurations that these strategies perpetuate or challenge (Bourdieu and Wacquant 1992, 8). Although it is true that social agents construct their social reality, the social structure they find themselves in, it is given and not created by them.

Thus, objectivism and subjectivism, structural necessity and individual agency constitute false antinomies. Each pole in these paired opposites actually reinforces the other. Bourdieu's social praxeology is, on the other hand, an excellent way to recapture the intrinsically double reality of the social world. Bourdieu's general social theory spans the whole range between subjective and objective conditions of practices, thus facilitating an appropriate understanding of these practices as *relations* between these conditions. Bourdieu's main theoretical concepts can be understood as a continuum between a subjective and an objective pole following the sequence *Habitus – practical sense – practical logic – field – social space.*

This clearly bridges the gap between signs and things, agents and structures, the symbolic and the material, dispositions and positions. Bourdieu's praxeology is, therefore, a plausible theory for the study of different social phenomena, and religious phenomena are not an exception.

3.1.2. Bourdieu and the Study of Religion: Towards a Religious Praxis

In general terms, Bourdieu fruitfully developed his praxeological approach in the field of cultural sociology, but he focused very marginally on the sociology of religion. In the late 1980s and early 1990s, he published "Legitimation and Structured Interests in Weber's Sociology of Religion" (Bourdieu 1987) and "Genesis and structure of the religious field" (Bourdieu 1991). Both articles may be taken as an attempt to interpret the cognitive structure of religious beliefs within the larger conditions of knowledge, framed by differentiation, domination, and practices. But his way to deal with religious praxis is problematic.

His approach provides an insufficient concept of religion since he only understands religious praxis as the consecration and disguise of social interests and, ultimately, of domination. This understanding is not completely mistaken. Religious praxis can work this way, but this is not the only way religious praxis works. As we saw in the previous chapter, there are many functions that can be fulfilled by religious praxis.

In order to overcome Bourdieu's constrains, Schäfer (2015) in his *Habitus Analysis* approach has adjusted the general praxeological theory to the empirical study of religious practices and beliefs. According to his study, Bourdieu's general praxeology offers very suitable theoretical concepts to inquire into the relations of religious beliefs and practices within a wider social structure (Schäfer et al. 2016a). In his view, religious praxis looks just like a specific kind of praxis that formally operates in the same way as other forms of praxis, whether economic, political, or any other. Hence, religion or, from a praxeological perspective, *religious praxis*, is not a *sui generis* experience, distinct from other dimensions of experience that we use to call "profane."

The study of religious phenomena following Bourdieu's praxeological approach entails a fundamental rethinking of what "religion" is and of what it means to be "religious." This particular analytical perspective implies a conception of religion as human praxis, in which one is concerned with what people do with religious practices, and what they make of themselves and their worlds as followers of these religious practices. Religion is praxis, mental and material praxis, operating through signs and material elements. It involves beliefs and practices as much as it involves the social conditions and struggles in which people live.

In this sense, a religious praxis is never a preexisting, external, and unreachable realm in relation to human activity, but rather a multifaceted, vibrant reality in constant interaction with its environment, continuously exposed to both internal and external resources, limitations, tendencies, and pressures (Maduro 1996). People are caught up—body, soul, and mind—in their religious praxis, an activity that people share (or dispute) with their neighbors.

At every concrete juncture of its history in a given time of society, a religious praxis is the singular outcome of an interaction between its own distinctive traditions and the surrounding conventions, conflicts, demands, and pressures (Maduro 1996). Thus, one side of a religious praxis is what people believe; the other side is the power and capability to act in relation to the social opportunities and constraints in which they are situated (Schäfer et al. 2016a, 153). Hence, the study of beliefs or "belief systems" apart from actual human activity is absurd because beliefs—even the most crucial—have no stable or intrinsic values that can be defined outside the context of their use. Religious agents are best characterized not only by what they believe but also by what they do.

Once the meaning of religious praxis is established, the question that emerges is related to how one can recapture the intrinsically double reality of the social world when studying religious phenomena. Following Schäfer and his Habitus Analysis approach, one way to combine cognitive and material aspects in a significant form is by looking at experiences of contingency and the interpretations that social agents give to them. Such experiences range from the perception of one's own finitude and the perspective of death to concrete social crises and threats such as economic scarcity, military repression, and ecological catastrophes (Schäfer et al. 2016a, 154).

Any human being reacts to such experiences by interpreting them, ascribing meaning to them. From a practical perspective, they do not carry out any intellectual and reflexive exercise, but rather they react spontaneously, and most often even unconsciously ascribe meaning to experiences. It is the process of meaning ascription that transforms social experience since ascribing meaning to it opens new perspectives of action. This is precisely the operation that generates identity and strategy (Schäfer et al. 2016a, 154).

Religious agents interpret social experience in the same operational mode as non-religious agents do: They ascribe meaning to it. The difference resides only in the fact that religious agents employ different semantic contents. It is precisely in these moments of contingency when a religious praxis gains significance. In a way, the particular "truth" of a religious praxis is especially apprehended by living it in the midst of a crisis; this is how, and where, God becomes real to religious people (Orsi 1997, 9). Religious praxis primarily copes with contingence and conflict by referring to transcendent beings or forces. It constructs religious meaning (Schäfer et al. 2016a, 152).

As religious agents, individuals and organizations interpret experience by means of a promise of "salvation," making reference to a transcendent entity (Schäfer et al. 2016a, 154). For them, "salvation" can be a ritual statement of authority, or a diviner's prognosis, or a miraculous healing in the expectation of a "new heaven and a new earth" (Schäfer et al. 2016a, 154). Invoking "salvation," they imagine a transcendent reality or entity, which can produce different social effects, from legitimizing domination and generating social cohesion to revolution and desires for radical social change (Schäfer et al. 2016a, 154).

The crucial point in the idea of salvation is the reference to a transcendent entity, to an "otherworldly" reality in Weber's sense. It is precisely the idea of a transcendent reality what marks the difference between religious movement and other modern social movement since religious agents do not primarily project social change into a more or less distant future, but rather, they derive their authority and orientation by referring to a transcendent entity, which they claim as existing, and to whom they ascribe certain properties. "Transcendence" in religious praxis is not an empty term. As Schäfer, Seibert, Tovar and Köhrsen (2016a, 155) point out, "religious agents tie the transcendent sphere to some idea of divine beings or 'superhuman powers.' They interpretively relate 'earthly' experiences to transcendent beings and realms, holding up the distinctions between each one of them. Transcendence turns into something concrete and practical."

From a praxeological perspective, it is precisely the relation between "earthly" experiences and "otherworldly" interpretations that creates religious identities, strategies, and finally the praxis itself. Therefore, references to transcendence can be conceived as "operators of practical sense and of practical logic" (Schäfer et al. 2016a, 155). The specificity of religious praxis does not lie in separating religious from nonreligious spheres or religious symbols from material processes; its specificity rather consists in interpreting non-religious and material processes in a religious way, emphasizing the distinction between "worldly" and "otherworldly" powers (Schäfer et al. 2016a, 155).

The reference to transcendence made by religious agents is, therefore, the analytical point that allows the identification of a discourse as religious. In every interview or speech given by a religious person, there are usually positive references to a transcendent entity—even if it is only referred to by the term "God." These reference points to the crucial element from which one can reconstruct the structures of meaning, and thus the forming of religious identities and strategies (Schäfer et al. 2016a, 156).

Nonetheless, the practical performance of religious agents does not rely simply on the semantic content of a given religious movement or disseminated institution. Religious praxis, instead, hinges on agent-specific positions within the social structure and the ascription of religious meaning to them (Schäfer et al. 2016a, 156). Hence, religious agents employ particular contents in response to particular events and circumstances. It is the relation between particular experience and specific religious content that makes agents develop their distinct religious identities and strategies, including their different understandings of the relation between transcendent forces and society or history and, of course, different strategies in social conflicts and competition (Schäfer et al. 2016a, 156). In this sense, religious identities are dependent on experiential contexts, and even if agents share the same semiotic inventory, each agent can develop different religious identities and strategies based on the context in which they live.

Taking into account that the process of interpreting experience and creating identities and strategies in religious matters is entirely the same as in any other form of social praxis, religious and non-religious perceptions, judgments, and action blend into one another, and religious interpretation and experience characteristically display different capacities in the face of the same social conditions and situations (Schäfer et al. 2016a, 156). In consequence, religious identities and strategies can provide an alternative and sometimes more effective ways of coping with challenges.

When immigrants are compelled to rebuild their worlds and themselves endlessly and relentlessly with constantly shifting grounds and in brutal economic circumstances, religious praxis has been the one primary way to achieve it. For instance, some of the most characteristic expressions of religiosity have been crafted in response to massive population movements due to modernization and industrialization processes not only in the United States (Orsi 1997, 9) but also in Latin America (Droogers 1998, 10).

Within hermeneutical and pragmatist readings of Bourdieu, the production of meaning is similar to both religious and non-religious praxis. Therefore, the two of them can be integrated into a theory and method of practical logic, which explains the cognitive dispositions, identities and strategies of the agents, as well as the similarities between the two forms of praxis and the particularities of each one of them. In order to better understand religious praxis, the concepts related to Bourdieu's praxeology and the form in which they are appropriated by the Habitus Analysis will be presented in some detail in the next section.

3.1.3. Between Embodied and Objectified Conditions of Praxis

In the introductory remarks, it was revealed that Bourdieu's praxeology suggests a theory design in terms of a continuum between embodied and objectified conditions of praxis, such as *habitus – practical sense – practical logic – fields – social space*. Following the concepts of this continuum, which go from the subjective side of the social agent to the objective side of the structural conditions, it is possible to explain how the convictions and beliefs of a person or a group relate to the distribution of material goods and power and thus to objective constraints and opportunities.

The View from the Agent: Habitus and Practical Sense

Bourdieu[7] conceived of *habitus* as a structured system of cognitive, emotional, and bodily dispositions which "integrating past experiences, functions at every moment as matrix of perceptions, appreciations and actions and makes possible the achievement of infinite tasks" (Bourdieu 1977, 214).

Habitus refers to dispositions, schemes of perception, judgment and action, language as well as strategies. This strategy-generating principle enables agents to cope with unforeseen and ever-changing situations, act-

7 See particularly Bourdieu 1990a, 53. See also Bourdieu 1977, 72–158; and Bourdieu 1998a, 75–91.

ing as a creative transformer of experience and a generator of partly stable and partly new, even novel, practices and strategies.

According to Bourdieu, people acquire their dispositions to perceive, to judge, and to act in persistent processes of socialization, through communication and interaction with others, under the condition of social differences in terms of interests and power, and in the flow of time (Schäfer et al. 2016a, 159). Feelings, words, concepts, and even mental images constitute, therefore, dispositions. Dispositions are never situated outside of praxis. They are not pure ideas, but rather they respond to experiences and are shaped by them. In turn, habitus dispositions form the experienced world through practices that follow a practical logic and may correspond equally to spontaneous impulses or strategic planning.

In addition, they are linked to one another. For example, perception activates judgment, and judgment activates action. One disposition is triggered by the activation of another, and so forth, following a certain logic. This is precisely true in the case of religious praxis in which religious dispositions may trigger feelings and actions with regard to politics, economy, or sexuality, and vice versa (Schäfer et al. 2016a, 160).

According to Schäfer et al. (2016a, 160), the concept of habitus is better understood in terms of a network of dispositions that are linked in manifold ways and are activated interdependently. Seen as a network, the dispositions of the habitus are able to transcend socially established discursive boundaries since interconnected dispositions provide cognitive content and emotional energy to guide the practical action of the agents.

Bourdieu introduces the concept of *practical sense* in order to define the relation between the social agent and the world. For him, this relation is not that between a subject (or a consciousness) and an object, but rather a relation of "ontological complicity" between habitus, as the socially constituted principle of perception and appreciation, and the world in which it is determined (Bourdieu and Wacquant 1992, 20).

This understanding serves to grasp the situatedness or involvement within a context, of the habitus in the concrete life-worlds of the agents. Leaning on Husserl (2014), Wittgenstein (2001) and Merleau-Ponty's (1962) phenomenological traditions, practical sense expresses certain social sensitivity, which guides the agents (Bourdieu and Wacquant 1992, 20). It refers to the situational affectedness of the dispositions of perception, judgment, and action, according to the social conditions and practices of other agents, as a given agent is immersed in practical relations with other agents. Hence, through the "sense of their place," agents exclude themselves from goods, places, or even contacts to persons, which they are excluded from anyway by the social structure (Bourdieu 2010, 473).

With their practical sense and feeling for the game, social agents partake in struggles in different fields of praxis (Bourdieu 1990b, 66). The practical sense is anchored in the dispositions of the habitus; it constantly deals with the conditions in fields that generate practices and discourses, according to the deep structure of its practical logic and to the logic that dominates the praxis in these fields. Thus, practical logic refers to the regular process of cognitive, and emotional, transformation between experience and interpretation that operates on the agent's side of praxis. In this process, interpretation does not mean an intellectual act of reflection but rather the more or less implicitly spontaneous cognitive appropriation of the "world" in everyday life (Bourdieu and Wacquant 1992, 20; Schäfer et al. 2016a, 161).

Following the Habitus Analysis approach, the practical sense can be understood from a theoretical point of view as the embodied disposition of the habitus in action. From a methodological point of view, the utterances of the practical sense—especially the semantics—are the material through which to explore the deep structures of meaning in the dispositions of the habitus—that is, the embodied conditions of discourse-production, and therefore the hidden logic of discourses (Schäfer et al. 2016a, 161). However, the objective conditions in which a discourse is produced are also indispensable for understanding its social effects and meaning.

View from the Objective Conditions: Fields, and Social Space

Bourdieu provides two widely known conceptions to deal with social structure: "field" and "social space." The concept of *field* addresses the functional differentiation of societies, highlighting that each differentiated "field" functions as an arena of struggle between specialists to win supporters from the non-producers' group. *Social space* refers, in turn, to social stratification through a model of differentiated distribution of capital in a given society in such a way that styles or habitus formations correspond to the spatial positions determined from the most important types of capital. According to him, a differentiated society is not a coherent totality integrated by systematic functions, a common culture, crisscrossing conflicts, or an overarching authority, but rather an ensemble of relatively autonomous spheres of "play" that cannot be collapsed under an overall societal logic, be it of capitalism or modernity (Bourdieu and Wacquant 1992, 20).

Following Weber's concept of life orders such as economy, politics, religion, or law, he points out that each *field* prescribes its particular values and possesses its own regulative principles. These principles define a socially structured space in which agents struggle, depending on the position they occupy in that space, either to change or to preserve its boundaries and forms (Bourdieu and Wacquant 1992, 20). Thus, a field consists of a set of objective and historical relations between positions anchored in certain forms of power (Bourdieu and Wacquant 1992, 16).

Based on this concise definition, three properties of the field should be highlighted. First, a field is a patterned system of objective forces (like a magnetic field), a relational configuration endowed with a specific gravity imposed on all the objects and agents that enter in it.

Second, when the field is a simultaneous space of conflict and competition, like a battlefield, in which experts endowed with different amounts of relevant capital with different field-specific power compete to establish a monopoly over the species of capital that are effective within it: cultural authority in the artistic field, scientific authority in the scientific field, sacerdotal authority in the religious field, and the power to decree the hierarchy and "conversion rates" between all forms of authority in the field of power.

In the course of these struggles, the mere shape and division of the field becomes a central stake because to alter the distribution and relative weight of forms of capital is equivalent to modifying the structure of the field. This gives any field a historical dynamism and malleability that avoids the inflexible determinism of classical structuralism. (Bourdieu and Wacquant 1992, 17). Lastly, as fields are conceived as relatively autonomous from one another, the conception of a field serves to understand the specific logics of the praxis that dominate a given field; religious reproduction thereby works differently from economic or artistic reproduction (Schäfer et al. 2016a, 163).

In order to model the religious field, Bourdieu's model of the field of cultural production (1983) constitutes an excellent example. Bourdieu's field of cultural production is designed as a two-dimensional model, with one axis representing the achievement of eminence (*arrivée*) and the other standing for authenticity (Schäfer et al. 2016b, 191).

Based on these two variables, achievement and authenticity, it is possible to represent a religious field. In the case of the religious field, the achievement of eminence points to the relation between the performers and the audience of a religious organization and can be described as its level of organizational complexity; while religious authenticity represents public credibility as an agent of religion. In Chapter 5, both variables are presented with more detail.

The conception of the *social space* (e.g., Bourdieu 2010) is presented in the idea of *Distinction*. It focuses on social power relations and models the overall social structure according to the distribution of economic and cultural capital. For Bourdieu (2010), the social space is made up of different dimensions, which can be political, economic, educational, cultural, or religious. These dimensions are constructed on the basis of principles of differentiation or distribution of the particular capital that is active in the social universe under consideration. Using this conception, one can locate the agents in the social power structure according to the volume and the structure of the capital they hold, understanding the possibilities and constraints at stake for the social agents in partaking of social life (Schäfer et al. 2016a, 163).

The conceptions of field and social space are especially relevant when they are related to the conceptions of practical sense and practical logic. By connecting these concepts, the embodied dispositions of given agents and the practical logic of their linguistic utterances and practices can be interpreted within the context of social differentiation and power relations. In methodological terms, the dispositions that form the habitus of a given agent can be projected onto these models of fields or of the social space, relating certain dispositions, practices, and discourses to specific positions in a field or within the social space (Schäfer et al. 2016a, 163).

In conclusion, this dissertation, based on a hermeneutical and pragmatist reading of Bourdieu, follows a theory and method, "Habitus Analysis," which serves to grasp and explain the cognitive dispositions, identities, and strategies of religious agents. This approach is applied to a semi-structured interview that aimed at capturing the religious production of meaning based on the specific logic where the agent relates to his beliefs and experiences in different areas of his/her daily life (Schäfer 2009). The forms of verbalization of both experiences and religious interpretations are understood as semantic operators of habitus dispositions.

Following this approach, it can be seen how symbolic-religious operations produce transformations of perception, evaluation, and strategy, adapted to the specific processes of identification, distinction, and formation of religious identities. The approach also distinguishes analytically between two types of transformations that constitute the productivity of habitus: those that go from the experiential to the interpretative, and those that go from the interpretative to the experiential. In the first case, we say that identity is produced, while, in the second, we talk of strategy.

The analysis of the correspondences between different religious habitus and social relations allows an understanding of the different ways of producing religious sense within the framework of the prevailing power relations on two levels: first, according to the position of a religious agent in the social space, measured by his economic and cultural capital (Bourdieu 2010); and second, by their individual participation and position in the power struggles of the religious field (Bourdieu 1998, Seibert 2010). With these concluding remarks, we finish the theoretical discussion. In the next session, we will turn to the methodological approach that will be followed in order to grasp the religious meanings and social position of Guatemalan transnational independent Pentecostal leaders.

3.2. Methodological Framework

The sociological inquiry into the impact of the current processes of globalization, transnationalization, and mobility in the production and transformation of religious praxis does not just enlarge and generate new fields of research about the dynamics of religious exchange, transfer, and interdependence. It also has methodological implications about which is the proper methodological approach to analyze these social transformations.

This is specially so in the case of the qualitative and ethnographic research approach. Social qualitative researchers and anthropologists have traditionally conducted fieldwork among people in small rural areas, often thinking of their informants as being part of the local habitat and usually considering that culture within a territorially confined and discrete unit that could be examined without paying attention to any interference from the outside world (Gupta and Ferguson 1997).

Taking this into account, an obvious question is what can bring an ethnographical perspective to the study of global mobility processes. In my dissertation, I argue that ethnography indeed provides the researcher with a highly relevant tool to study global processes such as transnational religious praxis and transnational religious leader's mobility. Nevertheless, I also suggest that the study of religious agents and practices in movement raises new and very different research questions to those of traditional ethnographic research. How do we study people in movement? How do we localize it in numerous physical settings and examine the relationships between these localities? How do we analyze people's movements between different places while observing their social practice and identity constructions in particular locations?

Next, I will present the methodological steps that I have followed in order to answer these questions. My intention is, thus, to elicit the methodology that has guided my research in an attempt to produce quality and transparency, allowing the reader to reconstruct the conditions under which the knowledge presented here was generated (Flick 1998, 243).

First, I will deal with the reconstruction of the process for developing appropriate methods and collecting relevant data. I have departed from the premise that every research process must be understood as an interactive process of knowledge production. I discuss in this section the issues of field entry, the research situation per se, and questions of trust and confidentiality. From a qualitative social research perspective, these processes already produce knowledge and reveal first insights into the structuration of the field under research. The second section deals with the most important type of data that I use in my research: biographical narratives. Last but not least, the third section addresses the process of analysis and writing, focusing on how different methods and data were integrated.

3.2.1. The Fieldwork

Between February and July 2013, I conducted fieldwork in Guatemala City and Los Angeles, CA, both urban settings where I implemented ethnographical research on the life of Guatemalan independent Pentecostal leaders in the inter-American space articulated between Guatemala and Los Angeles. This in itself brings to light the methodological challenge of such a project. How do I study Guatemalan independent Pentecostal leaders, who seem to be in movement most of the time because of the divine call they have received to expand the Gospel? How do I analyze people's movements between different places while observing their social practice and identity constructions in particular locations? And how can one be successful in this research enterprise following the principles, theories, and methodologies of qualitative research in an ethnographic tradition?

One of the aims of qualitative research is to reconstruct the meaningfully lived worlds of agents' daily lives, highlighting their "view point" (Flick 2007, 10). However, as I have already said, my research took a very different form than that of classical ethnographic research, which is based on permanent and long-term presence and participation in the field of research, usually in rural settings (Malinowski 2014). My research on the life of Guatemalan Pentecostal missionaries and their religious labor took place in the urban settings of Guatemala City and Los Angeles County. Both of them are physical settings for multisite research.

Being in these urban settings, I was confronted with fragmented environments, which many times only offered the opportunity to an "encounter" or meeting under unexpected conditions with a person/interviewee (Spiegel 2010, 35). Therefore, much of my work consisted in creating such encounters. For that purpose, I began following the logic of theoretical sampling. Theoretical sampling entailed selecting participants according to specific characteristics which are relevant for the research and the analytical framework of the study (Glaser and Strauss 2006, 48). This implied that before conducting research, researchers have to consider some dimensions to delimit who were the appropriate participants for their studies. In the case of this study, it was essential to analyze theoretical, geographical, and temporal aspects.

Regarding the theoretical dimension, I began by defining who is a missionary from the South and establishing the research goals, which as mentioned before were associated to the analysis of beliefs and their relation with the social positions of these religious leaders.

Concerning the geographical dimension, the research focused on missionaries from Guatemala working in Los Angeles. The reasons for this selection were that Guatemala is a country which has experienced remarkable religious transformations in the last decades. As described in the introduction, in the 1960s more than 90% of its population was Catholic. In 2014, more than 45% of its population recognized themselves as Protestants, particularly Pentecostals (Pew 2014). Los Angeles County has been the leading destination of Guatemalan migratory flows since the 1970s (Hamilton and Stoltz Chinchilla 2001). This combination of religious transformation, constant growth of Pentecostalism, and massive migratory flows made the case of Guatemalan independent Pentecostal leaders working in Los Angeles an excellent opportunity to analyze the experiences and the meaning of being a missionary from the South working in the North. Therefore, with respect to the temporal dimension, the study focused on the period between 1980 and 2014. These years are crucial for understanding the emergence of Guatemalan missionaries working in the United States.

Once these considerations were established, to generate "encounters" that facilitate the contact with potential interviewees, I reviewed the previous work carried out by CIRRUS by the University of Bielefeld. In these studies, I found information about Guatemalan Pentecostal leaders who were involved in the transnational expansion of their churches. Once in Guatemala, the original method to establish such "moments of encounter" were phone calls to the Guatemalan Pentecostal organizations where I was able to contact some Pentecostal leaders. They allowed me to carry out observations in their churches and talked to me about the history of the organizations and their life as missionaries. A particularly noteworthy contact was Alvaro Sanchez, pastor of a Pentecostal church with thousands of members and the person in charge of the international expansion of the church, which had already established congregations in El Salvador, Costa Rica, Mexico, and the United States. He invited me to travel with him to Los Angeles. Thanks to Alvaro Sanchez, it was possible to identify the next interviewee, implementing a snowball effect (Miles and Huberman 1994), which consisted of building networks and interactive linkages in the field itself, following the indications provided by former interviewees.

I used snowball sampling because the subjects of the study were limited to a very small subgroup and hard to locate. To acquire the appropriate information from the interviewees, it was necessary to create a trusting relationship with them. A good start was to have been introduced by someone they already trusted. It was also clear that snowball sampling implied some risks; for instance, there may be a bias in the sample. To reduce this risk, after the analysis of the initial interviews, other participants were selected. This time, I paid attention to specific characteristics such as gender, ethnic background, time of arrival in Los Angeles, and their legal status. I did so in order to interview leaders who could contradict the initial findings. The implementation of these sampling techniques helped to construct a diverse sample, making the collected information rich and wide-ranging. The concentration on pastors and church leaders allowed me, within a manageable sample, to deal with a significant variety of people from different ethnic and denominational backgrounds. As other studies tend to concentrate on one or two churches, I felt that a cross-sectional study focused on pastors and leaders of numerous churches could better illuminate what a missionary from the South might be.

Reflecting on my fieldwork, I can say that pastors and leaders were the people whom I knew best and with whom I interacted daily. Based on these everyday encounters, I was able to build trusting relationships with them and, therefore, I could expect that they would talk to me openly. Although many of them had to combine their religious activities with a secular job to be able to sustain their families and, therefore, had to attend their congregations, prepare the sermons, and deal with the bureaucratic and logistic work generated by their independent churches in their free time, they always offered me some hours to talk about their churches and their lives. My contact with other church members was much more limited due to their legal status and their fears of being reported to migration authorities and being deported. My role as an observer with a brief stay in Los Angeles did not help to assuage those fears.

Interviews and observations in their congregations constituted singular "moments of encounter" (Spiegel 2010, 35), which produced a dense fabric of different sorts of data. Nevertheless, the awareness of a social distance between myself and their social space remained every time I concluded an interview with a Pentecostal leader and every time I left the place of the reunion of a Pentecostal congregation. Although I have some similarities with my interviewees—I was born in Colombia, Spanish is also my mother tongue and I have a migratory experience in Spain and Germany—my Catholic background turned me into a potential convert in the eyes of my interviewees. They mostly obliged, devoting a lot of efforts in trying to convert me to their faith. These efforts took the form of long conversations about the state of my soul; affable suggestions to welcome the Holy Spirit into my life at every point during my research stay; or even numerous offers of baptisms in nearby swimming pools or even directly in the Pacific Ocean. I politely declined each offer, hoping that my unwillingness to convert would not create a distance between us. Quite the opposite happened—the more I politely declined offers of salvation, the more engaged my informants became in my research. They wondered how someone could make such probing questions about Pentecostal Christianity and spend so much time at the church if I were not actually on the way to conversion. Fortunately, the Pentecostal logic of conversion holds that only

God knows the time of salvation, and that salvation is always a possibility–even for the most skeptical person.

Facing a certain precariousness and fragmentation in my research field, questions about where to locate and how to operationalize the research "sites" that were relevant for my concrete research topic emerged. I decided to follow two strategies. On the one hand, I geographically focused my research site in the place of reunion of the congregations. On the other hand, I stretched the concept of "site" beyond the physical space to include elements of a multi-sited research methodology. In his article on "multi-sited ethnography," George Marcus (1995, 96-97) has argued that in order to "examine the circulation of cultural meanings, objects and identities in diffuse time-space" ethnography "has taken unexpected trajectories in tracing cultural formation across and within multiple sites of activity" and has developed "strategies of quite literally following connections, associations and putative relationships," which constitute the "very heart of designing multi-sited ethnographic research." Therefore, Marcus argues that the researcher herself has to follow the global flows and he develops a concise research program for multi-sited ethnography. The techniques of *follow the people* and *follow the biography* turned out to be quite relevant for my own research on Guatemalan Pentecostal missionaries.

First, in order to broaden the spatial dimension of my research field, I decided to use the technique *follow the agents*. As mentioned before, the contact with Brother Alvaro Sánchez allowed me not only to contact other international Guatemalan leaders in Guatemala and Los Angeles, but also to follow him in missionary campaigns. After some conversations, we arranged to travel together to the border between Guatemala and Mexico and then to Los Angeles, where he participated in preaching campaigns. Once in Los Angeles, I met another Guatemalan leader, Marcos Gonzalez. I travelled with him to Tijuana and participated in one of his preaching campaigns there. By doing this, I could follow the movements of these Pentecostal leaders. Following the people is one possible way to grasp the translocal nature of the field under study. If social agents who are engaged in the production, dissemination and transformation of the field under study are spatially mobile, and socio-religious practices are produced in several and distinct locations, our research has to consider these different sites of production.

Secondly, *following the biography* became a further method to grasp the connections between the different sites and arenas of Pentecostal praxis.

Numerous studies in migration have already shown that the focus on biographies and trajectories is a very fruitful approach as it shows how different localities were woven together by religious praxis and embedded into the biographical continuity of everyday life (see Paerregaard 2008; Levitt 2007).

In my research on Guatemalan independent Pentecostal leaders in Los Angeles, the analysis of biographies turned out to be an important method for gaining access to the trajectories and interdependencies of different socio-religious elements in the process of being a reverse missionary. More concretely, the focus on the diachronic character of agency makes biographical methods useful instruments for research on religious movements. Religious movements, like any social movement, entail the articulation of individual agency and collective action, of personal and social change.

Seven interviews were conducted in order to collect biographies and trajectories of individual Guatemalan Pentecostal leaders which shed light on their social backgrounds and motivations for engaging in the mission to expand the gospel beyond the borders of their country of origin. These narrative biographical interviews with Pentecostal leaders whom I met in Guatemala and Los Angeles were conducted mostly in the premises of their congregations. In three cases, I was invited to visit the leaders at their homes where I ended up conducting the interviews.

3.2.2. Biographical Narratives

There is a lively theoretical and methodological debate regarding the kind of insights that narrated life stories are able to generate and what kind of information can be gathered using a biographical approach (Schütze 1976; Rosenthal 2004, 2006; Cornejo, Mendoza, and Rojas 2008). This debate also became relevant for the analysis and reconstruction of biographical narrations of Guatemalan Pentecostal leaders collected for this study. Are these narratives a direct expression of the life experiences of the narrator, which grant the researcher with a chronology of a life and insights into the agent's frameworks of action in the past? Are these narratives entirely expressions of current cultural and social artifacts shaped by the narrator's location, which provide insights into the interviewee's strategies of self-image in her present situation? Or to put it into more practical terms: Do sequences about participation in missionary campaigns when they were young, which are part of biographical interviews with a Guatemalan Pentecostal missionary, generate insights into the youth of this religious leader, or do they generate instead knowledge about how this evangelist perceives his/her youth as an adult person? Or is the narrative of a Guatemalan Pentecostal missionary the history of a boy or girl who became a religious preacher? Or is it the story of a Pentecostal missionary who looks back on their youth and evaluates their life from the present location? These questions are linked to central issues in empirical social research: the dualism of agency and structure, the relation between experience and narrative, and the relation between life and the textual narrative of that life. The answers to the questions above will depend on the epistemological approach followed by the researcher.

From an objectivist perspective, the biographical narration constitutes a window on the objective facts of the agent's life, to be treated as a simple communicative act of a real chronology. This approach has been considered "a biographical illusion" by different authors (Bourdieu 1990a; Pereira Fernandez 2011). According to Bourdieu, biographical narrations suffer from a dangerous problem of subjectivism that leads the biographer to a series of pitfalls or illusions in the attempt to give an interpretive coherence to the life of his interviewee.

The first illusion mentioned by Bourdieu refers to the belief that one's trajectory might account for a unique historical process and is not in fact a product of structural constraints that weigh on the disposition of the subjects. The second illusion alludes to a tendency in objectivist biographers to consider that the trajectory of one individual has a chronological and lineal evolution, in which events are tied to one another and directed toward the fulfillment of a final end, giving the idea of a life as a teleological and mono-causal process. It is based on the assumption of a totally autonomous agent as a planner of his/her own biography. The third illusion refers to the belief that individuals have such identities, which are able to remain stable without considering the circumstances, times and places, denying, thus, the plurality of identities, contradictions, ambiguities, frictions and inconsistencies a person may have.

In short, all these illusions, which are characteristics of the interviewer or the biographer, could lead to the false conclusion that a person has a coherent life trajectory, forcing impossible articulations and connecting unrelated events with the aim of giving coherence to the life of his interviewee.

These criticisms of an objectivist and simplistic model of biographies and life stories are, in general terms, very convincing. Actually, they are crucial to underscore the constructed character of biographies as well as they correctly point out the dangers that a social researcher has to face when working with biographical narratives. Nevertheless, I find less convincing Bourdieu's arguments about how to face the epistemological problems of the biographical method (Bourdieu 1986). Accepting his proposal would amount to moving from the subjectivist risk to the reductionist danger of structuralism, eliminating what is specific to the biographical genre: its subjectivity, its concern for the particular, its irreducible anti-nomothetic character, and its special historicity.

As François Dosse states (2007, 213), "the goal is, therefore, to objectify the subjectivity and subjectify the objectivity", making efforts to escape the false dilemma between individual-structure, subjective-objective, particular-general, and so on. In an attempt to go further from these polar dichotomies, Dosse argues that it is necessary to understand that a good alternative to biography would be the use of medium-range theoretical models, that is, dynamic and flexible approaches, capable of capturing biographical trajectories without losing sight of the structural dynamics. Thus, the problems of subjectivity could be overcome, and the impoverishment of structuralist schemes about the analysis of a particular life might be avoided (Dosse 2007, 213-215). From a perspective that conceives of biography as a privileged ground for scientific experimentation, Dosse accepts the criticism of biographical subjectivism proposed by Bourdieu, but instead of seeing it as an epistemological dead-end, he conceives of it as a necessary crossroads to humanize the social sciences.

Taking into account that Bourdieu had not developed methods and models for qualitative research on human attitudes, especially not for research by means of interviews, my argument is that a study based on experience and agency can put Bourdieu's criticisms of biographical methods aside and draw instead on his concepts of habitus, practical sense, and practical logic as crucial instruments for developing medium-range theoretical models to grasp processes of social structuration, negotiation, and transformation related to Pentecostal reverse missionary flows. This is precisely the purpose of using the "Habitus Analysis Approach."

Pierre Bourdieu (1998) points to the way in which corporal and discursive sediments of social experiences shape current frameworks of action, allowing that biographical narratives might be conceived as important elements for the relationship between structure and agency. Human agency, manifested as cognitive, bodily, and emotional practice, is embedded into the continuity of the everyday life. Agents are situated within specific biographical situations constituted by specific experiences, and although each experience is individually discrete, it is always also a social experience.

This approach allows for a theoretical linkage between the concepts of structure and agency beyond a dualistic opposition. Based on Bourdieu's (2010) concept of habitus, it is possible to argue that the social agent within a specific biography becomes the main element for the articulation of structure and agency. According to Bourdieu, the habitus is socially and historically constructed, and it is based on individual and collective experiences. Habitus is formed through the internationalization and incorporation of external social conditions, which are transformed into internal structures of a cognitive, evaluative, motivational, and action-generating nature and materializes itself in the body. The habitus itself generates specific social practices without strictly determining their content, but rather the way in which they are performed.

The concept of habitus contains a dynamic dialectic and a co-constitutive relationship between agency and structure. On the one hand, habitus incorporates the social structure; on the other hand, the social structure does not have an ontological character and it is only realized through the social practices of the agents who generate social structures through their meaningful practices. From such a perspective, the agent is then the definite embodiment of general sociability and society.

After discussing the theoretical questions of agency and experience, the methodological question about the knowledge that biographical narrations produce appears in a different light. In this sense, biographical research and methods are one promising way to overcome the dualism of individual and society. Biographical narrations are a form of social reality that reflects the ambivalence of a unique individual's experiences and the structural patterns offered by society. Biographical self-representation gives us insights not only into the process of life history as a steady process of internalization and sedimentation but also into the rearrangement of biographical experiences within one's current location in society (Rosenthal 2006, 13). Life stories are more than an individual's endeavors. They constitute the product of the interactions with others and within specific institutions and stocks of knowledge. They can neither be reduced to the individual, nor to the settings and context that societies provide. Hence, biographical approaches constitute suitable tools for the reconstruction of specific cultural and social milieus and spaces and their processes of formation and transformation.

3.3. Process of Analysis and Writing

As mentioned above, the theoretical and methodological frameworks of this dissertation follow a praxeological approach. In turn, in order to systematically analyze the biographical narratives, this research relies on the "Habitus Analysis" approach. As mentioned before, this approach was developed by Heinrich Schäfer (2005; 2015) based upon the sociology of Pierre Bourdieu. The "Habitus Analysis" approach can be defined as a method of discourse analysis aimed at grasping the insider's accounts of one's experience and its interpretation. It is designed to structure the underlying practical logic according to very general formal categories. According to this approach, slightly structured interviews are considered the basic sources of information, since they evoke utterances of four different kinds: negative and positive experiences, and their interpretation. The method emerged from a reformulation of the model of logical transformations used in late antiquity by Aristotle, compiled by Apuleius and implemented with some changes for semiotic analysis by Greimas and Rastier (1971). For its use in the social sciences, Schäfer transformed the logical model into a "praxeological" model by introducing into it the levels of experience and interpretation, which he called "Praxeological Square" (Schäfer 2009)

According to Schäfer (2005; 2009; 2015), the basic idea is that everybody has negative and positive experiences and ascribes meaning to them. Social agents (individual or collective) perceive, judge, and act according to a (considerably but not thoroughly) coherent practical logic. The operations that take place in the related cognitive and affective processes involve positive and negative value ascription, as well as the interpretation of experience in a very general sense. This simple observation already leads to four terms: negative and positive experiences, and the interpretation of these negative and positive experiences. Therefore, the method simply helps to record people's accounts of their experience and their interpretations of them—no matter what these experiences and interpretations are (Schäfer 2009).

Thus, the "Praxeological Square" provides insights into the "cognitive maps" and the regularities of cognitive transformations of individual and collective agents (Schäfer 2009, 6) as well as into the processes of transformation from perception, through judgment, into action (Schäfer 2005, 267). In sum, the outcomes of this interpretative process are agent-specific models of the cognitive networks of dispositions that operate in the praxis of these agents.

Following the "Habitus Analysis" approach, the analysis of my empirical data started with the elaboration of codes differentiating between experience and interpretation as well as ascribing them with a positive and negative meaning. The administration of the data and the process of coding were significantly supported by MaxQDA—a program designed to facilitate and support qualitative, quantitative, and mixed methods research projects, particularly in the first phases of analysis when the "skeleton" of codes was being developed. This analysis showed that in the narratives there are more references to positive experience and interpretation than to negative ones.

At first glance, this was very striking considering the structural conditions that Guatemalans have had to face in Los Angeles, according to most academic literature. In addition, these biographical narratives tend to follow a similar pattern: in relation to the codes for experiences, the interviews showed in detail the religious involvement during their youth in their home country, during their first visits to Los Angeles and at present time. Most of them were living in that city and participated, to some extent, in transnational activities. Parallel to these references, accounts related to their everyday life in Los Angeles also emerged, particularly regarding the impact of the migratory policy of the United States on their lives. In relation to the codes for interpretation, the number of references to God was larger than other sources of interpretation.

The biographical narrative approach gives priority to "in depth holistic accounts for individual's experiences" (Hoskin and Stolz 2005, 96). It is also based on the idea that before one can understand the agent's rationality, it is necessary to know their social position in order to contextualize it and explore its "situatedness" or involvement in such context. In this approach, the agent is understood as the key liaison between structure and agency (Bourdieu 1985, 2010). However, the analytical process of the empirical data runs in parallel to the disaggregation of the primary research unit, a process in which the agent with a unique story is divided into units of meaning, code, categories, and dimensions as well as compared with other codes from other agents or from totally different types of data, such as documents or field notes.

This process of disaggregation and of disembodiment plays a crucial role in creating codes and reaching the necessary degree of abstraction.

The question that emerges is, then, how the different logics of the data could be reflected in the analysis. To solve this problem, this study opted for an intermediary solution. In Chapter 6, the presentation of the data follows the logic of the codification process. In Chapter 7, which deals with the multiple meanings given to God, natural accounts provided by the interviewees are presented because of their figurative power, choosing partly literal quotations from the interviews.

The methodological discussion of this study comes to an end with these concluding remarks and the presentation of the results. In the next chapters, I will proceed with the reconstruction of the social world of the Guatemalan independent leaders in Los Angeles.

4. Guatemalan Pentecostal Leaders in Los Angeles: Contexts of Departure and Arrival since the 1970s

As discussed in Chapter 3, this dissertation follows the Habitus Analysis approach, which focuses on the subjective as well as objective conditions of practices and discourses and studies them from the viewpoint of their practical logic. Hence, this chapter deals with the structural and material conditions (the social space) in which the Guatemalan Pentecostal leaders, who were interviewed in Los Angeles in 2014, are involved. In order to delineate the positions of these agents in the social space articulated between Los Angeles and Guatemala, the first part of this chapter addresses the demographical, economic, political, and religious context of Los Angeles in the 2010s, which has been the result of several long-term trends. After this contextualization, a brief historical description of the changing migratory flows of Guatemalans to Los Angeles from 1970 until 2010 is presented, using some biographical remarks of the interviewed individuals as examples for each period.

4.1. Los Angeles in the 2010s

Los Angeles County, or officially the County of Los Angeles, is the most populous county in both the state of California and the United States. It is home to more than one-quarter of California's residents and it is one of the most ethnically diverse counties in the United States.

In demographic terms, according to the 2010 United States Census, Los Angeles County has a population of 9,818,605. Figure 4.1 shows the racial make-up of the area.

The county has the largest population of Hispanic or Latino residents in the United States: 48 percent of Los Angeles County's population. 2.2 percent of them have a Guatemalan ancestry.

In economic terms, Los Angeles County is the third largest metropolitan economy in the world, with a GDP of over $700 billion (BEA 2011). It also has an extremely diversified economy, with established industry clusters ranging from aerospace, entertainment, and fashion to biomedical services, consumer products, and tourism. According to the 2015 American Community Survey, the median household income in the county was $59,134, and the median income for a family was $65,789. The county per capita income was $29,403. People from Hispanic or Latino origin had a median per capita income of $16,943 (see Table 4.1).

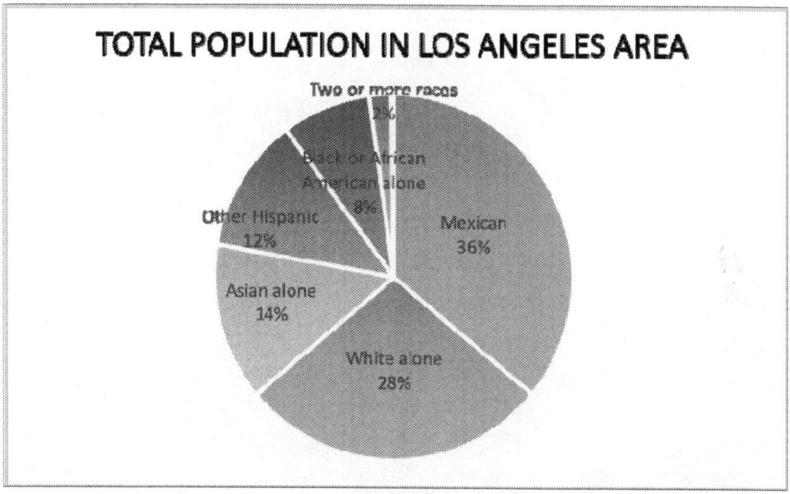

Figure 4.1: Ethnic composition in Los Angeles Area in 2010 (source: US 2010 Census).

Income in Los Angeles 2015	
Median Household Income	$59.134
Median Family Income	$65.789
Income per Capita	$29.403
Latino Income per Capita	$16.943

Table 4.1: Household income in Los Angeles 2015 (Source: American Community Survey 2015).

In spite of its affluence, Los Angeles County had the highest poverty rate in California, reaching 25.6% in 2013. Latinos' (28.8%) and African Americans' (20.2%) poverty rates were much higher than that of whites (14.0%) in 2014. The poverty rate among Asian Americans (17.0%) fell in between (Bohn, Danielson, and Levin 2013).

Poverty Rate in California 2013	
Latinos	28.8%
African American	20.2%
Asian American	17%
Whites	14%
Other	20%

Table 4.2: Poverty Rate in California 2013
(Source: Public Police Institute of California).

In political terms, Los Angeles County, as well as the state of California, has been characterized by paradoxical tendencies. While it is known as one of the most progressive counties of the United States, as the powerhouse of the entertainment industry and of innovative technology with a worldwide impact, it has also generated conservative—even reactionary—countermovements. On the one hand, the County has voted for Democratic candidates in most presidential elections in the past forty years, particularly in every election since 1988. However, at the same time, the property tax revolt of the 1970s and the nativist sentiments of the early 1990s resulted in the overwhelming support for Proposition 187, which aimed to restrict immigrant access to education and health care.

In regard to religious praxis, Los Angeles County has a vigorous religious presence that had actually increased over the last 30 years, despite its reputation as the paramount center of "secular" entertainment provided by their powerful show business and recreational industries (Flory 2012). Far from being a godless metropolis, Los Angeles is one of the most religiously diverse and pluralistic cities in the world. Nearly every religion and denomination that exists can be found in Los Angeles, and a number of fascinating (and even controversial) religious movements actually began here.

According to the Decennial Religious Congregations and Membership Study, there are currently 5,773 religious congregations in the city, which claimed a total of 5,214,110 adherents, or 53.1 percent of the population in 2010. Since 1980, the number of religious congregations has grown by 2,936 and the number of adherents by 2,285,970, an increase of around 14 percentage points, from 39 percent to 53 percent of the population. Nevertheless, Los Angeles is predominantly Christian. The Pew Research Center's 2014 Religious Landscape Study claims that 65 percent of its population identify themselves as Christian. Around 32 percent of the Los Angeles population is Catholic, making it one of the most heavily Catholic cities in the United States. The Los Angeles Archdiocese has approximately five million members and it is the largest in the United States. By contrast, in the city proper, fewer than one-in-five residents are evangelical Protestants.

The urban life of Los Angeles in the 2010s is, therefore, that of a multicultural and multiethnic region that has experienced deep demographic, economic, political, and physical transformations since the 1970s. These transformations were, in turn, the result of several long-term trends.

4.2. Historical Trends in Los Angeles

The first discernible long-term trend has been the demographic and ethnic heterogeneity growth. The population of Los Angeles has been the result of a vast and relatively continuous influx of migrants since the 1880s into what had originally been a predominantly Mexican area (Hamilton and Chinchilla 2001). At the end of the nineteenth century and the beginning of the twentieth century, the migratory flows included both domestic migrants (Anglo-Protestants from the Midwest and African Americans) and foreign immigrants (predominantly European and Mexicans in the early part of the twentieth century). These migratory trends dramatically changed in the 1970s and the 1980s due to global economic changes and geopolitical developments. There was both an increase in the number of immigrants and a profound change in the origin of those immigrants. Los Angeles became the destination of refugees from Vietnam, Cambodia, and Laos; of supporters of the Shah regime in Iran; of Jews from Russia; of Mexicans and South Americans uprooted by economic crises and restructuring processes in their respective countries; and of Central Americans escaping from political and economic upheaval in their region (Hamilton and Chinchilla 2001, 40). All in all, Los Angeles became a major destination for immigrants from Latin America, Asia, and other regions.

A second force behind this momentous transformation has been a dramatic economic change. Due to the global economic changes of the 1970s and 1980s, Los Angeles consecutively experienced deindustrialization and reindustrialization. Many traditional manufacturing firms moved abroad, which particularly affected black and Mexican American workers, erasing many of their former sources of earnings in which they had relied for decades. This process was also connected with a substantive increase in the number of firms in the electronics and aerospace industries, emerging from technological developments in communications and information industries and from increased defense spending in the 1980s (Hamilton and Chinchilla 2001, 38).

These changes were complemented with a restructuration of the labor market. On the one hand, professional, managerial, and technical employment in commercial, financial, trade, and other service activities expanded significantly. On the other hand, jobs in highly labor-intensive industries such as garment manufacturing and a variety of low-paid positions providing services for the newly affluent also increased. These new positions included janitors in office buildings, waiters and busboys in new restaurants or domestic servants and gardeners (Ong and Blumenberg 1996; Soja 1989). All of this led to the elimination of middle-income jobs in traditional industries such as the auto industry, leading to a growing income gap between a new affluent middle class and an impoverished working class, which was confronted by the disappearance of industrial jobs and also faced divisions within traditional minority groups (Hamilton and Chinchilla 2001, 39).

A third factor of change was the development of a decentralized pattern of geographic expansion characterized by the formation of suburbs on freeway-accessible urban peripheries, forming a polycentric structure (Dear 1996). While the city of Los Angeles maintained its central position as the core of political and administrative power, economic power was gradually dispersed, establishing centers of durable manufacturing, shipping, commercial, defense, and aerospace industries in peripheral areas of the Los Angeles County in the north, south, and west of the downtown city core (Hamilton and Chinchilla 2001, 37). This pattern also served to reinforce successive real estate booms, since along with the growth of industry and commerce, it produced residential growth in peripheral areas (Soja and Scott 1996; Soja 1989).

A fourth trend that left its mark on the demographic and ethnic composition of the Los Angeles population were the exclusionary polices of the dominant Anglo-European groups throughout the history of the region. Prior to the 1970s, conservative politicians—most of them descendants of Anglo-European migrants—were directly responsible for the pro-growth, anti-union character of the region. This gave rise to income inequalities and class distinctions, which reinforced ethnic/racial barriers. Due to the conservative nature of the power structure, African Americans, Latinos, and other minority groups have tended to occupy subaltern positions and to fight mainly defensive battles, impeding the achievement of better positions in the power structure (Anderson 1996). In addition, their struggle for better living conditions has been impaired by divisions between and within ethnic groups as well as between "old" and "new" immigrants (Anderson 1996; Ong and Blumenberg 1996).

Finally, the emergence of distinct ethnic communities living in particular neighborhoods is a fifth factor of change that resulted from several of the previously mentioned trends—the patterns of economic and demographic growth, spatial dispersion, discriminatory housing, real estate practices, and exclusionary politics. The immigration flows arriving since the 1970s heavily transformed the neighborhoods of Los Angeles, changing the predominant ethnic group in some cases, shifting other areas from ethnic to multiethnic. These demographic changes resulted in the growth of several areas of new interaction (and tension) between ethnic groups as Latinos became by far the largest ethnic community, amounting to nearly 38 percent of the population of Los Angeles County and 40 percent of the population of the city of Los Angeles proper in the 1980s. Areas with a high concentration of Latinos, predominantly of Mexican origin, such as East Los Angeles (95 percent), Huntington Park (92 percent) or Long Beach/Wilmington (88 percent) were deeply transformed as new immigrants arrived (Hamilton and Chinchilla 2001, 42). They settled initially in those areas, leading to a geographic concentration of the most impoverished Latinos and the move of many Mexican immigrants into other neighborhoods (Sotomayor 1991). They spread from Westlake into Koreatown and came to account for at least 50 percent of the population in South Central, displacing African Americans, who mostly moved to the west and south into formerly white neighborhoods such as Long Beach (Rocco 1996). According to Hamilton and Chinchilla (2001, 43), tensions among these groups rapidly emerged and were "exacerbated by the loss of well-paid, unionized jobs typically held by blacks and Mexican Americans." Nevertheless, the tension was not only interethnic, but issues within the same ethnic group have also appeared since low-paying nonunionized jobs in the manufacturing and services sectors began to be filled by the recent, undocumented Mexican and Central American immigrants.

As I will argue in the next section, all of these trends have heavily affected the life-trajectories of the Guatemalan Pentecostal leaders in Los Angeles, their decision to migrate, the conditions they encountered upon their arrival in the US, and even their religious outlook.

4.3. Guatemalans in Los Angeles: Changing Migratory Flows since 1970

4.3.1. The 1970s: The Beginning of Guatemalan Migration to Los Angeles

Various scholars have placed the beginning of a regular flow of Guatemalans coming to Los Angeles in the late 1970s. Although Guatemala had experienced internal and regional migration to other countries in Central America, according to the demographer Alicia Maguid (1999), it was in the 1970s when Guatemalan emigrants began to arrive in the United States. Hamilton and Chinchilla (2001, 45), following the census figures, considered that there were approximately 5,600 Guatemalans in the Los Angeles region in 1970, although some other estimations have suggested somewhat higher numbers in this period. The census figures also showed that the number of foreign-born Guatemalans increased almost by a factor of seven to 38,000 by 1980 (Popkin 1996; Hamilton and Chinchilla 2001).

Context of Departure

Some of these Guatemalan migrants arriving in the late 1970s were young middle- or upper-class men or women, often *ladinos* (mestizo or Hispanicized indigenous population), with business or professional backgrounds, who came to visit relatives or friends and ended up staying (Hamilton and Chinchilla 2001, 45). At first, they were dependent on low-paid industrial or service jobs, but frequently they were able to shift to better jobs compatible with their backgrounds and training. Professional training, skills, and contacts were certainly important aspects in this transition, but the context of their reception was also important, as in that period it was relatively easy to obtain legal status and some individuals could rely on family members who had arrived earlier (Hamilton and Chinchilla 2001, 45).

Parallel to the arrival of these middle- and upper-class Guatemalans, there was also a substantial increase in the number of poor or working-class Guatemalans coming to the United States.

It was during the 1960s and the 1970s that the Central American Common Market brought increased foreign, especially U.S., investment to the region, allowing the development of a small urban industrial sector. However, Guatemalan economic and political conditions did not evolve in a way that fostered population stability. The prevailing conditions of rigid social inequality, economic growth, and stability did not translate into better living conditions for the majority of Guatemalans, and this was particularly true for the large Mayan peasantry.

These conditions got even worse as the oil crisis of 1973 increased the cost of energy and ruined the chances of an export-oriented industrial growth (Jonas and Rodriguez 2014, 32). In fact, considerable numbers of Mayan rural workers, who migrated seasonally for harvest work in Mexico, began to arrive to Los Angeles after hearing of the job opportunities in that area while in Mexico (Loucky 1996). Some others had contacts with evangelical protestant organizations and were invited to spend some time in the United States. This was the case for Marcos González, who came to the United States in the second half of the 1970s.

Marcos González was born in the early 1950s in Chimaltenango, Guatemala, to a nominally Catholic family with indigenous ancestors. At the age of seventeen, he "found Christ" after attending a meeting in a small Pentecostal congregation in Guatemala City. At that moment, with no formal education whatsoever, he was working as a construction worker and was a heavy drinker. He began to attend the church, was baptized, and participated in some courses until he was finally appointed as an evangelist.

Marcos González's conversion years coincided with the period during which Protestant Christianity began to grow strongly in Guatemala. This growth is linked to the development of new and active evangelical missionary interest in Guatemala during the 1960s. In 1962 a new interdenominational fundamentalist faith mission group called Latin American Mission (LAM) began to work in Guatemala. In November of that year, the LAM launched a massive evangelization crusade based on a comprehensive program that combined door-to-door evangelization with media campaigns, revivals, radio programming, and church programs (Garrard-Burnett 1998, 109). Guatemalans believers were specifically trained for this door-to-door evangelism. During the LAM crusade of 1962, 15,000 Guatemalans converted to Protestant Christianity, and in the next years, Protestant membership continued to flourish (Garrard-Burnett 1998, 109). Nevertheless, in the late 1960s and early 1970s, the LAM lost importance as Guatemalan national churches began to grow. These churches were the spiritual descendants of the LAM crusaders, but with the caveat that they began to reject certain aspects of the American missionaries' evangelization codes as they matured (Garrard-Burnett 1998, 113). Nationalistic interests, doctrinal differences, and the divergent beliefs of a significant number of newly converted Protestants resulted in tens of small national congregations splitting from the older established churches (Garrard-Burnett 1998, 115).

Marcos González, as an evangelist and a member of a small national Pentecostal church, started to evangelize in Guatemala, married a woman who had already converted to Pentecostalism, and became the father of four children. Thereafter, he also participated in evangelist campaigns in other Central American countries as well as in Mexico. In 1976, while living with his wife and their four children in Mexico, he was invited to preach in Brownsville, Texas. Once in the United States, after preaching in Brownsville and with his family still in Mexico, he accepted work as a preacher with the Assemblies of God in the state of Oklahoma. Later on, he went to preach in the states of Colorado and California.

After being very successful in his evangelist campaigns, he decided to bring his wife and children to live with him in El Paso, TX. The context of reception and contacts played an important role in Marcos González's life. According to him:

> "En ese tiempo era muy fácil venirse para este lado. No era muy complicado como ahora."
>
> [In those times it was easy to cross to this side. It was not as complicated as it is now.]

A female pastor in Ciudad Juárez offered to bring his wife and children to the United States:

> "Hermano, no se preocupe, dígale a su esposa que no se martirice, que no ande buscando modo para pasar con visa, porque no le van a dar. Pero yo conozco un lugar … donde los puedo pasar ... ningún peligro van a pasar …"
>
> [Do not worry, my brother, just tell your wife not to suffer, tell her to stop looking for a visa to cross the border, because she is not going to get one. But I know a place to cross the border (…) without any danger …]

He also stressed the support that he and his family received from Pentecostal congregations after their arrival:

> "Luego en El Paso, la pastora de la iglesia nos dio un cuarto en la iglesia. Ahí vivíamos todos."

[Afterwards, in El Paso, the female pastor of the local church gave us a room in the church. We all lived there.]

Context of Arrival

As Marcos González's commentaries show, networks were formed as earlier arrivals sponsored relatives or friends. Guatemalan Pentecostal believers were not the exception, since they could receive at least temporary assistance in housing, job contacts, or other types of aid in Pentecostal organizations particularly in Latino congregations. Indeed, the growth of Guatemalan immigrant population in the United States during the 1970s was fueled by undocumented individuals, who took advantages of the scant control in the border and the ease of finding a job in certain niches in the service sector, characterized by highly labor-intensive and abundant low-paid positions.

Although Marcos González was very engaged in the "expansion of the Gospel," working as an evangelist in the borderlands, he claimed that "llegó una temporada en que a mí se terminaron los compromisos en las Iglesias" [a time came when my engagement in the churches came to an end], and as a husband and father of six children, he was forced to accept a secular job as a dishwasher in a Japanese restaurant. Although initially he earned less than 4 USD per hour, he highlighted that this job under a Pentecostal Japanese boss was the perfect chance to show his industriousness and the opportunity of being promoted to better positions. Thanks to his experience as chef in a Japanese restaurant, in 1982, Marcos moved with his family to Los Angeles. Better wages as a chef in an international hotel, better weather conditions and a recognizable community of Guatemalans and other Central Americans turned Los Angeles into an excellent destination where he was also able to continue working as an evangelist. In addition, as described later in this chapter, Guatemalan undocumented migrants that had arrived in the 1970s, like Marcos, found an opportunity for status adjustment in 1986, when the Immigration Reform and Control Act (IRCA) was passed, providing amnesty and legal status for tens of thousands of undocumented Guatemalan migrants (Jonas and Rodriguez 2014, 41).

During the last thirty years, Marcos has worked as an evangelist in his church, having also a secular job as an employee in Los Angeles's docks, as a photographer, and as a construction worker. He also has worked as an international missionary, helping pastors and churches in Guatemala and Mexico, especially in Baja California.

4.3.2. The 1980s: Economic or Political Immigrants? Social Turmoil in Guatemala

During the 1980s, increasing numbers of Guatemalans were still arriving to the Los Angeles area. According to the 1990 U.S. Census, the Guatemalan population in Los Angeles area reached 159,268 (a figure that once more undoubtedly underestimated the real one). Nearly 75 percent of them had entered in the previous decade (Hamilton and Chinchilla 2001). Although most of those who immigrated in the 1970s came for economic reasons, by the end of that decade an increasing number were coming for political reasons.

Context of Departure

In the late 1970s, the civil war that had begun in 1960 escalated. In 1978 with the military government of the General Fernando Romeo Lucas García, the persecution of participants in social protests increased. The social movements that emerged during the 1970s in response to worsening economic and political conditions became political targets of the military government (Jonas 1991). At that moment, participants in popular movements who came from a wide spectrum of society, including peasants, urban workers, teachers, university professors and students as well as priests and congregations oriented toward "Liberation Theology" were decimated through targeted extrajudicial assassinations and "disappearances" of leaders and members. Many survivors fled, seeking refuge abroad (Jonas and Rodriguez 2014, 35).

In 1981 and after the military coup led by General Efraín Ríos Montt[8] in 1982, state violence and repression in the Maya highlands worsened.

8 Efraín Ríos Montt was a born into a conventional Catholic middle-class family. He joined the army at the age of sixteen, advancing steadily in his military career until reaching the top ranks. After studying counterinsurgency tactics in the United States, he became President Arana's army chief of staff in 1970 and was promoted to general two years later. In 1974, he made his first incursion into politics as a Catholic presidential candidate of the UNO (United National Opposition) coalition led by the Christian Democratic Party and was defeated (Garrard-Burnett 1998, 139). During these years, in the midst of a ruined military career, Ríos Montt became a born-again Christian and joined a Pentecostal church called "The Church of the Word" or "Verbo" (Garrard-Burnett 1998, 139). On March 23, 1982, he

During his presidency, military belligerence articulated disconcertingly with evangelical reformation. He considered that the guerilla movement suffered a lack of moral values and explicitly intended to destroy Christian culture (Garrard-Burnett 1998, 141).

These arguments were a justification of sorts, one expressed in "religious" and "moral" terms, for the counterinsurgency campaign oriented to destroy the revolutionary movement, united in 1982 as the Unidad Revolucionaria Guatemalteca (UNRG, Guatemalan National Revolutionary Unity) (Jonas and Rodriguez 2014, 36). In fact, it targeted the civilian population in the highlands on the premise that the entire Mayan population was inherently "subversive" (Falla 1984 in Jonas and Rodriguez 2014, 36). Due to the *foquismo* techniques implemented by guerrillas to make the armed resistance indistinguishable from the civilian population, the army found the indigenous population an easy target for their reprisals (Garrard-Burnett 1998, 144).

On April 1, 1982, Ríos Montt initiated the National Security and Development Plan, also named "Victoria '82", under which the army dramatically stepped up the systematic scorched-earth sweep of the highlands (Garrard-Burnett 1998, 145). The army swept through the highlands burning homes, churches, and crops and killing livestock. According with surveys carried out in the affected areas, 440 villages disappeared from the map and more than a million people fled into exile between 1981 and 1984. In the Ixcán, the offensive either displaced or massacred nearly the entire population of 50,000 (Garrard-Burnett 1998, 148). In military terms, Victoria '82 was an outstanding military triumph. By mid-1993, the guerrillas were all defeated. However, it was an inhuman and infamous victory that Ríos Montt had always presented by invoking evangelical[9] terms (Garrard-Burnett 1998, 148).

---

participated with two other generals in a coup d'état, overthrowing the General Lucas regime. On June 9, 1982 he dismissed the other two coup leaders and declared himself chief of state, making clear that his military affiliation was going to be, at least rhetorically, subordinate to his evangelical identity (Garrard-Burnett 1998, 140).

9 Ríos Montt's declarations invoking religious terms to justify the high human cost of the campaigns were severely criticized not only by international human rights organizations but also by church groups, which criticized him for his hypocrisy in authorizing mass killings in the name of God and peace (Garrard-Burnett 1998, 148). A small group of Protestants in Guatemala

Amid this growing turmoil, the Guatemalan economy fell into shambles. Jonas and Rodriguez (2014, 36) point out that unemployment and underemployment rose from more than 25 percent in the mid-1970s to more than 40 percent in the mid-1980s; rural poverty reached 84 percent and urban poverty 47 percent in 1980. In addition, political violence severely restricted the agricultural economy, which employed the largest number of poor workers, as well as the artisan production of the Maya highland economy. The escalation of political violence affected not only conflict areas but also the economic activity of the whole country since the population restricted their movements beyond their local areas to avoid encounters with soldiers, guerrillas, or death squads (Jonas and Rodriguez 2014, 36).

Due to all of these events, the numbers of Guatemalans entering the United States increased significantly throughout the 1980s. Nonetheless, not every Guatemalan who came to Los Angeles in the 1980s had been directly victimized by war or violence. Substantial sectors of the population were threatened or at least indirectly affected as political violence and instability spread throughout the region and economic repercussions undercut the ability of many to sustain themselves and their families.

These are the cases of female pastor Francisca Arévalo and pastor Carlos Benítez, who arrived in Los Angeles in 1981 and 1984 respectively. Although neither of them suffered direct violence or military persecution, the economic and political conditions in Guatemala were a threat to their lives and possibilities for economic advancement. For instance, Pastor

---

City, for instance, conformed the Confraternidad Evangélica (Evangelical Brotherhood) in the late 1980s to protest against the government's systematic violation of human rights and to plead with the president to stop identifying the message of "Jesus" with injustice and inhumanity (Garrard-Burnett 1998, 149). Nevertheless, not all evangelicals in Guatemala protested against Ríos Montt's campaigns. Numerous Protestant organizations and agencies were directly involved in his civic action programs, had close ties to advisers in the Ríos Montt government, and operated primarily on money supplied by conservative Christian groups in the United States (Garrard-Burnett 1998, 149-50). Although there were suspicions that portrayed evangelists and their organizations as imperialist agents of the United States sent to divide and control the Guatemalan people, according to various experts in this topic, the existing evidence indicates that Protestants, like Catholic organizations, often cooperated with the army more for pragmatic than for ideological or theological reasons (Garrard-Burnett 1998, 151).

Francisca Arévalo, who was born in Guatemala City at the end of the 1950s to an already Pentecostal mother, emphasized in her narration that the years between 1978 and 1980 were a time when it was possible to find dead bodies in the streets:

> "recuerdo en el 78 o el 80 mucho, me recuerdo que empezó la guerra. Y entonces, en Guatemala aparecían muertos, por donde quiera."
>
> [I remember a lot about 1978 or 1980; I remember that the war began. And then corpses appeared everywhere.]

Similar reasons brought Pastor Carlos Benítez to Los Angeles, born in Jutiapa (Guatemala) at the end of the 1950s. Although Carlos Benítez was born into a poor Catholic family, thanks to the migration of his father to the United States in the 1960s, he finished high school and was able to enter the university in the capital to study civil engineering. During his years as a university student in Guatemala City, he converted to Pentecostalism and joined the Assemblies of God. After he finished his studies, he decided to migrate to Los Angeles. For him, the war put an end to his dreams of getting a job as a professional civil engineer, since nobody wanted to construct any houses or buildings in Guatemala any more:

> cuando yo me titulé, estaba todo el apogeo de la guerra civil, y de la carrera que yo estudié pues no había fuentes de trabajo, porque quién quería construir en la guerra, estaban destruyendo todo, estaban destruyendo las calles, carreteras, los edificios importantes, poniéndoles bombas, los inversionistas huyeron, no había nada.
>
> [when I got my degree, the civil war was at its height, and, well, there were no jobs for someone like me because, who would want to build something during the war? Everything was being destroyed, they were destroying the streets, the roads, the main buildings, bombing them, the investors fled the country, there was nothing left.]

The other two Guatemalan Pentecostal leaders interviewed arrived in Los Angeles in the 1980s. As it was noted above, during Ríos Montt's presidency, several evangelical organizations enjoyed more facilities to carry out religious activities in the country as the president's religious profile was evangelical (Garrard-Burnett 1998, 154). The new legitimacy and practical expediency enjoyed by Pentecostal believers also meant more opportunities to travel abroad to work together with other evangelical organizations. For instance, Pastor Martin Carmona arrived for the first time from

Guatemala with his band to give a concert in a Latino Pentecostal congregation in Los Angeles in 1980, when he was in his late teens, single, and with some experience as a Christian singer and music producer. Once in Los Angeles, he opted for a life of serving Christ and used his experience as a singer and missionary to stay in the United States, singing, recording, and travelling around the country for several years.

Another example is Alvaro Sánchez, who was able to travel to Anaheim, California to participate in a missionary conference organized by the famous Argentine evangelist Alberto Motessi in 1989. Pastor Alvaro Sánchez was born in the 1950s in San Pedro Sacatepéquez, Guatemala in a Catholic family. His mother died when he was only one year old. His father went to work in Quetzaltenango while his aunt took care of him. At the age of 15, he began to work in the production of traditional fabrics. Due to problems with his boss, when he turned 18, he moved to Guatemala City. There he lived with relatives and continued working in the textile industry.

Although he had a good job, feelings of loneliness led him to alcohol abuse, which cost him his job and his house. He was living and working in a marketplace when his drinking got worse until he followed the advice of Pentecostal preachers and converted to Pentecostalism. Once a member of a small Pentecostal congregation, he accepted different positions to become a pastor.

Due to Alvaro Sánchez's active involvement during the visit of international preachers in Guatemala, he was invited to go to California. Pastor Sánchez stayed for some months in Los Angeles, but he decided to return to Guatemala, where he still worked as a pastor in a church and married a Pentecostal-believer woman with whom he had five children. He also supported the missionary expansion of his church, opening congregations in Costa Rica, El Salvador, the state of South Carolina, and Los Angeles County. In the United States, he has been actively engaged in offering counseling to Latin American immigrants since 2008, travelling many times per year to both states.

Context of Reception: Work Conditions and Settlement Patterns in Los Angeles

For most Guatemalans coming to the Los Angeles area in the 1970s and 1980s, finding work in the expanding low-wage manufacturing and service sectors was not that difficult. Immigrant networks consisting of family members, friends, and former neighbors from their village or community often facilitated this process, which also helps explain the preponderance of Guatemalans in certain jobs such as garment workers, domestic works, garden workers, day laborers in the construction sector, or street vendors (Hamilton and Chinchilla 2001, 104).

Francisca Arévalo, the female pastor mentioned before, was able to get a job in a bakery through the intervention of her husband. There, she had to work nights and was forced to look for people to take care of her children during working hours. After some years of constant fighting and mistreatment, her husband finally walked out on her, leaving her in her late twenties with three children. Although Francisca Arévalo had to face the constraints of low wage and bad job conditions, she was able to develop survival strategies and improve her options. Despite the limitation of upward mobility in low-paying occupations, many Guatemalan workers like her got chances to improve their lot by holding more than one job or working two shifts, or by implementing household strategies in which two or more members of the family worked (Hamilton and Chinchilla 2001, 104).

With the support of her three brothers and one sister, she was able to shift from nighttime jobs to day jobs, resulting in better wages and more flexibility to take care of her children. Nevertheless, as a recently arrived immigrant, her participation in religious activities was less intensive in comparison with her years in Guatemala. In her country of origin, she was an active religious young woman, preaching, singing, and supporting her ex-husband as a pastor in a Pentecostal congregation. In Los Angeles, with three daughters and no support from him, she had to work to survive and satisfy the daily needs of her children before turning her full attention to her faith.

During the 1980s, along with other Central Americans, Guatemalan newcomers settled in low-income Mexican American neighborhoods, as well as other areas close to the downtown area (Hamilton and Chinchilla 2001). In these neighborhoods, Guatemalans could take advantage of low rents and proximity to jobs as well as a common language and the cultural familiarity of a Latino community. Regardless, the experience of arriving in Los Angeles in the 1980s was shattering.

In the large Central American settlement in the Pico Union section of Westlake, many Guatemalans settled in run-down, low-rent housing surrounded by crime and delinquency. In the nearby parks, Guatemalan immigrant families with small children attended family festivals and other social events while drug dealers openly conducted their illegal business (Jonas and Rodriguez 2014). Trying to evade this situation, Guatemalans as well as other Latinos also moved into the predominantly black neighborhoods of South Central, which had declined with the exodus of members of the black middle class and the deterioration in schools and other institutions. This was the case, for instance, of Inglewood, a predominantly black neighborhood that with the years transformed itself into the home of a substantial Central American community. Transformations in the ethnic compositions within black neighborhoods led to tensions between Latinos, who sometimes identified African Americans with drugs and crime, and the latter, who saw Guatemalans and Central Americans as taking control of their neighborhoods and sometimes their livelihoods (Hamilton and Chinchilla 2001, 58).

All of these circumstances may reflect the fact that predominantly Guatemalan and Central American neighborhoods were mostly depressed areas but, at the same time, also offered many opportunities for the religious work of Guatemalan Pentecostal leaders. During the 1980s, there was also an increase in Evangelical churches and services in Westlake and South Central, since significant numbers of Guatemalan Evangelicals also arrived in Los Angeles (Hamilton and Chinchilla 2001, 66).

Meanwhile, Guatemalan Catholics expressed concern at the increasing rates of conversion of co-nationals to Evangelical, Pentecostal, and Charismatic churches and organizations (Popkin 2005). Most of the Guatemalan Pentecostal leaders interviewed had lived or worked in these neighborhoods, and all their churches were located in these areas, particularly in the South-Central area.

Responses to Guatemalan Immigration

The majority of Central American newcomers arriving in Los Angeles during the 1980s were undocumented immigrants. This generated two basic responses from the American public, depending on how they saw the U.S. military intervention in Central America in the 1980s. Those who viewed the intervention as a form of U.S. support for right-wing governments recognized and associated Guatemalans and other Central American immigrants as refugees displaced by political violence and deserving of asylum. This opinion was held by some activists, religious organizations as well as local communities.

In contrast, those who viewed the intervention as a necessary means to prevent a Soviet-supported leftist takeover of Central America tended to consider Central American newcomers as economic migrants or as dangerous leftists and reacted with opposition to the settlement of these immigrants in the United States (Jonas and Rodriguez 2014).

These different viewpoints materialized into different actions. In the early 1980s, a "sanctuary movement" of religious leaders and organizations emerged to support the immigration of undocumented Salvadorans and Guatemalans. The actions of the sanctuary movement consisted of transporting and housing these migrants and in making public their cause for asylum (Crittenden 1988; Davidson 1988). In 1982, the First Unitarian Church of Los Angeles was the first in the city to declare itself as a sanctuary church. By the mid-1980s, some forty other local churches joined it.

Nationwide, 400 churches officially declared themselves as sanctuaries. Declarations of sanctuary in the Los Angeles area were not limited to churches and synagogues; several university campuses, such as, for instance, the University of California, Riverside campus, were also declared as safe havens for Central Americans fleeing repression. And after an intense battle, on November 27, 1985, the city of Los Angeles became one of the largest U.S cities to publicly declare itself as a sanctuary (Hamilton and Chinchilla 2001, 146).

Simultaneously, the opposition of the U.S. government appeared in two ways. One way was to infiltrate the sanctuary movement and arrest its members (Davidson 1988). A second way was the attempts to avoid the petition of asylum of Guatemalans and Salvadorans at the detention centers at the moment of their arrival in the United States (Hamilton and Chinchilla 2001, 142) as well as the frequently denial of asylum status to Central American petitioners, with the exception of some Nicaraguan cases (Gzesh 2006). Analysts have related the denial of asylum for Central Americans during the Reagan administration to the financial and military resources that the administration was providing to the governments fighting leftist movements in Central America (Hamilton and Chinchilla 2001; Gzesh 2006).

Granting asylum to large numbers of Salvadorans and Guatemalans could have meant ending the military cooperation between the U.S. and Central American governments, since Congress during the Reagan administration had also banned U.S. aid to governments that violated human rights. The extremely low approval rates for Guatemalan and Salvadoran asylum applicants were addressed in the class-action *American Baptist*

Churches v. Thornburgh filed in 1985 by religious organizations against the INS (see next section of this chapter). It was not until the ABC lawsuit (as it was called) was settled in the late 1990s that the U.S. government began granting asylum to significant numbers of Guatemalans (Hamilton and Chinchilla 2001, 143)

The second part of the 1980s was characterized by the U.S government's enactment of IRCA (Immigration Reform and Control Act) in 1986. After years of debate in Congress during four presidential administrations, IRCA, which was signed under the Reagan administration, offered amnesty and the possibility of legalization for undocumented migrants who met the residential and work criteria specified by the law (Jonas and Rodriguez 2014, 44). Concern about illegal immigration rose among U.S. government officials when undocumented Mexican immigrants surged in the late 1960s after the U.S. Congress shut down the so-called "Bracero Program," causing increasing numbers of former *braceros* and other Mexican migrants to cross the border yearly without visas to work in agricultural fields and other worksites where U.S. employers eagerly awaited them.

As a solution to this situation, the IRCA proposed two programs to deal with undocumented immigration. The first, Section 245A, offered amnesty and the opportunity to acquire legal status for undocumented migrants who had lived continuously in the United States since before January 1, 1982. The second one, the Special Agricultural Workers Program, provided legalization for migrants who had worked in seasonal agricultural jobs for a minimum of 90 days in the year preceding May 1986. This law also provided penalties against employers who continued to hire undocumented migrant workers after the passage of the law. In any case, sanctions against employers were not rigorously enforced until the late 1990s (Jonas and Rodriguez 2014). Guatemalans in Los Angeles and the Southern California region viewed IRCA with uncertainty and suspicion rather than as an opportunity to gain legal resident status. The Spanish-language sources of information, frequently only rumors, tended to emphasize the employer's sanctions of the law more than its amnesty measure. Even if the new law brought an opportunity for amnesty, the requirement that applicants must have lived in the United States since before 1982 could only be met by a small percentage of Guatemalan migrants, precisely by those who had a longer history of migrating to the United States, which, at the end of the day, were the upper- and middle-class Guatemalans who arrived in the 1970s (Jonas and Rodriguez 2014, 48).

In the Los Angeles region, only 70,953 Guatemalans applicants were able to improve their legal situation through this amnesty according with the 1991 INS Statistical Yearbook (Hamilton and Chinchilla 2001, 124). Because of their year of arrival, four of the Guatemalan Pentecostal leaders interviewed—Marcos González, Martin Carmona, Francisca Arévalo, and Carlos Benítez—could obtain legal resident status through this amnesty and, as a consequence, gained more opportunities for their settlement in Los Angeles.

Regardless of this, many Guatemalans did not have the same chances. The amnesty offered close relatives of beneficiaries the opportunity to travel and settle legally in the United States and increased the legal resources for Guatemalan immigration (Jonas and Rodriguez 2014, 45). In addition, visas obtained through the IRCA enabled thousands of legalized Guatemalan migrants to visit their families in Guatemala as often as their incomes and free time permitted.

Through periodic return visits, legalized Guatemalans dramatically increased their interaction with their home communities. The growth of Guatemalan migrants' periodic visits also served to increase the volume of monetary, material, and symbolic remittances they brought for their families and for friends and relatives (Jonas and Rodriguez 2014, 47). For the Guatemalan Pentecostal leaders analyzed in this study, their new legalized status allowed them to travel to Guatemala, bringing with them what can be called *religious remittanc*es (Ramírez 2015, 29), that is, symbolic goods sent or brought home by migrants to prompt or maintain a religious identity, in this case a Pentecostal identity, among their relatives and friends. This was the case for pastor Martin Carmona, who thanks to his legal residence could use his free time to evangelize through music in Guatemala. These return visits also aroused the interest of many young men and women in Guatemala to migrate to the United States, as the visiting migrants were usually seen as examples of success (Jonas and Rodriguez 2014, 48).

Finally, in relation to social mobility, legalization through the IRCA gave former undocumented migrants new opportunities in the labor market. For instance, after the legalization brought by amnesty in Los Angeles, some Guatemalan migrants left their jobs in garment sweatshops for better positions in other industries (Jonas and Rodriguez 2014, 46). With their new legal status, and with the English training required by the IRCA to advance from temporary to permanent legal residency, some Guatemalans also underwent job promotions in the firms where they worked. In addition, in the life narratives of the Pentecostal leaders, there are numerous references to the fact that a more established life in Los Angeles also allowed for a more active participation in congregational life.

In the case of Pastor Martin Carmona, who was already married with a Pentecostal woman, he acquired a better position as a business administrator and began to serve in churches close to their home. After some years, he started to feel the "call to pastorate" and decided to "go back to the origins" and established a ministry between Guatemala and Los Angeles in alliance with his mother. In Los Angeles, he began the ministry in his home with the support of his wife and brother. Afterwards, they found a place in a restaurant to meet with the members of the congregation and soon they could rent a theater. With his brother's support, they decided to open a new congregation, allowing each of them to work as pastors. In May 2014, the ministry was composed of three congregations, each one with approximately fifty to one hundred members. In Guatemala, there is a congregation with more than one hundred members, where her mother is the pastor.

In the last years, Pastor Martin Carmona was focused on the counseling of other pastors. He has also worked as an international missionary, helping the planning of churches and advising pastors in Guatemala, Mexico and Spain. In the 2000s, his reputation as a respected pastor got him elected as Secretary of the *Alianza Ministerial Hispana* [Hispanic Ministerial Alliance] in South California. Under the cover of this organization, he organized numerous events calling for respecting the rights of immigrants in California. In addition, he was also interviewed on radio and TV programs.

Pastor Francisca Arévalo also improved her living conditions as she got their legal residence. In 1987, she met her second husband, like her, a Guatemalan divorcee with two children, while visiting an Assemblies of God congregation. After that, she went to study missionary work at the Assemblies of God's Bible Institute and was sent as a missionary to other places. In 2000, she was invited to sing and preach in a Pentecostal church in Compton, where the ailing pastor asked her to lead the congregation. She accepted the position and immediately began to pastor the congregation that was then composed of six families. In May 2014, her independent Pentecostal congregation had approximately seventy members, one-third of them children and teens, including her children and grandchildren.

Nevertheless, not every Guatemalan migrant arriving in the 1980s experienced the same improvement. For a substantial number of Guatemalans, living in the United States was still problematic. Since most of those who arrived in the 1980s were not eligible for the amnesty program, some felt more vulnerable as a result of IRCA regulations (Jonas and Rodriguez 2014) and were confined to the low-wage manufacturing and service sectors (Hamilton and Chinchilla 2001, 104).

4.3.3. The 1990s: Changing Context, Shifting Expectations

For the Guatemalan immigrants in the Los Angeles County, a region that by 2000 had the largest Guatemalan concentration in the United States (181,419 individuals) (Jonas and Rodriguez, 2014, 57), the 1990s was an ambivalent decade.

Context of Departure

For those who had come because of war, persecution, and political instability, with the expectation of returning when the war ended and political conditions improved, the peace process in Guatemala did not open the option to return, since political conflict and economic deterioration largely remained.

Despite the military advantages in its war against the leftist insurgents in the mid-1980s, the Guatemalan government was not able to annihilate the uprising. Consequently, some insurgent groups, mainly the Unidad Revolucionaria Nacional Guatemalteca (URNG) [Guatemalan National Revolutionary Union] based largely in the Mayan highlands, redefined their objectives and interventions and became reinvigorated in the late 1980s, causing more casualties among the Guatemalan army and leaving the fight closer to Guatemala City (Jonas 1991).

Although the possibilities for peace increased as more civil society organizations became involved in the public arena and as the UNRG increasingly saw its struggle in political rather than military terms, the economic situation remained discouraging. After thirty years of authoritarian rule, a climate of civil war, unemployment, lack of supplies, loss of foreign currency due to military expenditures, fuel shortages, international isolation and, in general, all the symptoms of a deep economic recession, Cerezo Arévalo's neoliberal policies implemented since 1985 brought prosperity only to the speculative capitalist class, while the parallel burdens of austerity cuts and high inflation fell on the vast majority of the population of workers, peasants, and the urban middle-class (Jonas 1991).

According to Jonas and Rodriguez (2014) following the reports of the World Bank, the country reached a population of 9.2 million by 1990 with a poverty level of about 65 percent, and with about 40 percent of the population living in extreme poverty. These economic conditions demotivated the return of Guatemalans settled in Los Angeles, at least in the short term.

Context of Reception

For those who obtained legal residence, although opportunities for social mobility began to emerge, the economic conditions in Southern California worsened. Cutbacks in defense-related industries resulted in the loss of thousands of jobs, which had repercussions in the other sectors of the economy, and by the early 1990s the state of California, and particularly Southern California, was immersed in a severe recession, which led to a decline in employment at all levels (Hamilton and Chinchilla 2001, 153). For Guatemalan immigrants, who had not been covered by status adjustments, not only did work opportunities worsen, but they also remained stuck in deteriorated inner-city neighborhoods characterized by high levels of crime, delinquency and acute racial and ethnic tensions (Jonas and Rodriguez 2014). Westlake, for instance, had become a major center of drug dealing, and increasing gang activity, drawing Guatemalan youth into delinquency (Jonas and Rodriguez 2014).

In addition, immigrants from Mexico and Central America continued to arrive in the late 1980s and early 1990s, increasing competition even for low-wage jobs. This difficult situation is well illustrated in the case of Antonio Rodríguez, who was born in Guatemala City in the 1950s. In spite of being born into a Pentecostal family, he preferred to develop a secular career as a manager of a soccer team, he married a Pentecostal woman and became the father of four children, all the while keeping himself away from the church.

In 1985, he and his wife offered to devote their lives to Jesus if his youngest son's life were spared from what seemed to be an unknown illness. Upon their son's recovery, he joined a congregation near their home. Some years later, Antonio Rodríguez resolved to heed God's call to the pastorate and opened an independent congregation. In 1989, as a pastor of a congregation with 200 members who met four times per week, he was invited to participate in Pentecostal preaching events in Latino congregations in Los Angeles, receiving a visa as a religious worker. After this successful stay in Los Angeles and upon his return to Guatemala City, he decided to go back to Los Angeles in 1991, but this time with his wife and children and with the goal of opening his own congregation there. Once in the United States, he was not able to find any work as a pastor and was forced to accept a job in a pizzeria instead.

Finally, for undocumented Guatemalan immigrants arriving in Los Angeles during the 1990s, in contrast to the experience of legalized migrants, who could travel freely, the land journey to the United States, which began in the southernmost region of Mexico, was riddled with bandits, gangs, and corrupt police waiting to victimize migrants (Rodriguez 2007). Additionally, transmigrants faced the increasing enforcement of immigration laws by the Mexican government. The U.S. government expanded its efforts to prevent Guatemalans and other Central Americans from reaching the U.S.-Mexico border in the early 1990s by providing training and financing for Mexican interdiction and deportation campaigns.

Responses to Guatemalan Immigration

Some options regarding status adjustment for undocumented Central American immigrants also materialized in the 1990s. The 1990 Act authorized the provision of Temporary Protected Status (TPS) for the safety of migrants who would otherwise be deported to countries where they would be persecuted or experience armed conflict, natural disasters, or other extraordinary and temporary dangerous conditions (Jonas and Rodriguez 2014). TPS was granted to many Salvadorans in 1990 and provided relief for Hondurans and Nicaraguans in 1999. However, it was never used to help Guatemalan migrants. More important for Guatemalans migrants was the settlement of the ABC v. Thornburgh lawsuit in the late 1990s, which gave Guatemalan and Salvadoran asylum seekers the chance to have their cases individually readjudicated (Jonas and Rodriguez 2014).

Pastor Antonio Rodríguez and his family could legalize their stay in the United States thanks to the measures implemented as a result of that lawsuit to force the U.S Government to recognize the asylum status of the people coming from Guatemala and El Salvador. This new legal status gave Pastor Antonio Rodríguez the opportunity to get a better job, this time in the office of lost baggage in the Los Angeles airport, while his wife found work as a receptionist in a hotel.

As middle-class immigrants who had been forced into low-wage jobs due to their lack of English-language skills on arrival, they could now move into higher-skilled and better-paying positions thanks to the recognition of their asylum status and to their degrees and technical or professional credentials. With half of their combined salaries, they could pay the expenses to rent a space for religious services of their congregation in a building of an African American Pentecostal church.

Due to some schedule-related problems and the need to use musical instruments, they decided to move to a more convenient location within the building of a Latino church. They remained there until 1995, at which point they had enough savings to buy a place where their church is now located, achieving the dream of establishing their own congregation. By June 2014, theirs was a vibrant Pentecostal congregation with nearly fifty people. In the last twenty years, with more faith in their mission than material means to make it real, Pastor Antonio Rodríguez has raised a family of six and a Pentecostal congregation, which has been supporting Latin American immigrants without legal status in the United States, particularly in cases of family reunification while still finding the means and time to go on missions from Los Angeles to serve communities as a missionary in Guatemala.

In spite of these advancements in migratory polices, in the 1990s, a rising concern over what many perceived to be an uncontrolled wave of immigration, particularly of undocumented migrants, also emerged, culminating in attempts to pass propositions which called for the denial of services, including education and health care, to undocumented immigrants and their children (Hamilton and Chinchilla 2001, 154).

In November 1994, California voters decided on a highly controversial state referendum, Proposition 187, which was designed to severely restrict the lives of undocumented migrants in the State (Jonas and Rodriguez 2014). Although Proposition 187 was passed, it never became effective since Federal Judicial Review deemed it unconstitutional, ruling that it infringed on legislative powers that were reserved for the Federal Government (Jonas and Rodriguez, 2014, 56). Nevertheless, its restrictive spirit was reflected only two years later in the enactment of a new immigration law, the Illegal Immigration Reform and Immigrant Responsibility Act (IIRIRA), which increased the resources for immigration enforcement measures and significantly curtailed immigrant rights. (Jonas and Rodriguez 2014, 57)

Due to the implementation of this Act, some Guatemalan migrants became more vulnerable since the IIRIRA facilitated the deportation of non-citizen immigrants and provided measures to ban deported migrants from reentering the country for several years or permanently. Deportation also meant permanent separation from their families and homes in the United States and the termination of U.S. employment, which for many Guatemalan families in the United States and Guatemala was the means to have a relatively middle-class lifestyle (Jonas and Rodriguez 2014, 57) The number of Guatemalan immigrants removed from the United States after the enactment of the IIRIRA in 1996 rose sharply. In 1996, 2,106 Guatemalan migrants were formally deported, but in 2003 the number more than tripled to 6,848 (U.S. DHS 2003), turning Guatemalans into the group with the second highest number of deportations among Central American migrants, with Honduras occupying the first place with 7,884 deportations (Jonas and Rodriguez 2014, 57)

This serves to illustrate that the economic, political, and social conditions during the 1990s in the Los Angeles metropolitan area were largely averse to Guatemalan immigrants, who, facing these difficulties, began to move to rural-based industries located in southern areas of the United States, as rural recruiters came from these places to look for migrant labor in the Los Angeles area (Jonas and Rodriguez 2014). The Los Angeles region no longer held the promise of employment for migrants as it had done in the 1980s.

4.3.4. From 2000 to the Present: Inclusion and Exclusion Conditions for Guatemalans in a Megalopolis

At the beginning of the twenty-first century, significant numbers of Guatemalans have settled in the Los Angeles area. A total of 1,044,209 individuals of Guatemalan origin resided in the United States in 2010, according to the U.S Census. From those, approximately 23 percent (243,655 individuals) lived in the Los Angeles region, which remained the region with the largest concentration of Guatemalans, who, in turn, have followed numerous and diverse paths in their quest for social incorporation.

Context of Departure: Guatemala in the 2000s

During the 2000s, numerous and significant structural changes could be observed in the context of both Guatemala and the Los Angeles region. In Guatemala, the national scene was greatly changed from that of the late 1970s and early 1980s. The Peace Accords were signed in 1996, formally ending the military confrontation and the massive political violence that had largely motivated migration prior to the mid-1990s. Nonetheless, emigration to the United States did not stop. The end of the war did not mean the establishment of "peace" but rather the emergence of new postwar problems such as increasing inequality, common crime, and environmental disasters, which became the motivation for migratory flows during the first years of the new century (Jonas and Rodriguez 2014, 61).

Although in macroeconomic terms Guatemala has done well in comparison with other Central American countries, postwar Guatemala has remained among the most unequal countries in the world, with a Gini index of more than 50 during this period, according to World Bank data.[10] According to Jonas and Rodriguez (2014 61), crucial provisions of the Peace Accords regarding the improvement of the socioeconomic situation of the majority of Guatemalans and economy modernization were not implemented, since the economic elites were able to resist paying taxes that could have financed social programs or prioritized the creation of decent jobs. In addition, the employment situation was characterized by increasing exclusion from the labor market, combined with greater informalization of labor (Perez Saínz 2001).

Although the Central American Free Trade Agreement (CAFTA) that took effect for Guatemala in 2006 was designed to alleviate this situation, at the end it actually exacerbated economic and social problems by implementing and institutionalizing new neoliberal economic policies (Jonas and Rodriguez 2014, 61). Additionally, Guatemalans suffered a variety of environmental disasters such as the 2005 Hurricane Stan in western Guatemala and the Guatemala-Mexico border; a calamitous drought in eastern Guatemala during part of the 2000s, which caused large numbers of deaths, widespread destruction in the country, and a crisis of hunger and nutritional precariousness (Jonas and Rodriguez 2014, 61).

Having as a backdrop this structural context of socioeconomic crisis, common crime increased significantly in Guatemala, turning citizen securi-

10 https://data.worldbank.org/indicator/SI.POV.GINI?locations=GT.

ty into a major concern as violence from organized crime, drug trafficking, and complicity from state institutions became everyday events. Meanwhile, in urban neighborhoods, social violence also emerged in association with the growth of gangs, some of which recruited deportees from the United States who were unable to find work in Guatemala. Among the crimes committed by gangs, attempts to extort money from business owners and families receiving remittances from migrant members in the United States were common (Ribando Seelke 2014).

Facing these devastating conditions in their own country and witnessing the large volume of remittances that the migrants sent to Guatemala, Guatemalan workers also continued migrating to the Los Angeles area. Francisco Quiacaín, who came to Los Angeles in 2004, is an example of the newcomers arriving in the twenty-first century. He was born in the town of San Pedro La Laguna, Guatemala, in 1954 to a Tz'utujil family converted to Pentecostalism and member of the Assemblies of God.

When he was 23 years old, he got married, became a father of five and, along with his family, joined the Church Bethel, a Pentecostal church founded by a Tz'utujil pastor. He participated actively in this church, taking numerous responsibilities or "privileges" such as singer and leader of the men's group, and some years later he became the president of the church association of his town. During those years, he also developed his own business, making and selling ice to the increasing flows of tourists and expatriates, who came to learn Spanish and develop small businesses. In 2004, because of economic problems in Guatemala, he migrated to Los Angeles, crossing Mexico in a complicated journey by car and train, leaving his wife and children in San Pedro.

When in Los Angeles he began to serve in a Latin Pentecostal church as well as in a Korean Pentecostal church. He has assumed responsibilities in both of them. At the same time, he has been employed as a construction worker. Although he has no legal documents to reside in the United States, he has economically supported his family and church at home.

Context of Reception: Los Angeles since 2000

During the period 2000-2014, Guatemalan immigrants in Los Angeles, particularly undocumented immigrants like Antonio, had to face unfavorable political and economic conditions. In the political sphere, the enactment of IIRIRA in 1996 significantly increased the spatial restrictions on Guatemalans as it enlisted the cooperation of state and local police agencies in the enforcement of immigration policies, increasing at the same time the number of local norms to restrict the presence of undocumented immigrants (Jonas and Rodriguez 2014, 21). In addition, as a result of the terrorist attacks in New York City and Washington, D.C. on September 11, 2001, the U.S. immigration policy began to be concerned primarily with immigration as a subcategory of national security and antiterrorist issues.

Jonas and Rodriguez (2014, 21) note that more than 1,300 state and local police agents from 19 states had been trained by the U.S. Immigration and Customs Enforcement (ICE) in the enforcement of immigration policies, resulting in more than 300,000 identifications of "potentially removable" immigrants since 2006. In the economic sphere, although the first years of the 2000s were characterized by real estate booms, during the Great Recession (2008-2010) unemployment rate reached 12.7 percent in Los Angeles, exceeding the national average by 3 percentage points (Myers 2012). This especially affected undocumented migrants, who worked in the housing and construction sector and were effectively very vulnerable to economic shifts.

Regardless of being exposed to these restrictions in their everyday lives, many Guatemalan migrants—particularly undocumented newcomers like Francisco Quiacaín—still see major opportunity in Los Angeles rather than Guatemala. Even if they have limited chances for integration in the United States, it remains their main reference point.

Having a family in Guatemala, they focus all of their energy on improving their livelihoods and their families for when they return, working as much as possible and sending back an important share of their low U.S wages, which is still significantly more than what they had received or would receive in Guatemala. Thus, Francisco Quiacaín, a day worker in the construction sector, expressed pride in the fact that with the money sent back home he had bought two houses in Guatemala, his youngest daughter has been able to study architecture in Guatemala City, and his wife is in charge of a fund to help people from the church in need due to health problems.

Context of Departure: Social, Economic, and Political Features of Guatemalans in 2010

Apart from individual efforts, it is important to point out that the social, economic, and political integration of Guatemalans in the United States remains a pending issue. Since the 1970s, Guatemalans have migrated to Los Angeles after crossing the borders of Mexico and the United States and many of them have arrived in often difficult, and sometimes unwelcoming environments in which they have faced the pressures of finding a job, working long hours, and coping with the problems of a megalopolis like Los Angeles.

In 2010, the Pew Hispanic Center elaborated a statistical profile of Guatemalans in the United States, which compares the demographic and economic characteristics of the Guatemalan population with the characteristics of all Hispanics and with the U.S. population overall. Key facts in this study were, for instance, that in relation to immigration status, seven-in-ten Guatemalans (69.4%) in the United States were foreign born compared to 38.1 percent of Hispanics as a whole and 12.5 percent of the U.S. population overall. Seven-in-ten immigrants from Guatemala (69.6%) arrived in the U.S. in the 1990s or later and nearly one quarter of Guatemalan immigrants (23.8%) were U.S. citizens.

In relation to educational attainment, Guatemalans have lower levels of education than the Hispanic population overall. 53.6 percent of Guatemalans ages 25 and older—compared with 39.2 percent of all U.S. Hispanics—have not obtained at least a high school diploma.

Regarding income, the median annual personal income for Guatemalans ages 16 and older was $19,349 in 2008; the median income for all U.S. Hispanics was $21,488. The share of Guatemalans who live in poverty, 20.6 percent, is higher than the rate for the general U.S. population (12.7 percent) and similar to the share for all Hispanics (20.7 percent). Furthermore, by the end of the 2000s, the employment situation of Guatemalans was remarkably similar to that in the 1980s and 1990s. It seems clear that low levels of education, limited English-language skills, and undocumented legal status still play important roles in their concentration in low-income jobs with limited mobility.

Social Participation: The Case of Pentecostal Independent Churches

Despite these negative conditions, the twenty-first century has also brought new opportunities for Guatemalan immigrants, particularly for those with legal residence. Thanks to their legal status, Guatemalans and their descendants, who were already U.S. citizens, have had more opportunities to participate in more established organizations, pursuing educational and religious goals or fighting for immigrant rights.

The Pentecostal independent churches founded by the religious leaders analyzed in this study are good examples of this engagement. Using the assistance offered by the U.S. government to open and register religious and cultural organizations, five out of seven interviewed leaders had registered their congregations by 2000. In addition, the seven visited congregations had similar characteristics: They were independent congregations with a membership between 50 to 500 devotees of Latin American origin, particularly from México, El Salvador, or Guatemala, or else second-generation immigrants that were already U.S. citizens. However, the majority still did not have legal status in the United States.

Religious services are usually held in Spanish, given the limited English-speaking skills of the members of the congregation. These congregations provide important material help to their members, besides the more obvious spiritual support. This includes English courses, Bible-reading courses in Spanish especially oriented to second-generation immigrants, and music classes for those willing to play an instrument or even to form a band.

Interviewing members in these churches has allowed a look into the complex lives of Guatemalan Pentecostal believers, particularly those of religious leaders. As the life narratives presented above have shown, Guatemalan Pentecostal religious leaders spend long days and nights accommodating responsibilities of (often multiple) time-consuming jobs, extended families, fragile congregations, and problem-ridden neighborhoods.

These realities contradict long-established ideas that associate Pentecostal growth with investments from outside the congregations or the supposedly profitable character of the establishment of a congregation by religious entrepreneurs. As Maduro (2012, 202) has pointed out, looking into the Guatemalan Pentecostal leaders' migratory trajectories and their congregations, one can see, on the contrary, that Pentecostal growth in Los Angeles is the result of single-handed and often heroic hard work of strong-willed, tenacious individuals, highly convinced of being the recipients of a divine and urgent call to start a new church with very few resources, to attempt to radically transform their lives and the lives of others, and of being blessed with a God-given power to do so against all material, social, and/or educational odds.

Through such hard work, it is possible to witness the ability of dozens of Guatemalan immigrants of meager resources to launch difficult religious initiatives, keeping afloat lives and congregations for years amid innumerable obstacles and challenges, generally overseeing not just their congregations' growth, but also their expansion, even beyond the U.S. borders.

4.4. Conclusions

This chapter has explored the range and complexity of the Guatemalan migratory experiences in Los Angeles since 1970, presenting the changing structural conditions of the context of origin and of the context of the arrival of migrants. Since the 1970s, Guatemalans have migrated to Los Angeles, leaving a country hit by successive economic, political, and military crises. They have crossed the borders of Mexico and the United States, facing hardships and dangers, and ending in often difficult, and sometimes unwelcoming environments, in which they had faced the pressures of finding a job, working long hours, and coping with the harmful effects of anti-migratory policies. These are the structural conditions of the transnational space articulated between Guatemala and Los Angeles.

At the same time, this chapter was concerned with Guatemalan Pentecostal leaders' trajectories, delineating the social position of the agents in the social space articulated between Guatemala and Los Angeles. It has shown that the changing conditions of their context, particularly the opportunities for a legalized stay in Los Angeles, together with the social-ethnic background of each leader, which have led to the attainment of economic, social, and educational resources after many years in Los Angeles, have generated opportunities to launch tenacious and perdurable religious initiatives. In the next chapter, I will present the positions held by the seven Guatemalan independent leaders and their religious initiatives in the religious field of Los Angeles.

5. The Religious Field in Los Angeles in 2014: The Scene of Latino Pentecostalism

In the previous chapter, the social, economic, and political context of Los Angeles was presented. Los Angeles is usually depicted as a county with no ethnic majorities. However, one ethnic group is predominant, although its numbers are not reflected in the civic infrastructure of the county.

Latinos are almost 50 percent of the population of the county, but it seems as if Latinos inhabit a parallel universe; they have relatively little political, social, or economic power. Something similar happens in the religious field. Latinos are usually in the periphery of the power structures, despite being important players in the changing religious landscape due to their numbers and religious commitments. In religious terms, Latinos constitute the single largest and fastest growing ethnic group of the Los Angeles Roman Catholic population. At the same time, they are also the single most important source of converts to the Protestant and other Christian denominations in the United States, in many of which they represent if not the largest, then indeed the single fastest growing portion of their constituency (Maduro 2012, 199). That is particularly the case of Latino Pentecostals, who are influencing the shape of Protestant denominations and even the Roman Catholic Church.

This chapter aims to portray the religious field in Los Angeles and the impact of Latino Pentecostalism following a praxeological approach. This allows an understanding of religion as praxis and, at the same time, to set any religious praxis in an identifiable, relatively autonomous field within the ever-changing domains of action, interaction, and friction of agencies striving to define what is sacred and to manage the relationship between the sacred and a given community.

In order to trace the impact of Latino Pentecostalism in Los Angeles, this chapter follows the dimensions pointed out by Bourdieu regarding the field of cultural production, which were adjusted by Schäfer et al. (2016b, 190) for the study of the religious field. These two dimensions are "achievement of eminence" and "authenticity." The first dimension, "achievement of eminence," refers to the relation between the performers and the audience of a religious organization and the level of religious complexity. The second, "authenticity," refers to the public image of being an agent of the "true" religion, that is, to the credibility of a religious organization, to its presence, autonomy, and resilience. The chapter begins by presenting the religious affiliations among Latinos, with particular regard to Central Americans in Los Angeles, then it explores the dimension called "achievement of eminence" by presenting some characteristics of Latino Pentecostal churches. It also examines the dimension of "authenticity" by looking into the connection between Latino Pentecostal praxis and politics. Finally, it offers a conclusion.

5.1. Latino Pentecostalism in Numbers

The population with a Latin-American origin or "Latinos" became the largest minority group in the United States during the first decade of the twenty-first century. The Latino presence is even more pronounced in Los Angeles. They represent almost 50 percent of the city and 48 percent of the county population. According to the 2010 United States census, approximately 4.7 million Latinos live in Los Angeles County. This demographic weight is not reflected in a similar amount of political, social, or economic influence. In the religious field, in turn, where Latinos have a higher Christian commitment than the rest of the population, their role is limited, at best.

The Pew Research Center's 2014 National Survey of Latinos and Religion finds that a majority (55%) of the nation's estimated 35.4 million Latino adults identify themselves as Catholics, down from 67% in 2010, a steep decline that is part of a long-term trend in the erosion of Catholicism among Latinos in the United States. About 22% are Protestants, and 18% are religiously unaffiliated.

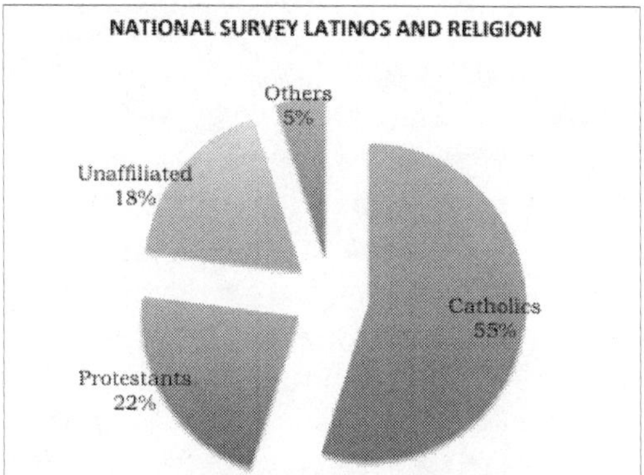

Figure 5.1: Latino's religious affiliation in the US.
Source: Pew Research Center (2014).

That means that in Los Angeles County, there are currently about 2.5 million Latino Catholics and over 1 million Latino Protestants, while 800.000 Latinos are secular. About 75 percent of the Protestants are members of evangelical or Pentecostal churches, and 22 percent belong to mainline denominations. It is also worth noting that according to the Pew (2014) study, 52 percent of Latino Catholics identify themselves as charismatic and 28 percent identify themselves as born-again Christians. So, even though the majority of Latinos call themselves Catholics, many of them also identify with religious practices that are more commonly identified with evangelicals and Pentecostals. Based on this data, it is possible to say that the share of Latinos who identify as Catholic has decreased incrementally in the last decades but also that a growing number of Catholics identify themselves with "Protestant" religious categories.

The Pew study also points out that the long-term decline in the share of Catholics among Latinos may partly reflect religious changes that are currently underway in Latin America, where evangelical churches have been gaining adherents, and the share of those with no religious affiliation has been slowly rising in a region that historically has been overwhelmingly Catholic. Also, it reflects religious changes taking place in the United States, where Catholicism has had a net loss of adherents. Many Latinos leaving Catholicism have tended to become born-again or evangelical Protestants, a group that exhibits very high levels of religious commitment. On average, Latino evangelicals—many of whom also identify themselves as either Pentecostal or charismatic Protestants—not only report higher rates of church attendance than Latino Catholics but also tend to be more engaged in other religious activities, including Scripture reading, Bible study groups, and sharing their faith.

Furthermore, concerning the religious background of Latinos in Los Angeles, it is argued that the county represents an exception to the national religious profile of the Latino population. Due to the composition of the Latino population of Los Angeles County—75 percent of Mexican origin and 14 percent of Central American origin—the percentage of Catholics and Protestants vary in comparison to the Latino population at large. Thus, the percentage of Mexicans that identify themselves as Catholics is higher (61%) than the percentage of the Latino population as a whole, and the percentage of Central Americans that identify themselves as Protestants is higher (37%) than among the average Latino population.

Most likely, this is because these figures reflect the religious preferences in their country of origin. Because a more significant percentage of the Central American population is Protestant than in other Latin American countries, Central American immigrants going to Los Angeles are much more likely to be, and they are also more likely to remain Protestant once they are there. The cases analyzed in this study reflect this trend. All the Guatemalan Pentecostal leaders interviewed were already Pentecostal before traveling to the United States for the first time. Martin Carmona, Francisca Arévalo, Antonio Rodríguez, and Francisco Quiacaín were all born into a Pentecostal family or else their families were converted when they were just a few years old. The rest, Brother Marcos González, Brother Alvaro Sánchez, and Brother Carlos Benítez did so in their youth.

Besides, considering the prevalence of religious practices such as Bible study groups and sharing their faith among Pentecostals, Central Americans are more likely to engage in missionary activities (Martínez 2012, 3). There are good examples of this tendency in the present study. Brother Marcos González, who arrived in the 1970s, commented that he is a missionary and that evangelization was his reason for traveling to the United States, a place in which he had participated in evangelistic campaigns. Brother Martin Carmona, in turn, described his experience as a musician and founder of a Pentecostal rock band, doing evangelical work from his youth through tours in different countries. Francisca Arévalo referred to the concerts and preaching she gave at the beginning of her career both in Guatemala and in the United States. Brother Carlos Benítez spoke of his preaching in missionary campaigns in different areas of Guatemala only a few weeks after his conversion. Brother Alvaro Sánchez narrated his first trip to Los Angeles to participate in an international conference in which he learned of the importance of missionary work, and how, as a result of this experience, he participated in evangelizing campaigns in different countries. Brother Antonio Rodríguez referred to his commitment to evangelization and the opening of new congregations in Guatemala and the United States, and Francisco Quiacaín described his experience during his trip to the United States, in which each time he and other migrants paused to rest, he took the opportunity to introduce them to God and pray for their successful arrival in the United States.

Last but not least, the observed trend among many Christians to identify themselves with independent churches or to downplay or reject traditional denominational labels is also apparent among Latinos. It is likely because Latinos do not have the same type of representation in most Protestant denominations. Although their numbers are on the rise in most Pentecostal and evangelical churches, they are not the leaders in traditional denominational churches (Martínez 2012, 10). Some of these churches behave as if Los Angeles was never a Mexican city and also ignore the fact that half of its population is made of Latinos.

Latinos' preference for independent churches is reflected in the growth of another type of organization that is usually disregarded, the ever-growing Latin American or Latino-based Pentecostal churches in Los Angeles. Some of these churches were founded in the Los Angeles area almost a century ago. However, most of them are much more recent. Latino Pentecostal churches led and funded by Latinos are thriving throughout the city. Some of them are as transitory as some of their members. They often have to move to new locations when they lose their leases. Nevertheless, these congregations are growing. The Guatemalan Pentecostal independent leaders analyzed in this dissertation are working in the frame of these transitory organizations. A brief characterization of these congregations is presented in section 5.2 below. Finally, there are also larger Latino Protestant churches in the city which are Pentecostal. Regardless of their size, Latino Pentecostal churches are an example of religious transnationalism (Martínez 2012, 16). The next pages deal with this issue.

5.1.1. Pentecostal Churches' Ties to Latin America

The study of the religious experience of Latinos usually tends to focus on what happens north of the border, though the Pew study (2014) recognizes that "religious affiliation in Latin America is very relevant to any examination of Hispanics in the United States." Globalization, legal and undocumented migration, and transnationalism are changing the U.S. Latino religious field. Hence, it is important to think about the impact of these new social conditions on religious practices and affiliation both in Latin America and among Latinos in the U.S.

According to the Pew Research Center's 2014 National Survey of Latinos and Religion, nearly six-in-ten Latino churchgoers (57%) say that their church maintains close ties with Latin American countries by sending money or missionaries to them or by receiving clergy from countries in the region. About one-in-five Latinos say that their place of worship does not maintain close ties to Latin American countries (21%) and the same percentage says that they do not know if this is the case (21%). Among religious groups, churchgoing Protestants are more likely than Catholics to say that their church maintains close ties with Latin America (71% and 54%, respectively). Protestants are also significantly less likely than Catholics to say that they are unsure of their church's ties to Latin America (10% to 26%).

Moreover, there are many Latin American pastors, conference speakers, and musicians who regularly live in the Los Angeles area. Cross-fertilization of influences also occurs because many Latino pastors travel to Latin America to preach and give conferences on a regular basis (Martínez 2012, 17). The transnational character of Pentecostalism can be mainly seen in Los Angeles County: At the dawn of modern Pentecostalism, Latino converts went from Los Angeles to their places of origin, becoming informal missionaries among their relatives and friends. Now the movement is in both directions. A variation on this transnational theme is when a church such as Robert Schuller's Crystal Cathedral in Garden Grove brings someone like Dante Gebel to pastor its Spanish-language congregation.

Regarding the ties to Latin America, this study follows a *transnational perspective*, which underlines, above all, social phenomena and social relationships extended over several local units in different nation states, which are relatively durable and involve comparatively dense interactions, considering the role that transnationalism plays in the articulation of religious praxis of the Guatemalan Pentecostal leaders interviewed.

As mentioned in Chapter 2, religious convictions and practices disregard national frontiers. Several scholars (Rudolph and Piscatori 1997; Vásquez and Marquardt 2003; Levitt 2004) have argued that because most religions usually seek to link individual and community renewal with global transformation in the name of universal values, they have a long tradition of operating transnationally, a fact that is reflected not only in their beliefs and symbols but also in their practices and forms of organizations.

All of the Guatemalan Pentecostal leaders interviewed provided numerous accounts connected to activities such as preaching and missionary work, founding new congregations in other countries and providing material aid for people in need in other countries. They offered detailed descriptions of the times when they were invited to preach and to participate in numerous missionary campaigns in other countries. Guatemalan independent Pentecostal churches in Los Angeles do not exist as isolated islands. Instead, they are bound into dense, multiform, and flexible networks of communication, cooperation, and exchange that connect them not only to churches in the country from which their members originally came, but also to the transnational networks that make up the global Pentecostal movement.

Although leaders of smaller churches are usually limited to travelling short distances in North and Central America due to financial constraints, pastors of larger churches often engage in intercontinental travel. The countries mentioned by the interviewees were Guatemala, Mexico, El Salvador, Costa Rica, Argentina, Peru, Chile, and Spain. Two of the pastors also referred to the opening of new congregations in other countries. For instance, Alvaro Sánchez described the origin and current functioning of congregations of his church in Costa Rica, El Salvador and in North Carolina in the United States. Likewise, Martin Carmona talked about his church congregation in Guatemala. Regarding the provision of material aid for people in need in other countries, Francisca Arévalo referred to her efforts collecting clothes and toys for children in Guatemala. Francisco Quiacaín mentioned his endeavors collecting money alongside other Pentecostal believers from his town in order to create a fund to offer economic assistance for ill people there.

For the analysis of these results, it was clear that specific indicators for the description of transnational relations were required since current definitions of transnationalization are focused on the intensity of cross-border interactions and how they are structuring social spaces (Pries 2010, 29). For instance, Pries distinguishes among transnational relations, transnational networks, and transnational spaces. Transnational relations emerge from the exchange of participants in an internet community like a music forum or student forum, who, thanks to a technical artefact system relation, share symbols and experiences in a specific field of practices (Pries 2010, 29). Transnational networks are based on more intensive exchange, which allow the development of binding cross-border relationship since interaction shapes cross-border symbols systems, which are adapted to the different locations of the participants. Although transnational networks function without a clear organizing core and the local social spaces are of decisive importance, in some cases these networks can reach a substantial weight, influencing the local everyday world (Pries 2010, 29). Finally, transnational social spaces constitute cross-border social interdependencies in which social practices, system of symbols, and social and cultural structures are interlinked (Pries 2010, 39).

Considering Pries's conceptualization, it is possible to argue that the references provided by Guatemalan independent Pentecostal leaders reflect the type of transnational networks. Since the descriptions depict a more or less intensive exchange, which allow the development of fluid cross-border relationship and influence the local everyday world of the agents. Nevertheless, this classification does not focus on the power conditions inside a particular field, denying any consideration about how transnational exchange transforms the position of the agent in the field. To overcome this limitation, to analyze these results, it is not only necessary to consider the durability, frequency, and importance of transnational exchanges, but also other indicators like the degree of institutionalization of these exchanges. Based on the conceptualization that Sarah Mahler and Katrina Hansing (2005) developed from the analysis of Catholic transnational relations established between Cuba and Miami, I elaborated a set of indicators.

The first of these indicators is the frequency of transnational activities, which measures how often people participate in transnational activities and indicate their degree of commitment (Portes, Guarnizo, and Landolt 1999). The second indicator is the degree of institutionalization of transnational activities. Considerations about the size of the organizations or number of agents involved, how formally or informally these people operate, and the quality (close or distant) of the transnational relationship provide information regarding the degree of formalization of transnational activities. The third indicator is the mediation of the relations. It refers to the type of interactions people have. Are they face-to-face? Do they involve direct contact without face-to-face exposure (such as through telephone calls, mail, or e-mail)? Alternatively, do agents relate through intermediaries, such as physical, written, visual, or electronic devices?

Once these indicators were examined, it was possible to differentiate Guatemalan independent Pentecostal leaders of this study in two groups: Those who have *transnational missionary work through family and friends* and those who have *transnational missionary work through organizations.*

The first group, *Leaders with a transnational missionary work through family and friends*, is composed of five leaders: Marcos González, the female pastor Francisca Arévalo, Antonio Rodríguez, Carlos Benitez and Francisco Quiacaín. In this group, the frequency of transnational activities is not very intensive, with trips and contacts mainly taking place between California and Guatemala, although sometimes other countries would be included. The frequency of these trips is one or two times per year, occurring on holidays. Also, interviewees stated that they participate as individuals. The amount of economic resources devoted to these trips seems to be limited since they rely on family members or friends. Due to this personal component, the transnational activities have an informal character.

Finally, although many of these activities involve face-to-face encounters, others, such as the creation of financial funds to support people in need, take place through electronic devices that allow communication and sending money. Nevertheless, these activities are cross-border phenomena and allow these interviewees to expand their ministry beyond Los Angeles, connecting them with other Pentecostal ministries in the Americas through family and friends. They travel and establish contacts in Guatemala and the United States aiming to form a broader community. Besides, in the case of Antonio Rodríguez and Francisca Arévalo, a legitimation process takes place due to the invitation to preach in other countries. Both of them stated that they accept invitations to preach in other churches in other countries. The very fact of being asked to preach in other countries enhanced their authority as a pastor, since that serves to prove that they are in demand by other churches and countries. At the same time, they invite speakers, who usually come from abroad. In this way, they can expand their ministry and connect with other churches in different places and countries without generating significant competition.

Pastors Alvaro Sánchez and Martin Carmona are included in the group *Leaders with a transnational missionary work through organizations*. These two leaders work in the frame of more established organizations and usually develop their missionary work as a full-time job. Additionally, their religious organizations have churches in different countries. Therefore, the frequency of transnational activities serves to constitute cross-border social networks in which the similar dispositions, social practices, and communication systems have developed so intensely that they have become a significant social and spatial reference unit for everyday life practices. Besides, these transnational activities not only take place between Guatemala and the United States, but also between other countries. From this expansive character of the organizations derives the transnational exchange, which is much more formalized and institutionalized, leaving less space for emotional proximity. As leaders and executives, they travel to evangelize with the idea of furthering the missionary expansion of their churches. The background of their clientele is largely low and low-middle class, often with migratory origins. Therefore, the miraculous triumph over the impediment in achieving a modest economic stabilization through faith and coaching by a religious specialist with divinely granted powers is the paramount pastoral strategy.

5.2. Pentecostal Latinos and Their Churches: The Dimension of "Achievement of Eminence"

Considering this overview of the religious affiliations among Latinos in Los Angeles, the influence of religious practices and affiliation both in Latin America and among U.S. Latinos, and the transnational character of Latino Pentecostalism in Los Angeles, the following offers a description of Latino Pentecostal churches according to the "achievement of eminence" dimension.

Achievement of eminence refers to religious complexity—that is, the relation between the performers and the audience of the organization (Schäfer et al. 2016b, 191). According to Schäfer et al. (2016b, 191), this is related to Weber's distinction between church and sect. While the former is a well-established organization with a small number of performers and a large number of laypersons, the latter consists of activists, with no real laypersons among them. Yinger (1970, 259-262), in turn, introduced the subtler concept of "religious complexity," something that is probably much more similar to the current situation in Los Angeles County. From an agent-centered perspective, we can say that the higher an organization's complexity, the more significant the potential public impact of the experts working on it. Complexity thus denotes the purpose, stability, and operating distance of religious organizations.

The greater Los Angeles area constitutes an excellent location to look at how Pentecostalism has developed among Latinos in the United States. Modern Pentecostalism began in Los Angeles and spread through the world, but now new generations of adherents are bringing Pentecostalism back to Los Angeles in various forms. Hence, some forms of Latino Pentecostalism in Los Angeles are the churches linked to traditional American Pentecostal churches. All of the U.S. Pentecostal denominations have Latino churches in Los Angeles, including traditionally African American denominations (Martínez 2012, 17). These religious organizations tend to have a high level of complexity and the experts working for them can exert a genuinely public impact.

There are also many churches from Latino Pentecostal denominations such as the Apostolic Assembly, the *Concilio Latino Americano de Iglesias Cristianas* (CLADIC) [Latin American Council of Christian Churches], the *Concilio Latinoamericano Internacional de la Iglesia de Dios Pentecostal de Nueva York* (CLANY) [New York International Latin American Council of the Pentecostal Church of God] or the *Asamblea de Iglesias Cristianas* [Assembly of Christian Church]. There are also many churches from Latin American Pentecostal denominations such as the Elim Pentecostal Church. Although these religious organizations tend to have some level of complexity and the experts working for them can have a public impact, they are less significant in comparison to the U.S. Pentecostal denominations.

Finally, it is also possible to see various forms of immigrant-based Latino Pentecostal movements in Los Angeles. Most of these churches are small, transitory, and many have part-time pastors. Some of them try to imitate the larger churches, while others see them as threats. Networks of small churches sometimes affiliate themselves with one of the large churches. Others complain that the large churches grow at the expense of the smaller congregations in the area. Some of the small churches see themselves as alternative congregations, while others would like to grow into megachurches (Martínez 2012, 17). As mentioned above, the Guatemalan Pentecostal independent leaders analyzed are working in the frame of these small and transitory organizations. The seven visited congregations were independent congregations, with a membership between 50 to more than 500 devotees of Latin American origin, mainly from México, El Salvador, or Guatemala, or else second-generation immigrants that are already U.S. citizens. Religious services are in Spanish, given the limited English-speaking skills of their members. These congregations provide important material help to their followers, besides the more obvious spiritual support. Help includes English courses, Bible reading courses in Spanish especially oriented to second-generation immigrants, and music classes for those willing to play an instrument or even to form a band.

These religious organizations tend to have a low level of complexity and the experts working for them have almost no potential public impact. Although there are no official numbers regarding these independent churches in Los Angeles,[11] some authors argue that they are challenging the

---

11 Most of the estimations about the number of Latino Pentecostal churches refer to the United States. For instance, Espinoza (2004) calculated that

official religious order, not by directly confronting the religious powers, but by offering counter-narratives that are more compelling and that allow people to be active participants in "God's work" in the world (Martínez 2012; Maduro 2012). These churches grow among Latinos because they speak to a lived and practical experience of God. Most Latinos experience God as someone who walks with them in the journey of life. That experience is precisely encouraged in Latino Pentecostal worship and church life. Besides, these congregations are one of the few places where Latinos can express their faith in their way and lead their congregations (Martínez 2012, 17).

For many immigrants, these churches also become their new extended families. Because of these characteristics, Latino Pentecostal congregations are increasingly attractive and many non-Pentecostal churches imitate their styles. Immigrant-based Latino Pentecostal movements in Los Angeles are producing changes in the religious field of Los Angeles as their style and massive conversion from one religious institution into another put pressure on the conditions and structures of more established religious institutions.

---

there were more than 10,000 non-Catholic Latino Christian congregations in the United States (most of them headed by Latino ministers), but only 1,441 (14%) of these are mainstream Protestant churches, which means that more than 8,500 are Pentecostal congregations. Another study referring to the Chicago metropolitan area is the Chicago Latino Congregations Study (CLCS) carried out in 2010 by the Center for the Study of Latino Religion at the University of Notre Dame. In this study, researchers solicited lists of Chicago Latino churches from a wide variety of organizations such as denominational or church councils, pastoral associations, coalitions, parachurch organizations, community organizations, the Mayor's office, and the office of a local alderman; and from other research studies on Chicago-area churches. Due to the temporary and informal character of many independent Latino Pentecostal churches, most of them could not be considered. Until 2018, I could not find any study about Latino Pentecostal churches similar to the Chicago Latino Congregations Study for Los Angeles.

5.3. Who is in Charge? The Dimension of "Religious Authenticity"

Religious authenticity is a less objectively addressable notion, as it mostly stands for the image of being an agent of the "true" religion. Credibility denotes a religious organization's presence, autonomy, and resilience concerning compromise (Schäfer et al. 2016b, 191). Credibility is elicited by the connection between Latino Pentecostal praxis and politics. The variety in the type of churches described above also represents opportunities for new positions and leadership roles among the Latino population of Los Angeles. Historically, Latinos have been in charge of very few institutions in Los Angeles. Until recently, they were even at the margins of Catholicism in the region. The significant exceptions have been the Latino Pentecostal churches.

According to Martínez (2012, 11), Pentecostal and evangelical growth has created an unusual situation in Los Angeles. Even though there are almost three times as many Latino Catholics as Latino Pentecostals, there are many more Latino Pentecostal pastors than Latino priests. According to him, part of the difference has to do with ordination requirements; becoming a Catholic priest is much more complicated and demands a much higher commitment than becoming a Pentecostal preacher. Besides, the Catholic Church is a hierarchical transnational organization that appoints its priests from Rome, leaving little room for local initiatives. In contrast, Latino Pentecostalism provides spaces for otherwise marginalized people to learn and practice leadership. People who have a sense of calling can become pastors, even if they have not had access to formal theological education or cannot qualify as such because they do not have enough formal education, cannot study in English, or are undocumented. Because the churches depend on lay leadership, many working-class people have the opportunity to develop leadership skills even though they might never have a similar opportunity in other settings. In many churches, the central leader is literally a person who comes from the people. This is also one of the reasons for the growth of Pentecostalism among the Latino community: it attracts people from other Christian expressions. Hence, Pentecostalism becomes a challenge for the official religious order, not by directly confronting the religious powers, but by offering a counter-narrative that is more compelling and that allows people to be active participants in God's work in the world (Martínez 2012, 17).

Due to these new opportunities for leadership, some aspects have changed regarding the relationship between religion and politics. Historically, most Latino Pentecostal leaders followed the Latin American Pentecostal model and considered that they should be apolitical. This trend began to change both in Latin America and in the United States as the community grew and attracted the attention of political parties looking for new constituencies. Nevertheless, for many years, Latino religious leaders continued to play a limited role in local politics and many Latino Protestants were largely apolitical (Martínez 2012, 9). The credibility of Pentecostal churches with a Latino leadership still remains doubtful. This is the case for six of the Guatemalan Pentecostal independent leaders interviewed. They did not refer to any political involvement and tended to avoid talking about political issues. As will be explained below, only one, Brother Martin Carmona, commented on his political involvement.

This situation changed for many Latino Pentecostal leaders after December 2005 when Congressman James Sensenbrenner proposed the *Border Protection, Antiterrorism, and Illegal Immigration Control Act* (HR4437). According to this bill, supporting undocumented immigrants in the United States constitutes a felony. This measure directly affected pastors, social workers, medical personnel, and others who regularly interact with the undocumented immigrants. As most Latino pastors and priests regularly serve the undocumented, many of them decided that they had to work in favor of a fair and comprehensive immigration reform that should include a path for the legalization of the undocumented (Martínez 2012, 9). Fighting for immigration reform put them at odds with the politically conservative leadership of many Protestant denominations as well as forcing many theologically conservative Latino leaders to rethink their understanding of the pastoral ministry. It also led to the creation of many organizations like *La Red de Pastores y Líderes del Sur de California* (LA RED) [The Network of Pastors and Leaders of Southern California], which brought together many Latino Protestant leaders who had never been politically active before, working together towards immigration reform and the protection of undocumented migrants. Reflecting his concern for political involvement, Martin Carmona talked about his involvement in defense of the right of migrants, articulated through protest in front of official buildings in Los Angeles and his support in the creation of other organizations to gather Latino American pastors and leaders.

As a consequence of these increasing opportunities for leadership and links with Latin American churches, the Latino Pentecostal organization's presence, autonomy, and resilience is growing. According to Martínez (2012, 18), this is due to the numerous points of encounter highlighted by the Latino Pentecostal movement in Los Angeles. For instance, they are between North America and Latin America. They offer a religious praxis between Euro-American Protestantism and Latin American Catholicism. Thus, Latino Pentecostal movements emerge between a dying Christendom and the vital new Christian expressions of the Global South, reflecting the difference between the First World and the majority world and the changes in notions of the nation-state and the new transnational reality of migrant peoples.

5.4. Where Can the Guatemalan Pentecostal Independent Leaders of this Study Be Placed in Los Angeles's Religious Field?

As it was presented above, the Guatemalan Pentecostal independent leaders here analyzed are working in small congregations. Regarding the dimension of "achievement of eminence," these congregations exhibit a low level of complexity. Additionally, concerning the dimension of "religious authenticity," which refers to credibility (Schäfer et al. 2016b, 191) the leaders interviewed can also be positioned as low-ranking with regard to the general public.

Based on these two dimensions, it is appropriate to argue that Guatemalan Pentecostal independent leaders occupy insignificant positions in the Los Angeles religious field and have almost no potential public impact as religious experts. Nonetheless, some features of the leaders such as their dedication to religious work, their social involvement, and their type of transnational ties with Latin America not only serve to redefine their identity but also to challenge the official religious order, not by directly confronting the religious powers but by offering counter-narratives in which people are seen as active participants in "God's work" in the world.

The marginal position of these leaders in the Los Angeles religious field can be interpreted by several of Max Weber's (1963) concepts that Bourdieu (1991) used with regard to the religious field. Weber's concepts of "priest" and "prophet" allow for a better illustration of the positional differences between weak and strong positions in the field. It is possible to say that the leaders of this study tend to resemble Weber's "prophet." For Weber, the prophet is an "individual bearer of charisma" (1963, 46) who appears seemingly out of nowhere, proclaiming a message from the gods. His authority has nothing to do with tradition or office, but with personal revelation- that is, from a unique divine call. The prophet is not paid for his preaching but lives on his own manual labor and by unsolicited alms. So are the Guatemalan Pentecostal independent leaders, who emerge from nowhere, put a lot of effort in presenting a message coming from their God, and have lived on their secular work. They are not priests who dispense spiritual resources in an office for which they are remunerated (Weber 1963, 46).

In our former sketch of the religious field, we have positioned the Pentecostal leaders as a homogenous marginal position distinct from the hegemonic Catholic Church and other well-established churches. Now, we distinguish between two groups of leaders within this field position: those who are in a definitely marginal position and those who are positioned a bit higher. This positional distinction is not very significant if it is seen in the context of the entire field. Yet, from the point of view of the agents, their practices, and their self-concepts (as evident in the Habitus Analysis), the difference between these positions counts indeed. Features like the intensity of the dedication to religious work, the social involvement, and the type of transnational ties with Latin America render this distinction significant for the religious practices and self-understanding of each of the groups.

Those in the more marginal position understand their activities as a result of "divine consecration." They are pastors and leaders that work in the frame of religious organizations with 50 to 100 devotees, carry out transnational religious work through their personal network, and do not have social involvement beyond the boundaries of their near neighborhood. Those agents who are in the higher position are leaders who came with a missionary project to the United States and feel like "professional consecration." This group includes pastors who work full time in the frame of religious organizations with more than 500 devotees, tend to have social and even political involvement, and carry out transnational religious work through the official network of their own organizations, which have satellite-congregations in other countries.

Interestingly, these self-ascriptions and the life histories of these two groups of agents correspond to the theoretical distinction between "expatriates" and "migrants" (see Introduction and Chapter 6), which we will take up in the next chapter.

5.5. Conclusion

The last pages have shown the religious impact of the Pentecostal praxis among the Latino population in Los Angeles. In the last years, Latino Pentecostalism has redefined a specific domain—what is sacred and transcendent—generating different dynamics that are transforming the religious field of Los Angeles.

Even though the Catholic Church still has the most substantial impact in the religious field, combining credibility and organizational complexity, there are important competitors in the religious field. The U.S. Pentecostal denominations with Latino churches in Los Angeles have quite a high score for credibility, competing with the Catholic Church. They compete not so much through their religious organizational power as their compromise and religious credibility. Finally, the small, independent Latino Pentecostals, like the Guatemalan leaders analyzed in this dissertation, occupy a weak position in the field concerning their financial capital and organizational complexity. However, they are generating significant changes in the religious field since they are offering a very personal and practical experience of God in spaces where Latinos can express their faith in their own way and lead their congregation—in short: they enjoy a good deal of credibility among the migrants.

The next chapter analyzes the biographical narratives of the Guatemalan independent Pentecostal leaders according to Habitus Analysis, delineating their identities and strategies, distinguishing between the groups of "leaders by divine consecration" and "leaders by professional consecration." Further, we will relate our findings to the theoretical distinction between migrants and expatriates.

6. Immigrant or Expatriate? The Self-Perception of Guatemalan Independent Pentecostal Missionaries in Los Angeles

Chapter 4 dealt with the social context in which the religious life of Guatemalan Pentecostal independent leaders has developed, highlighting the structural conditions of this context. Chapter 5 showed the position of these leaders in the Los Angeles religious field. This step allowed a distinction between two groups of Guatemalan Pentecostal independent leaders. The first group consists of leaders who present themselves as "leaders by divine consecration." They are pastors and leaders who work in religious organizations with up to 50 or 100 devotees, carry out transnational activities through their personal network, and do not have political involvement. The second group, denominated "leaders by professional consecration," is composed of pastors that work full time in the frame of religious organizations with more than 500 devotees, tend to have social and even political involvement, and carry out transnational religious work through the official network of their organizations, which has satellite-congregations in other countries. In this chapter, the biographical narratives of these two types of religious leaders are examined.

The chapter is articulated in four parts. The first part presents some methodological considerations regarding Habitus Analysis and its praxeological square, which is the approach implemented to assess the biographical narratives provided by the leaders of this study. This part also presents the overall results of the Habitus Analysis, showing the thematic areas of the four positions of the praxeological square, which are *a negative experience, negative interpretation, positive experience* and *positive interpretation*. The second part deals with the contents of each thematic area according to the results obtained from the interviews, distinguishing between "leaders by divine consecration" and "leaders by professional consecration." The third part provides reasons for which is the most important result of the analysis of the biographical narratives, namely that there is a significant majority of positive experiences and interpretations in comparison with negative experiences and interpretations. Finally, some conclusions from these results will be discussed.

6.1. Methodological Considerations Regarding Habitus Analysis

This dissertation follows an analytic approach to the religious praxis that relates the worldviews of agents—especially their religious beliefs—to the social structures and processes in which they are involved in order to capture the *practical sense* of the agents studied. Practical sense (Bourdieu 1980) expresses a very concrete "being in the world." It refers to the situational affectedness of dispositions regarding perception, judgment, and action, according to the social conditions and practices of other agents, as a given member is immersed in practical relations with those other agents. Besides, the concept denotes the constant process of cognitive and emotional transformation between experience and interpretation that operates on the agents' side of praxis as it is anchored in the dispositions of the habitus (Schäfer et al. 2016a). Precisely, this chapter aims to delineate the cognitive, emotional, and bodily dispositions of the Guatemala Pentecostal leaders investigated.

In order to grasp the cognitive, emotional, and bodily dispositions that articulate the practical sense of religious agents, the Habitus Analysis approach (Schäfer 2015), particularly its method of the praxeological square (Schäfer 2009) was implemented as a method to analyze the operators of the practical sense. Described in Chapter 3, the model of the praxeological square results from various theoretical ideas linked to Bourdieu's concepts of habitus, practical sense, and practical logic as it follows some basic and common assumptions. Social agents perceive, judge, and act according to a (considerably but not thoroughly) coherent practical logic. The operations that take place in the related cognitive and affective processes involve positive and negative value ascription as well as the interpretation of experience in a very general sense. This simple description serves to present its four terms: positive and negative experience, and the interpretation of these positive and negative experiences. The praxeological square transforms the Aristotelian logic into a *praxeological* model by introducing and distinguishing the levels of experience and interpretation, facilitating the capture of the "cognitive maps" and the regularities of cognitive transformations of individual and collective agents (Schäfer 2009, 6). The praxeological square also shows the processes of transformation from perception, through judgment, to action (Schäfer 2005, 267). In other words, an agent's utterances turn out to be operators of praxis (Schäfer 2005).

In this study, the analysis of the biographical narratives using Habitus Analysis followed the approach of Leif Seibert (2018). According to him, the first step consists of a critical reading of the material as a whole, relating the collected information to appropriate secondary information (Seibert 2018, 256). The second step was collecting and highlighting free primary codes, according to the four positions of the praxeological square. The term "code" is used to denote an elementary unit of meaning used by the interviewees. Such a code may be a singular word, e.g. "GOD," but it is frequently a set of words, e.g. "FACILITIES TO ENTER AND RESIDE IN THE UNITED STATES." At the same time, its denotation and its connotation may be explicit and direct, e.g. "God's call" or implicit and only discernible from its context, e.g. "God's plan" (Seibert 2018, 256). For Habitus Analysis's purposes (Seibert 2018, 257), codes are located in precisely one position in the praxeological square. Its means that the praxeological codes belong to one of the four families introduced earlier:

- Positive experience
- Positive interpretation
- Negative experience
- Negative interpretation

In the cases of positive or negative interpretation, the distinction follows the value judgments of the interviewees who distinguish between favorable, agreeable, satisfying, or good, and unfavorable, adverse, sad, or bad. In the case of the experiential or interpretational distinction, experience refers to particular and concrete acts, events, or incidents, while interpretation indicates meaning that attribute causes and purposes to experiences. It is also important to note that all codes belong to at least one "quotation." Quotations cover larger units of meanings, i.e., sentences or even short paragraphs. Also, these codes indicate the practical operators running in the biographical narratives of the Guatemalan Pentecostal leaders.

After an exhaustive process of coding, the analysis of the entries using the Habitus Analysis approach generated the following results: 530 quotes have been found containing 716 entries referring to their lives, religious practice and beliefs, which were collected in thematic areas ascribed to "positive experience," "positive interpretation," "negative experience," and "negative interpretation." The category "positive experience" has 315 quotes, while "negative experience" has 115. Therefore, references to positive experiences are more than twice the references to negative experiences. Regarding the interpretations, the number of references follows a similar pattern. "Positive interpretation" has 202 quotes while "negative interpretation" has just 79 (see Table 1). Each of the categories derived from Habitus Analysis serves to delineate elements that help to interpret the biographical narratives in a thematically ordered and therefore comparable manner.

Each thematic area, which was sorted out by *semantic fields*, is presented as a subchapter offering a brief description of the meaning of each semantic field and the most important links to other thematic area categories. Semantic fields are written in italics. These subchapters follow the above-mentioned distinction between "leaders by divine consecration" and "leaders by professional consecration." The methodological procedure consists of indicating to which group the interviewee belongs, then naming the thematic area within the framework of the position of the praxeological square (e.g., Economic Problems as negative experience) with its corresponding thematic fields and then clarifying it with information from individual biographical narratives.

Figure 1 shows which are the thematic areas in each position of the praxeological square, along with the *total* number of (salvageable) entries for each one. In other words, the following table shows the entries of *all* interviews; it is still not divided up into the two sub-samples.

Before turning to the two types of actors, the thematic areas and their semantic fields, it is pertinent to mention some general remarks about the results. First, it is astonishing the vast number of references to positive experiences and interpretations, which reflects that Guatemalan Pentecostal independent leaders working in Los Angeles have a very positive outlook about their lives. That is particularly striking given the problematic structural conditions that Guatemalan migrants have faced in the United States, and particularly in Los Angeles since the 1970s, as presented in Chapter 4.

Guatemalan independent Pentecostal leaders: Habitus Analysis Overview			
Interviews 7		Quotes 530	
Positive interpretations	**202**	**Negative interpretations**	**79**
God	118	Causes critical situations in missionary life	27
Importance of missionary praxis	41	Living away from God	18
Importance of religious beliefs and practices	26	Migrants' lack of interest in following Pentecostal beliefs	16
Personal value	9	Causes leaders' problems	11
Importance of studying	8	Downfall in U.S.	7
Positive experiences	**315**	**Negative Experience**	**115**
Missionary work	182	Problems in missionary life	31
Family	77	Conflicts with other pastors	15
Economic success	33	Everyday life problems	15
Studies and degrees	15	Problems during arrival in U.S.	14
Entry & residency in U.S.	8	Migrant problems in L.A.	14
		Economic problems	11
		Family problems	10
		Problems of public order	5
Total entries 716			

Table 6.1: Guatemalan independent Pentecostal leaders' overview

The above result is also related to the fact that a large part of what was narrated by the interviewees, regardless of the group to which they were assigned, is mainly connected to two themes, as can be seen in Table 6.1. The first theme is missionary life in both positive and negative experiences and the second is Pentecostal beliefs and practices as a basis for interpretations of experiences. That is already an indication that the way Guatemalan Pentecostal independent leaders' view is particular and profoundly influenced by the beliefs and practices of Pentecostalism as shown by the considerable high number of references to the thematic areas "God" and "Religious beliefs and practices." In the next pages, this particular way of re-signifying the migratory experience will be analyzed, presenting the results of Habitus Analysis obtained by "leaders by divine consecration" and "leaders by professional consecration."

6.2. Results of the Habitus Analysis

6.2.1. Leaders by Divine Consecration

This group is composed of pastors and leaders who work in the frame of religious organizations with up to 50 or 100 devotees, carry out transnational work through their personal networks, and do not have political involvement. Two of them, Francisca Arévalo and Carlos Benítez, are founders and chief pastors working full time for their small congregations. Antonio Rodríguez is the founder and leading pastor of his congregation, but he works part time. Marcos González and Francisco Quiacaín are both preachers and musicians in Latino Pentecostal congregations in Los Angeles. Although they were all introduced in Chapter 4 according to the time of arrival in the United States, the next paragraphs provide a brief description of each one.

Francisca Arévalo is a charming and very dignified woman, approximately 60 years old, from Guatemala City. She is the only woman and female pastor of this study. She has been living in Los Angeles for almost thirty years and holds U.S. citizenship. She grew up with her mother carrying out missionary campaigns throughout Guatemala. In her late teens, she married a Pentecostal man in Guatemala, with whom she had three daughters. In 1978, her husband moved to Los Angeles, and three years later, she rejoined him with the children there. After some years of fights and mistreatment, her husband walked out on her, leaving her alone with the children. Facing this situation, she had to work and take care of the children, abandoning any active participation in a church. Four years later, she met a Guatemalan divorced man while visiting an Assemblies of God congregation. A year and a half later, they were married. She decided to go to study missionary work for three years at the Assemblies of God's Bible institute and afterwards she was sent as a missionary. For ten years, Francisca Arévalo was a missionary combining her domestic responsibilities and child rearing, the life of the Pentecostal congregation, and her missionary activities focused primarily in the United States and Guatemala. In 2000, she began to pastor a Pentecostal church in Compton due to the chief pastor's illness. In May 2014, her independent Pentecostal congregation had approximately seventy members. I met Francisca Arévalo in Los Angeles, and the interview was recorded at her home there.

Carlos Benítez, a former civil engineer, is a rather shy, soft-spoken man in his sixties who changes into a fiery, humorous preacher once in front of a congregation. He has lived for more than thirty years in Los Angeles and holds U.S. nationality. Born in Jutiapa (Guatemala) from a nominally Catholic family, he converted to Pentecostalism and joined the Assemblies of God during his years as a university student in Guatemala City. His conversion generated a lot of problems with his father. After he finished his studies in the 1980s, facing the difficulties of finding a job in his profession due to the war, he migrated to Los Angeles, crossing Mexico without any visa to enter in the United States. After some years living there, working as a preacher in a Pentecostal congregation, he got married and fathered four children. Once he and his wife could legalize their stay in the United States, he founded his congregation. In June 2014, he was the head pastor of a congregation with approximately 100 members and was able to acquire a lot and build a church with an adjacent community center. I met Carlos Benítez in Los Angeles, and the interview was recorded there.

Antonio Rodríguez is a quiet, soft-spoken Guatemalan in his sixties who has been living in Los Angeles for about twenty-five years at the time of the interview. Although he was born into a Pentecostal family in Guatemala City, he preferred to develop a secular career with his wife, away from the church. In 1985, he and his wife promised to dedicate their lives to Jesus if his youngest son's life were spared from what seemed to be an unknown illness. Upon their son's recovery, he joined a Pentecostal church and assumed some responsibilities there, leading a satellite congregation of that church. After two years and some misunderstandings with the leading pastor, Antonio Rodríguez resolved to pay heed to God's call to the pastorate and opened in the same place his independent congregation. In 1989, as a pastor of a congregation with 100 members, who met regularly four times per week, he was invited to participate in Pentecostal preaching events in Latina/o congregations in Los Angeles, receiving a visa as a religious worker. After his return to Guatemala City in 1990, he decided to go back to Los Angeles, but this time with his wife and children and with the goal of opening his congregation there. Once in the United States, he did not find any job as a pastor and was forced to accept a job in a pizzeria. When he and his family could legalize their status in the United States, Antonio Rodríguez found a better job in the office of lost baggage at the Los Angeles airport, a job that allowed him to open his own shipping company, while his wife got a job as a receptionist in a hotel. In 1995, they had enough savings to buy a small establishment for their church. In June 2014, nearly fifty people attended religious services there. Also, Antonio Rodríguez has supported Latin American immigrants without legal status in the United States, particularly in cases of family reunification while still finding the means and time to go on missions from Los Angeles to collaborate with Pentecostal churches in Guatemala. The interview was recorded in Los Angeles.

Marcos González is a U.S citizen of Guatemalan origins in his sixties. Small and of nervous intensity, he charms people around him with his peculiar sense of humor. He was born into a nominally Catholic family with indigenous ancestors. At the age of seventeen, facing problems with alcohol and drugs, he converted to Pentecostalism. He was baptized and participated in some courses until he was finally appointed as an evangelist. Some years later, he married a woman who had already converted to Pentecostalism and became the father of six children. He has participated with his wife in evangelist campaigns in other Central American countries as well as in Mexico. An evangelist in an independent Latino Pentecostal church, he had been living in the United States for forty years at the time of the interview, thirty of them in Los Angeles. During these years, his work as an international missionary, helping pastors and churches in Guatemala and Mexico, has been complemented by his secular work in different economic sectors such as the catering business, the construction sector, and the port industry in Los Angeles. I met Marcos González in Los Angeles in June 2014, where he invited me to visit him at home and recorded the interview there.

Francisco Quiacaín is a quiet and formal man in his sixties with Mayan origins. He has been living in Los Angeles for ten years at the time of the interview. He was born in a small village in the highlands of Guatemala from a family converted to Pentecostalism some years before his birth. When he was 23 years old, he got married, and became the father of five. He continued attending and actively participating in Pentecostal churches with his wife, taking numerous leadership positions or "privileges" such as singer or leader of the men's group. Some years later, he became the president of the church association of his town. In 2004, because of economic problems in Guatemala, he migrated to Los Angeles, crossing Mexico in a complicated journey by car and train, leaving his wife and children in the Guatemalan village. In Los Angeles, he has been working as a construction worker and has participated in numerous independent Pentecostal churches, not only Latino but also Korean. He has assumed some leadership positions in both, particularly a musician. He is the only interviewee of this study who did not have any legal documents to reside in Los Angeles. I met Francisco Quiacaín in Los Angeles in June 2014 and recorded the interview in a cafeteria close to his home.

In the next pages, the analysis of the thematic areas and semantic fields deals with these individuals collectively.

Negative Experiences

According to the Habitus Analysis approach, the category *negative experience* groups together statements about experiences that were perceived by the interlocutors as adverse both in the past and in the present. In the case of the Guatemalan Pentecostal "leaders by divine consecration" presented above, the negative experiences were related to thematic areas such as: Problems during the arrival in the United States; Everyday life problems; Economic problems; Family problems; Problems in the missionary life; Conflicts with other pastors; and Problems of public order. Nonetheless, references to negative experience were few and an important part of them dealt with problems related to the religious work carried out by the leaders, and frequently appeared connected to "God" as a way to positively interpret these experiences. Next, I will elucidate these thematic areas in more detail.

Problems During the Arrival to the United States

Regarding negative experiences during their trip to Los Angeles, one thematic area displayed in the interviews is called "Problems During the Arrival to the United States," which is associated with the following semantic field: *Dangerous journey to Los Angeles without documents through Mexico, Detention in a deportation center, Encounter with migration agents.* As mentioned in Chapter 4, some of the Guatemalan leaders did not get a visa to come to the United States and had to go through Mexico under dangerous conditions. For instance, Marcos González had to travel by night; Carlos Benítez had to cross through treacherous rivers and Francisco Quiacaín had to cross the desert hidden in a truck with other people. In addition to situations such as paying the *coyotes* (as people dedicated to smuggling illegal migrants into the US are colloquially called), the fear of being caught by migration authorities and encounters with migration agents were mentioned. In particular, Marcos González narrates his unpleasant encounter with a migration agent, who denied him a visa to go to preach in a small town in Texas. Francisca Arévalo also recounts her capture and detention in a deportation center, a place that she could leave only when a female migration agent allowed her to change some information in her application. For her, the very unlikelihood of this happy outcome was proof of its miraculous character. Therefore, this negative experience was in the end connected to a favorable interpretation as a result of God's will.

Everyday Life Problems

The thematic area "Everyday Life Problems" emerged in the interviews as the leaders recalled negative experiences during their first years living in Los Angeles. These experiences are connected to *health problems*, *difficulties due to working conditions*, *mobility problems*, *language problems*, and *violence in Los Angeles*, particularly in the neighborhood in which the congregations are located. Interestingly, these negative experiences appeared connected to "God" as a positive interpretation. For example, Francisca Arévalo mentioned her sufferings because of cancer and how she was healed thanks to God's intervention. Similar connections emerged regarding working conditions. Antonio Rodríguez, who arrived in the 1990s, remarked that at the moment of his arrival, he only got a job as a pizza deliveryman with a below-minimum wage. According to his narrative, these deplorable working conditions even led him to blame God for bringing him to Los Angeles until he realized that these negative experiences were a test by God. According to Antonio, once he went back to God, He gave him a better job, which facilitated the purchase of his own house after a couple of years.

Economic Problems

Another thematic area alluded to by the religious leaders is "Economic Problems," although references to this topic are less frequent. Two leaders in this group, Marcos González and Antonio Rodríguez, claimed that they went to Los Angeles in the first place because of religious reasons such as an invitation to preach or to participate in missionary conferences. In contrast, two other leaders mentioned economic reasons to settle in Los Angeles. Carlos Benítez stated that due to the war in the 1980s, he could not find a job as a civil engineer and decided to migrate to the United States. Similar motives brought Francisco Quiacaín to Los Angeles almost 20 years later, when economic problems in post-war Guatemala forced him to incur unaffordable debts, impossible to repay on his meager salary. Also, Francisco Quiacaín referred to his uncertain income due to the 2008 economic crisis.

Family Problems

The thematic area "Family Problems" is connected to misunderstandings with some member of the family, in this case, a husband or a father. As mentioned before, Francisca Arévalo had to face a complicated relationship with her first husband. Mistreatment and other abusive behaviors characterized her marriage. A critical part of her narrative revolves around problems with her first husband and his strategies to deal with them. As a religious leader who had to face difficulties due to marital problems in a migratory context, in her interview Francisca Arévalo frequently highlights the role of her Pentecostal faith to overcome family problems, emphasizing that genuinely Pentecostal believer husbands are less likely to be unfaithful, use drugs, abuse alcohol, or physically abuse their wives.

Carlos Benítez, who also arrived in the 1980s, mentioned the problems with his father due to his conversion. Studies in Pentecostalism (Droogers 2001, 45) have already pointed out that confrontations between members of the same families can occur after the conversion of one of the members. Conversion often implies a rupture of kinship ties with non-converts since Pentecostal believers depict the "world" or their surrounding society as lost and corrupt and some aspects of his or her culture are considered sinful and demonic, and, at the same time, the non-converted members of the family tend to see the new behavior of their converted relative as extravagant. As a Pentecostal pastor, Carlos Benítez mentioned with sorrow fighting episodes with his father when he was young. There are numerous connections between "Family problems" references and the negative interpretations "Causes for leaders' personal problems" and "Living away from God."

Problems of Public Order

There are also some references to "Problems of Public Order." Although most of the leaders by divine consecration (four of them) arrived for the first time in Los Angeles during the war in Guatemala, references to war, guerrilla or criminality are scant. Therefore, it seems that these events played a minor role in the articulation of the biographical narratives of the Guatemalan Pentecostal leaders analyzed in this study.

Problems in the Missionary Life

The negative experiences of "leaders by divine consecration" were mainly connected to "Problems in the Missionary Life." This thematic area includes semantic fields such as *Difficulties in the opening and maintenance of Pentecostal congregation in Los Angeles* and *Difficulties of "living by the faith*." The semantic field *Difficulties in the opening and maintenance of Pentecostal congregation* was mentioned regarding the disadvantages of many Latino leaders who had to accept secular jobs or had to rely on an uncertain income. Carlos Benítez explicitly remarked that he had accumulated debts in order to acquire a lot and construct a church building there. Marcos González mentioned the *Difficulties of "living by the faith."* For him, missionaries should only depend on God's mercy to obtain what they need to survive in missionary campaigns. Nevertheless, there were occasions in which what he received was not enough to cover the expenses of going on missions. It is significant in light of what Max Weber (1963, 46) said about the "prophet," arguing that what distinguishes the prophet from other types of religious leaders is that prophecy is unremunerated and obviously the criterion of voluntary service can generate problems in the maintenance of any religious endeavor. The thematic area "Problems in the missionary life" is connected to the negative interpretation included in the thematic area "Causes of critical situations in missionary life."

Conflicts with Other Pastors

"Conflicts with Other Pastors" is also a thematic area related to negative experiences. For those leaders with experience as pastors and founders of their congregation in Guatemala before their arrival to Los Angeles, the process of opening their congregations in Guatemala was plagued with plenty of conflicts with other pastors. The schism-proneness of Pentecostalism has often been mentioned as one of the reasons for its expansion. Leaders have to face competition from aspiring members who seek to build new congregations (Droogers 2012, 98). This was the case for Antonio Rodríguez who, after having many problems with his pastor, abandoned the congregation altogether to open his own. Besides, the religious leaders interviewed mentioned problems with pastors at the moment of their arrival in Los Angeles. For example, Antonio Rodríguez had conflicts with Afro-

American Pentecostal pastors and Latin-American Pentecostal leaders who used the same building for their pastoral mission. *Conflicts with pastors while being a Pentecostal leader in Los Angeles* is implicit in remarks about other pastors; for instance, their lack of interest in religious studies or doctrinal misunderstandings of the role of women in congregations. Finally, the interviewees also referred to *Conflicts with other pastors as a consequence of their transnational religious praxis*. Sometimes, the mere fact of visiting other congregations can generate conflicts, particularly when the host pastor sees in the guest preacher a competitor. This thematic is connected to the negative interpretation "Causes of critical situations in missionary life."

Negative Interpretation

Following the Habitus Analysis approach, the term *negative interpretation* is linked to statements that provide a cause to a bad or unfortunate experience. In relation to "leaders by divine consecration," negative interpretations allude to the following thematic areas: Causes of critical situations in missionary life; Living away from God; Migrants' lack of interest in following Pentecostal beliefs; Causes for leaders' personal problems; and Downfall in the U.S. In the next pages, I will analyze these thematic areas in more detail.

Causes of Critical Situations in Missionary Life

As a significant part of the interviews revolved around "Problems in Missionary Life" and "Conflicts with Other Pastors" as negative experiences, it is not surprising that "Causes of Critical Situations in Missionary Life" came up as a negative interpretation. This thematic area revolved around semantic fields such as *Pentecostalism in the U.S. is not as Pentecostalism in Guatemala*; *Modern breed in US Pentecostalism*; and *Desire to abandon the pastorate.* Guatemalan Pentecostal leaders included in the group "leaders by divine consecration" tend to consider that *Pentecostalism in the U.S. is not as Pentecostalism in Guatemala*, remarking that Pentecostal praxis is better in Guatemala because people attend church, fast, and pray more often. Particularly, Marcos González argued that there is a "Modern breed in US Pentecostalism," which allows the use of alcohol and drugs and does not foster fasting and prayer. In line with the need to combine both secular and religious work as independent leaders, Brother Carlos Benítez expressed a *desire to abandon the pastorate* as he is unsure of whether he would be able to get a pension in his old age.

Living Away from God

Another thematic area related to negative interpretations is "Living Away from God." Interviewees alluded to awkward moments in their lives when they put God aside or when they were *reproaching God.* They also referred to the *need to ask God for forgiveness* and to occasions when they *followed other roads away from God.* For the interviewees, it is not social, political, or economic problems that cause their negative experiences, but life away from God.

Migrants' Lack of Interest in Following Pentecostal Beliefs

As negative interpretative operators, Guatemalan Pentecostal leaders also referred to the thematic area "Migrants' Lack of Interest in Following Pentecostal Beliefs." According to all of them, immigrants prefer to rely on *alcohol and drugs*, rather than convert themselves to Pentecostalism to cope with their problems. Immigrants also tend to *blame God for problems.* Particularly, Marcos González and Francisco Quiacaín argued that all of these issues would happen because of *the Intervention of The Enemy (the Devil).*

Causes for Leaders' Personal Problems

"Causes for Leaders' Personal Problems" is another thematic area related to negative interpretations. The interpretative operator is connected to a negative personal state of being or mood when he/she was young such as *Desire to maintain a relationship with an abusive spouse*; *Innocence when young*; *Exaggerated faith when young*. Francisca Arévalo exposed how her innocence when she was young led her to marry a man who had no real Pentecostal praxis and how she wanted to stay attached to him despite the suffering this relationship caused her. Carlos Benítez talked about his *Exaggerated faith when he was young,* recounting how his big misunderstanding of the principles of Pentecostalism caused personal problems with his family and friends.

Downfall in the U.S.

The last thematic area brought up by Guatemalan Pentecostal leaders which is related to a negative interpretation is Downfall in the U.S. Some of the leaders specifically mention *Licentiousness* and *Homosexuality*. According to them, in the United States, there is materialism, rampant and visible sexuality, and disregard of the Christian faith.

Positive Experiences

Based on the Habitus Analysis approach, the category of positive experience refers to particular and concrete acts, events, or incidents that were understood by the interviewee as favorable, agreeable, or good. Hence, the positive experiences mentioned by Guatemalan Pentecostal independent leaders by "divine consecration" were related to the following thematic areas: *Missionary work*; *Family; Studies and degrees*; *Economic success*; *and Facilities to enter and reside in the U.S.* The following pages explain these thematic areas in more detail.

Missionary Work

"Missionary Work" is the most central positive experience referenced by the Guatemalan Pentecostal leaders interviewed, the primary focus towards which their efforts are aligned. All of the interviewees refer to their missionary work in Guatemala before coming to the United States, at their arrival in Los Angeles, to their current missionary work in Los Angeles and, finally, to their current missionary work in other countries.

The missionary work in Guatemala before going to the United States includes events and activities inside Pentecostal congregation such as *Position as a leader in groups inside the congregation*, *Pastorate and congregation opening* and activities related to what they consider as a requisite for the expansion of Pentecostalism (*concerts and evangelization campaigns*). In the narratives connected to the process of relocation of religious praxis from Guatemala to Los Angeles, most interviewees present themselves as religious agents committed to preaching the Gospel since their youth in Guatemala. Marcos González and Antonio Rodríguez claimed that their missionary work facilitated the arrival at the United States since their engagement in preaching activities brought them to Los Angeles. Similarly, these two interviewees talked about the missionary work at their arrival in Los Angeles, which consisted primarily of preaching in missionary campaigns.

Regarding their missionary work in Los Angeles, the following semantic fields emerged: *Position as a leader in groups inside the congregation*; *Pastorate and Congregation opening*; *Evangelism*; *Coaching*; and

Participation in social activities. All the interviewed leaders mentioned some semantic fields like *Leadership, Pastorate and congregation opening* or *evangelism*. Other semantic fields like *Coaching* or *Participation in social activities* were mentioned only by one of the leaders, Francisca Arévalo. She mentioned her involvement in coaching families. Ostensibly a consequence of the family problems she had to face in her life, the topic "family" plays an essential role in her narrative. Concerning the family counseling offered by Francisca Arévalo, she mentions that it has two pillars: relationships with children and marital relations. About relationships with children, the interviewee considers that the role of parents is to teach their children how to love and spend time with them. In her opinion, time with the family is more important than the accumulation of money. She also emphasizes the importance of promoting the study and implementation of leisure activities such as music, as these are an excellent method to avoid drug addiction. Regarding marital or couple relationships, she emphasizes the importance of a respectful relationship, showing her rejection of any kind of abuse in the family. According to her comments, she is a supporter of divorce in domestic abuse cases. About drug use by a member of the couple, she is in favor of rehabilitation promoted through active participation in the church, and the maintenance of marriage, since in her opinion children have the right to have a father and a mother. Regarding social participation, as one of the most critical tasks she performs as a religious leader is family counseling, she also mentioned her involvement in conferences and radio programs dealing with family concerns.

The numerous references found in the biographical narratives demonstrate that leaders "by divine consecration" interviewed described themselves as counselors, social workers, and helpers with bureaucratic procedures. Sometimes these tasks are the complement of a secular job.

To conclude, "Missionary work" is connected to positive interpretations such as *God's Call*, *God's will*, *God's blessings*, *God as a facilitator*, *opening doors* and *an opportunity to Serve God* and to the positive interpretation thematic area "Importance of missionary praxis."

Family

Another crucial thematic area mentioned is "Family," which is addressed in two different ways. On the one hand, it refers to members of the leaders' family unit. In the narratives, there were positive references to mother, siblings, and wife. They appeared as facilitators or supporters of the trip to the

United States. In this study, there were also positive references to husbands and wives as well as to their children. From these accounts emerge an ideal family picture, with the nuclear family as the minimum reproductive social grouping. On the other hand, the interviewees reflected on the familial support they got from their religious praxis, more concretely to experiences in which a member of the family has taken an important role in supporting their religious praxis. This role may be as a transmitter of Pentecostalism, as a promoter of preaching activities or as an assistant inside the congregation. Women, particularly mothers and daughters, seem to have played an essential role in the interviewees' religious involvement. "Family" is related to the positive thematic area "God," specifically to *God's call* and *Serve God.*

Studies and Degrees

Another significant thematic area is "Studies and Degrees." Before outlining the semantic fields of this thematic area, some points require consideration. In Chapter 2, some essential features of Pentecostalism were presented. One of these features was the claim that the Bible can be understood merely through the guidance of the Holy Spirit and by plain charisma, disregarding any kind of theological training. Is the intervention of the Holy Spirit relevant in order to become a Pentecostal leader? Or is some training required? The narratives provided by the interviewees shed some light on the way they assessed theological training. Most of the interviewees did not discuss theological or professional training as a precondition to becoming a Pentecostal leader. For them, a Pentecostal leader only needs to be called by God.

Nevertheless, during the interviews, Antonio Rodríguez mentioned *the possession of university degrees* (BA) in religious studies, while Francisca Arévalo and Carlos Benítez talked about their informal theological *training*. Francisca Arévalo referred to her training as a missionary by the Assemblies of God. These references serve to illustrate that studies were to some extent significant for the Guatemalan Pentecostal leaders, as they can be useful tools in order to be a good or acknowledged pastor. This point will also be illustrated in the next section, as all "leaders by professional consecration" working in established organizations claimed the possession of university degrees in religious studies.

The thematic area "Studies and Degrees" also emerged as a positive experience in the stage of being a Pentecostal leader in Los Angeles. This time concerning their children's studies. Most of the interviewees stressed the importance of having children who were able to go to the university in Los Angeles and get a university degree.

Economic Success

"Economic Success" is also a thematic area in the category "positive experience." After living and working in Los Angeles for more than ten years, Guatemalan leaders by divine consecration alluded to "Economic success," which they associated with *real estate ownership, higher incomes*, and *better working conditions*. Antonio Rodríguez and Francisco Quiacaín explicitly mentioned *house ownership.* Antonio Rodríguez mentioned one house in Los Angeles, while Francisco Quiacaín mentioned two houses in his native town in Guatemala. Besides this, the religious leaders interviewed also mention the achievement of a higher income and better working conditions, which allowed two of the leaders, Francisca Arévalo and Carlos Benítez to turn all their attention to their congregation and their religious work. "Economic success" is also connected to the positive interpretation of "God" related to the semantic fields *Thank God* and *God as a provider of material goods.* These references reflect an idea of economic prosperity as an earthly blessing. Prosperity does not refer to a measure of excessive wealth, but as certain stability derived from the proper integration in the socioeconomic context of Los Angeles.

Secular Work

The thematic area "Secular Work" is also included in positive experiences, although with fewer references than "Missionary Work." "Secular Work" is connected to experiences that they have had in order to obtain money and which are not directly related to religious activities. Regarding their occupation in Guatemala, Marcos González mentioned that he was working as a construction worker when he was not preaching. Antonio Rodríguez recounted his experiences working as a business manager of a soccer club and his transportation firm in Guatemala, while Francisco Quiacaín talked about his small ice-cream factory. During their first years of living in Los Angeles, they referred to their occupations as employees in the service, agricultural, or construction sectors. These activities are positive experiences to the extent that they allow active religious participation. There is, therefore, a connection between these entries and the entries of "God" as positive interpretation such as *God as a provider of material goods*. On the contrary, as discussed above regarding negative experiences, sometimes a secular occupation is considered as a negative experience when *job conditions* do not grant the time, energy, or money necessary to foster religious participation. Also, when "Secular work" constitutes a positive experience, it is connected to the positive interpretation of "Personal value," particularly to the semantic field *Industriousness.*

Facilities to Enter or Reside in the United States

The thematic area "Facilities to Enter or Reside in the United States" is related to the procedures carried out by the leaders in order to obtain a legal status to enter, stay, and work in the United States. As mentioned in Chapter 4, three of the Guatemalan Pentecostal leaders of this study got a visa the first time they traveled to the United States. One of them is Antonio Rodríguez, who recounted that he was able to obtain a visa to travel as a missionary and he also remarked how he got his legal documents to reside and work as a political refugee. Although the other leaders, Marcos González, Francisca Arévalo, and Carlos Benítez, mentioned that they arrived without a visa, they remarked that they obtained their legal documents thanks to the 1986 Amnesty. For the leaders who successfully entered the United States, "Facilities to enter or reside in the United States" is connected to "God" as *God's will* and *God blessing* as positive interpretative operators.

Positive Interpretations

Positive interpretation in the framework of the Habitus Analysis approach indicates statements in which the interviewee attributes causes and purposes to good and favorable experiences and in which he also expresses desires and goals for the future. Positive interpretations include the following thematic areas: God; Importance of religious beliefs; Importance of their missionary praxis; Personal value; and Importance of studying. These thematic areas are illustrated in the next pages.

God

The thematic area "God" functions as the most important positive interpretative operator. As an interpretative operator, "God" is the main point of reference for every experience in the life of the leaders. Most of them understood their "Missionary work" as *God's call.* They *thank God* and saw

God as a material goods provider connected to their "Economic success." They also consider God as the Almighty, a facilitator, and a door opener, who makes things happen at the right time for the benefit of His believers. The speakers commented that is *God's blessings* allowed them to travel frequently to other countries to preach. They recounted that such trips to Los Angeles or other places happened because of *God's will.* Some leaders also referred to God as a healer, while others indicate that *God gives them the wisdom* to conduct their life. Although it is notable that the discursive reference to God is abundant and connected with several social experiences, there is one element in common: These accounts show that the interviewees see God as an answer to their existential and physical concerns, providing tangible material results in their lives.

"God" is the primary reference to a transcendent entity in this study. According to the Habitus Analysis approach, references to transcendence made by interviewees are crucial to reconstruct the structures of meaning, and thus the forming of religious identities and strategies of the meaning of religious agents (Schäfer et al. 2016a, 156). Given its evident importance, in the next chapter, the reference to GOD will be exposed in more detail.

Importance of Religious Beliefs

The thematic area "God" was also complemented by the positive interpretations concerning "Importance of Religious Beliefs." The interviewees not only consider "God" as a crucial interpretative operator, but they also pointed out the *Importance of the Gospel.* All the interlocutors in this study present the Gospel as the fundamental pillar of their faith, highlighting the time they spend reading it. Although the literature on Pentecostalism points out the importance of the Holy Spirit, not all of the interviewees make explicit references to the *Importance of the Holy Spirit.* Only two of the interviewees, Marcos González, and Francisco Quiacaín make references to the Holy Spirit. Francisca Arévalo, Carlos Benítez, and Antonio Rodríguez alluded instead to the *Importance of prayer.* In the accounts related to prayer, prayer represents a way to intertwine directly with the material dimension, generating health and prosperity.

Importance of Missionary Praxis

"Importance of Missionary Praxis" also represents a significant thematic area of positive interpretation regarding the role of Guatemalan Pentecostal leader in Los Angeles. Concerning the positive judgment of being a missionary, Francisca Arévalo remarked the joy she experienced counseling women and families. Likewise, Antonio Rodríguez highlights the *Importance of his transnational missionary work* as he received some recognition as a religious leader in other countries.

Personal Value

Some religious leaders also attached positive interpretations to the thematic area "Personal Value," more specifically to their *industriousness* and, less frequently, to their *lack of interest in luxury.* Regarding industriousness, Francisca Arévalo, Marcos González and Francisco Quiacaín remarked that their success in the United States comes from their will to work and fulfill their duty, as God had ordered.

Importance of Studying

Another thematic area for positive interpretation in their endeavor to become a Guatemalan leader in Los Angeles is the "Importance of Studying." Francisca Arévalo mentioned the *importance of studying for children,* highlighting her efforts in motivating the children of their congregation to go to school and finish their studies. Meanwhile, Antonio Rodríguez referred to the *Importance of studying for religious leaders*, since he considered that a well-trained leadership is a significant asset for Latino congregations.

6.2.2. Leaders by Professional Consecration

Martin Carmona and Alvaro Sánchez are the Guatemalan Pentecostal independent leaders included in the group called "leaders by professional consecration." They are pastors that work full time within religious organizations of more than 500 devotees, which tend to have a significant social and even political involvement and carry out transnational religious work through the official network of their organizations, which, besides, have satellite congregations in other countries.

Martin Carmona, an ebullient U.S. citizen of Guatemalan origins in his fifties, has been living in Los Angeles for more than thirty years. Born in a Pentecostal family, he came with his Pentecostal rock band in the 1970s to Los Angeles. After working as an assistant evangelist in a large international Latino-led church for several years, he started his congregation after accepting a call into full-time ministry and became the founder and head pastor of an international church with branches in the United States, Guatemala, and Spain. Martin Carmona is also the secretary of the *Alianza Ministerial Hispana* (Hispanic Ministerial Alliance), an organization formed by Pentecostal leaders with Latin American origins sited in Southern California. I met Martin Carmona in Guatemala City when he was preaching in an independent Pentecostal church, but the interview was recorded in Los Angeles.

Alvaro Sánchez is a quiet man who transmits much warmth with his words. He was born in a small village in the Guatemalan Highlands to a Catholic family. In his teens, having had severe alcohol problems, he converted to Pentecostalism. Once a member of a small Pentecostal congregation, he accepted different positions until he finally became a pastor. In his early sixties, he is a pastor working for the same Guatemalan independent Pentecostal church, supporting the missionary expansion of his church in Central and North America for more than 30 years. He is the only Pentecostal leader in this study who did not live in Los Angeles, but he traveled there regularly to counsel Latin American immigrants as well as Latino Pentecostal leaders. In Guatemala, he is very well known due to his international ministry in the United States. I met Alvaro Sánchez in February 2014 in Guatemala City, where in addition to the coordination and supervision of the missionary work mentioned above, he was the chief pastor of a congregation of the same church and hosted a radio program every Monday. Due to his multiple occupations, we had to meet several times in order to record his interview. We contacted each other again in Los Angeles, where I was allowed to accompany him in his preaching in numerous Latina/o congregations. As of 2017, Alvaro Sánchez was the general director of the Samaria Churches, an organization with congregations not only in Guatemala City but also in North Carolina, El Salvador, Costa Rica, and Mexico. In the metropolitan area of Los Angeles, he cooperated with leaders of other Latino Pentecostal organizations, assisting them in evangelistic campaigns.

Negative Experiences

Regarding statements on experiences that were perceived by the interlocutors as unfavorable or adverse in the past and the present, "leaders by professional consecration" referred to thematic areas such as "Problems in the missionary life," and "Problems of migrants in Los Angeles." These thematic areas are explained in the following sections.

Problems in the Missionary Life

The thematic area "Problems in the Missionary Life" includes semantic fields such as *Difficulties of Latino Pentecostal churches in Los Angeles* and *Difficulties in maintaining a transnational Pentecostal praxis*. Regarding *Difficulties of Latino Pentecostal churches*, Martin Carmona reflected on the conditions of the members of the congregation. Most members do not have a residence permit, some of them lack a motivation to learn the language or to attend school, others show resistance to changes in the congregation and, finally, there is a kind of distrust towards any form of leadership among Latina/o immigrants. The semantic field *Difficulties in maintaining a transnational Pentecostal praxis* was explicitly noted by Alvaro Sánchez, who had his residence in Guatemala City and was not able to travel to the United States as frequently as he wanted. He also alluded to some tensions derived from his transnational Pentecostal praxis since each congregation had its dynamics and deserved his attention. He was often anxious because, as he had to attend congregations both in the United States and Guatemala, he was not able to dedicate enough time and effort to each of them. "Problems in the missionary life" is connected to the negative interpretation included in the thematic area "Causes of critical situations in missionary life."

Problems of Migrants in Los Angeles

Another thematic area mentioned by the Pentecostal leaders by "professional consecration" was "Problems of Migrants in Los Angeles." This area includes *Solitude*, *Infidelity*, *Fear of being deported*, *Discrimination*, and *Materialization after arrival in the United States* as some of the problems faced by immigrants in Los Angeles. Some of these references are connected to negative interpretations included in the thematic area "Migrants' lack of interest in following Pentecostal beliefs."

Regarding negative experiences, there are some similarities with the above-mentioned "leaders by divine consecration." For instance, both mentioned similar problems and conflicts derived from their missionary life. By contrast, "leaders by professional consecration" did not refer to problems in secular life such as "Problems during the arrival in the United States," "Everyday life problems," "Economic problems," "Family problems." Instead, they talked about the problems of migrants in Los Angeles. That surely has to do with the fact that both obtained a visa to travel to the United States as religious workers and they have always worked within the framework of established religious organizations in the United States, reflecting some of the features of their professional career as religious leaders. At the same time, this also shows that, as full-time consolidated Pentecostal leaders, the church and its members are critical points in the articulation of their narratives.

Negative Interpretation

Negative interpretations or statements regarding causes of adverse experiences were connected to the following thematic areas: Causes of critical situations in missionary life and Migrants' lack of interest in following Pentecostal beliefs.

Causes of Critical Situations in Missionary Life

The thematic area "Causes of Critical Situations in Missionary Life" was articulated around semantic fields such as *Criticism to other Pentecostal leaders*; *Pentecostalism in the U.S. is not as Pentecostalism in Guatemala*; and *Need of counseling*. Both leaders by professional consecration interviewed expressed some *Criticism of other Pentecostal leaders* since not all Latin American religious leaders tend to support the undocumented members of their congregations. They also mentioned that *Pentecostalism in the U.S. is not as Pentecostalism in Guatemala* as leaders prepare their preaching better in Guatemala, even though they do not have as many technological resources. Particularly Alvaro Sánchez, who resides in Guatemala, stressed the *need of counseling* in the United States since Latin American religious leaders have no time for *counseling,* because they have to combine a secular job with their missionary work.

Migrants' Lack of Interest in Following Pentecostal Beliefs

As negative interpretative operators, Guatemalan Pentecostal leaders also referred to the thematic area "Migrants' Lack of Interest in Following Pentecostal Beliefs." According to both, immigrants prefer to rely on *alcohol and drugs* in order to cope with their problems rather than convert themselves to Pentecostalism and they also *tend to blame God for problems.*

Positive Experiences

Concerning particular and concrete acts, events or incidents which were seen by the interviewee as favorable, agreeable, or good, Guatemalan Pentecostal leaders by professional consecration mentioned the following thematic areas: Missionary work; Family; Studies and Degrees; as well as Facilities to enter or reside in the United States. These thematic areas are explained next in more detail.

Missionary Work

As mentioned before, concerning "leaders by divine consecration," "Missionary Work" is the main most positive experience referenced by the Guatemalan Pentecostal leaders interviewed, regardless of their position in the religious field. Through the description of their *position as leader or pastor* and of activities related to what they consider as a requisite for the expansion of Pentecostalism (*concerts and evangelization campaigns*), both interviewees presented themselves as religious agents committed to preaching the Gospel since their youth in Guatemala. Thanks to their missionary work, they could arrive in the United States since their engagement in preaching activities brought them to Los Angeles, even with a visa.

Regarding their missionary work in Los Angeles, the narratives offered ample descriptions of the opening of their congregations as well as numerous examples of the social and political activities that Guatemalan Pentecostal leaders carried out as pastors. For instance, Martin Carmona depicted the extent of his involvement as secretary of the *Alianza Ministerial Hispana* (Hispanic Ministerial Alliance), an organization created by Pentecostal leaders of Latin American origin in Southern California. He also alluded to his appearances on Latino television channels and his participation in meetings with candidates for public positions in Los Angeles and his engagement as a religious leader in migratory reform, organizing events such as vigils in front of immigration authority buildings. Similarly, Alvaro Sánchez talked about his participation in radio programs in Guatemala and Los Angeles.

Another important semantic field is *Coaching.* Alvaro Sánchez, who is the president of an international Pentecostal church, with congregations in Guatemala, El Salvador, Costa Rica, and the United States, highlighted how his work in Los Angeles consisted of presenting himself as a friend with whom immigrants could talk about their problems and get counsel. He also mentioned his involvement as a *counselor* in Guatemala, working not only with the members of his church but also with other religious organizations and with the Guatemalan Police Department. Martin Carmona also alluded to counseling to other religious leaders as an essential part of his religious work. Notably, in both cases, coaching consists of references and recommendations aligned with management literature based on positive thinking and leadership.

As we can see, the list of activities mentioned by these leaders is more extensive and covers many more fields than the list provided by "leaders by divine consecration." Particularly notable are the numerous references to media participation, political participation, and involvement in associations.

Studies and Degrees

Another significant thematic area is "Studies and Degrees." Martin Carmona and Alvaro Sánchez mentioned the *possession of university degrees* in theology explicitly, underlining that they have a Ph.D. and a Master's degree respectively. In both cases, university degrees function as symbolic capital in order to be considered a good or acknowledged leader. According to him, it is not possible to be a genuinely religious leader without university studies. In this respect, they differ from the "leaders by divine consecration," who did not consider professional theological training as a precondition to become a Pentecostal leader.

Facilities to Enter or Reside in the United States

The thematic area "Facilities to Enter or Reside in the United States" is related to the procedures carried out by the leaders in order to obtain a legal status to enter, stay, and work in the United States. As mentioned in Chapter 4, three of the Guatemalan Pentecostal leaders of this study got a visa the first time they traveled to the United States. Two of them were Martin Carmona and Alvaro Sánchez. Both offered detailed descriptions of how they obtained the visa as a religious leader. For both of them, the successful entry into the United States is connected to "God" with *God's will and God's blessing* as positive interpretative operators.

Positive Interpretation

In regard to positive interpretations or statements regarding the causes of good and favorable experiences, the following thematic areas emerged: "God," "Importance of their missionary praxis" and "Importance of the gospel and prayer."

God

Similar to the "leaders by divine consecration" analyzed above, the thematic area of God constitutes an essential positive interpretative operator, with God being the crucial point of reference in the life of the leaders. Martin Carmona and Alvaro Sánchez conceived their "Missionary work" as the realization of *God's call.* They commented that it is *God's blessing* that allowed them to travel frequently to other countries to preach and to open new congregations. They recounted that such trips to Los Angeles or other places happened because they are *God's will.*

Importance of the Gospel and Prayer

These two leaders also referred to the "Importance of the Gospel and Prayer." For them, the Gospel constituted the fundamental pillar of their faith, underlining the time they spent reading it. Furthermore, they invoked the *Importance of prayer,* prayer being an active way to cope and deal with worldly concerns.

Importance of Missionary Praxis

References to the "Importance of Missionary Praxis" also constitutes a crucial thematic area of positive interpretation in the biographical narratives of the "leaders by professional consecration" interviewed. Both leaders expressed a confident judgment about being a missionary. In particular, Alvaro Sánchez stressed positive feelings such as *blessing and joy derived from their missionary work* in Los Angeles. He also highlighted the *importance of coaching* in the migratory context. Meanwhile, Martin Carmona noted the *Importance of pastors' involvement in migratory reform*, consistent with the disproportionally large number of undocumented immigrants in their congregations.

6.3. Interpreting the Results

This chapter has aimed to inquire into the practical sense that articulates the everyday life of the interviewees. Through this practical sense, agents situate themselves regarding goods, places, and relationships with other people. The questions that emerge are: How do the interviewees of this study see themselves? What kind of biographical accounts do the Guatemalan Pentecostal leaders convey? To answer these questions, I have to consider which are the spatial, biographical, and spiritual processes mentioned in these narratives. They are primarily narratives of spatial displacement: The narrators, who have moved from Guatemala to Los Angeles, describe how these displacements came about and what sense they make of them. Their narratives are the stories of a journey and describe both spatial and psychological movements and developments.

In the dominant North Atlantic discourse, two terms are used to denominate people involved in such movements (Währisch-Oblau 2012, 136). One is "migrant/immigrant"; the other one is "expatriate." According to Währisch-Oblau (2012, 137), the term "migrant/immigrant" is applied to people who move out of need. They are refugees, asylum seekers or economic migrants fleeing from war, poverty, and deprivation. In this account, migrants come from the South to the North, they are usually dark-skinned, tend to work in low-skilled jobs, and usually have a lower financial status than the indigenous population. Besides, they are expected to adapt and integrate. For its part, the term "expatriate" alludes to wealth, power, and glamour: Expatriates move as an act of personal agency. They move to a foreign country (commonly from the North to other parts of the world) with a sense of purpose, to do a specific job, or to fulfill an ideal. They move freely and can go back home (or to yet another country) if they chose to do so. According to Währisch-Oblau (2012, 138), expatriates are well-educated people who work in highly specialized fields for which no locals are available, and international companies or organizations employ them. They tend to live in much better financial circumstances than most indigenous people around them and they are usually white. Expatriates are expected to show some "cultural sensibility" and local language skills, but they are not supposed to integrate or accommodate to the new culture, but rather to keep some distance from the local population: They are international, belonging to a culture that is not defined within national borders.

Which of these types fit best into the biographical narratives of the interviewees? Admittedly, in the case of "leaders by divine consecration," some of the negative experiences enumerated before, particularly those related to "Problems during their arrival in the United States," "Economic problems" and "Everyday life problems" seem to fit better into the "migrant" type. Most of the "leaders by divine consecration" did not get a visa to come to the United States and had to go through Mexico under dangerous conditions. Besides, situations such as paying the *coyotes*, the fear of being caught by migration authorities, and encounters with migration agents and the severe consequences appeared in their narrations. They also recalled negative experiences during their first years living in Los Angeles such as difficulties due to working conditions, mobility problems, and/or language problems. Finally, two of them mentioned economic reasons to settle in Los Angeles since both had problems getting a well-paid job in Guatemala.

Nevertheless, a close consideration of narratives provided by "Guatemalan Pentecostal leaders by divine consecration" shows that they do not follow the structure of the migrant/immigrant type. Most of their narratives analyzed are not about a search for a better life or a struggle for integration. As exposed above, most quotations coded as positive experiences referred to their missionary work, mainly to preaching in missionary campaigns, presenting themselves as active religious agents who go from one place to another. Similarly, as the positive interpretations showed, their narratives carry a sense of "God's calling" to the country to which they have moved. That means that they see themselves as "missionaries," something that resonates much more to the expatriate type.

References to missionary work allows leaders by "divine consecration" to give meaning to their displacement to Los Angeles. It also serves to articulate a narrative in which their stay there finds a religious reason, arguing that they have a divine order to spread the Gospel and a congregation to serve. Invoking such an understanding of their situation in Los Angeles, they transform the meaning of space. Missionary work, thus, emerges in the biographies as a symbolic operator for space where the experiences of crossing borders are creatively re-signified by appealing to religious metaphors based on biblical texts. By invoking evangelism and missionary work, Guatemalan Pentecostal leaders by "divine consecration" can establish and strengthen a particular position, tapping a mechanism of empowerment. Their missionary work is proof of their infinite personal value, not in the eye of the law, but in the eye of the author of all law, the Lord.

Second, this change in the meaning of space is explicitly presented as an effort to improve "U.S. society" through the socio-moral effect of such conversions; this action is combined with the hope of a better social environment following the logic: the more "Christians," the better society is. It is particularly significant in the case of "leaders by divine consecration" working in the "impacted ghettoes" and the "ungovernable spaces" of megacities. In these areas, the domestic order based on the traditional family and the church support systems create social capital out of nothing.

Third, missionary work also plays a vital role in giving meaning to their relation with people in other countries. Thanks to their faith, leaders by "divine consecration" could establish transnational relations as they were invited to pray or had created small financial funds to support people in need in other countries. Particularly in the cases of pastors and founder of small Pentecostal congregations, they can prove that they are "someone" in the religious field and that their churches are expanding.

Regarding Guatemalan Pentecostal leaders "by professional consecration," it is clearer that they see themselves as "expatriates." As the thematic areas of their positive experiences such as "Facilities to enter or reside in the United States" and "Missionary work" have shown, facts such as having a visa to travel to the United States and their continued work in established religious organizations there reflect that their move to the United States was due to professional reasons as is usually the case for expatriates. In their case, the abundant references to missionary work not only allows a transformation in the meaning of the space as it was pointed out in relation to Guatemalan Pentecostal leaders by "divine consecration," but also missionary work can be combined with the hope of political change and thus transformed into political action (e.g., through civic participation in political parties). Leaders "by professional consecration" refer to involvement in defense of the right of migrants, articulated through protests in front of official buildings in Los Angeles and supporting the creation of other organizations to gather Latino American pastors and leaders.

The interlocutors of this study could have held the same jobs and experienced similar conditions as other Guatemalan immigrants in Los Angeles, yet their perception of their daily life struggles was radically different. Their worldview was remarkably positive, especially in light of the conditions of Guatemalan immigrants in Los Angeles outlined in Chapter 4. In the biographical narratives of Guatemalan independent Pentecostal leaders, there are no traces of feelings of helplessness in the midst of constant hardship, rather a firm belief in divine purpose, high personal value, hope in the outcome of their trials and faith in the miraculous power of God to overcome all obstacles.

So, what is it that makes the migrant exhibit such self-perception and allows him/her to act in this way? As the results of the analysis showed in this chapter, the religious beliefs of Latino Pentecostalism instilled through active participation in the church play an essential role in this peculiar understanding of their displacement to Los Angeles. The interviewees did not tell their stories as narratives of contingency. While in some cases, seemingly contingent factors influenced their actions and movements, in the end, all biographies were interpreted as the unfolding of a pre-ordained divine plan. The narrators went to Los Angeles because God sent them there: Divine agency merely used the political contingency. Rebecca Pierce Bomann (2011) has shown in a different context how Pentecostal Christians gain a new sense of power and direction by transferring all agency to God. That liberates them to act and think creatively in situations where there seems to be no possible way out.

In short, when it comes to their practical sense, the interviewees in this study described themselves as missionaries. Hence, both groups of Guatemalan Pentecostal leaders invoked in their biographical narratives features of "expatriates." All leaders of this study have claimed that they move to a foreign country with a religious purpose, and therefore, Guatemalan Pentecostal leaders in this study tend to present themselves as missionaries coming to the "rich North" from the "poor South." Evidently, some have been more successful than others through their involvement in preaching, teaching and the opening of new congregations, but both groups of Guatemalan Pentecostal leaders consistently reinforced their belief that God was their infinitely loving provider, protector, healer, and friend, who has brought them to other places to share their faith with other people.

Guatemalan independent Pentecostal leaders' religious beliefs form certain habitual dispositions, according to which a habitus is articulated. With the formation of this habitus, there is a change in the identity of believers. Their self-conception, which is articulated around their faith, allows them to develop a way of seeing the world oriented towards professionalization in religious life, even before they become professionals. Following the reconstruction of the religious field for Los Angeles, a distinction has been made between leaders by divine consecration and leaders by professional consecration. This distinction refers to an objective position in a given field and social space. The consideration of the elements linked to the terms "migrant" and "expatriate" in the formation of the practical sense of the interviewees allows for a better understanding of how the interviewees perceive themselves; where they situate themselves according to their habitual dispositions, particularly those with a religious content or an idea, the idea of divine beings or a "transcendent entity." Thus, the interviewees can be clustered in a new way:

Leaders by "divine consecration" in intermediate leadership positions, reflecting the migrant type as in the cases of Marcos González and Francisco Quiacaín, who presented themselves as preachers and singers in small Pentecostal churches in Los Angeles, illustrating the first step in a professional career.

Leaders by "divine consecration" who are pastors of their own congregations and see themselves as "expatriates" as illustrated by the biographical narratives of Francisca Arévalo, Carlos Benítez, and Antonio Rodríguez. These leaders have taken further steps in their professional careers as religious leaders because they are founders and head pastors of their own churches, having a social impact in their neighborhoods.

Leaders by "professional consecration" who are expatriates as exemplified by Martin Carmona and Alvaro Sánchez. They move freely in a foreign country and are well-educated people who work full time in the frame of their religious organizations with more than 500 devotees.

This differentiation makes sense when reconstructing the religious habitus formations, which will be presented in the next chapter, in which the statements connected to the idea of divine beings or a "transcendent entity" are analyzed in depth.

6.4. Conclusions

This chapter has illustrated how Guatemalan Pentecostal independent leaders place themselves concerning goods, places, and relationships with other people. Through the exhaustive examination of their biographical narratives using the Habitus Analysis approach, it was possible to show that they do not see themselves as simple migrants, but rather as people that move to other countries because of a religious reason connected to "God's calling." Appealing to their involvement in preaching, teaching, and the opening of new congregations, the Guatemalan Pentecostal leaders analyzed in this study give a positive meaning to their lives in Los Angeles as they consistently reinforced their belief that God was their infinitely loving provider, protector, healer, and friend, who brought them to other places to share their faith with other people.

This form of self-perception and action reflects how the beliefs and practices of Latino Pentecostalism allow its believers to develop a habitus oriented towards professionalization as a religious agent. Hence, in this case, three examples regarding the development of a professional career were found. Migrant leaders by "divine consecration" in intermediate leadership positions; Migrant leaders by "divine consecration" who are pastors of their own congregations and see themselves as "expatriates;" and leaders by "professional consecration" who are expatriates.

Considering the numerous references in which missionary work, and particularly evangelism, is presented as the reason for their displacement to other countries and their stay in Los Angeles, it is possible to argue that Guatemalan Pentecostal independent leaders tend to interpret their migration experience spiritually, regardless of whether they are leaders by divine consecration or by professional consecration. It means that the Guatemalan leaders interviewed retain a strong sense of agency: They are not victims but people whom God called upon to achieve his aim of worldwide evangelism. The fact of migration is a divine commandment, not something to be avoided. Even if the war, or its political, social, and economic consequences, partly explains their decision to leave their countries, such political and economic realities are only seen as "outside" factors: The real reason for their migration was that God made them move, sometimes using unexpected means. In the next chapter, this particularly spiritual way of interpreting migration is analyzed in more detail, illustrating what "God" means to the studied Guatemalan Pentecostal independent leaders.

7. The Centrality of God

The results of the habitus analyses presented in the previous chapter showed that the Guatemalan independent Pentecostal leaders interviewed made numerous statements connected to the idea of divine beings or a "transcendent entity." This transcendent entity usually is God and in some other cases the Holy Spirit. Additionally, they related their "earthly" experiences in an interpretive way to transcendent beings and realms. For instance, they continuously thanked God and saw God as a provider of material goods, connecting God's direct intervention to their economic success. Some leaders also referred to God as a healer to whom to turn in moments of illness. Finally, the understanding of an idea of God is closely related to the missionary work of the interviewees since they referred to their religious involvement as an opportunity to serve God. These statements are an excellent example of how transcendence turns into something concrete and practical (Schäfer et al. 2016a, 155).

In Chapter 6, it was also noted that the religious beliefs of Guatemalan independent Pentecostal leaders of Los Angeles form certain habitual dispositions, according to which habitus formations are articulated. These habitus formations entail a transformation in the self-conception or identity of the believers. Their self-conception based on their religious beliefs helps them to develop a way of seeing the world oriented towards professionalization in religious life, even before they become professional religious leaders. Besides, the consideration of the elements linked to the terms "migrant" and "expatriate" in the formation of the practical sense of the interviewees allows for a better understanding of how the interviewees perceive themselves and where they situate themselves according to their habitual dispositions. Hence, the interviewees were clustered in the following way: Expatriate leaders by "professional consecration" who correspond to the classic definition of "expatriate" since they move freely in a foreign country and are well-educated people who work full-time for their religious organizations; migrant leaders by "divine consecration" who are pastors of their congregations and see themselves as "expatriates"; and migrant leaders by "divine consecration" in intermediate leadership positions. This differentiation allows a better reconstruction of the religious habitus formations, which emerge from the statements connected to the idea of divine beings or a "transcendent entity."

From a praxeological perspective, it is precisely the relation between "earthly" experiences and "otherworldly" interpretations that creates religious identities, strategies, and the praxis itself. Therefore, references to transcendence made by interviewees mark the crucial element from which one can reconstruct the structures of meaning, and thus the forming of religious identities and strategies (Schäfer et al. 2016a, 156). Nonetheless, the practical performance of religious actors does not rest solely on the semantic content that a given religious movement or institution disseminates. Religious praxis, instead, hinges on actor-specific positions within the social structure and the ascription of religious meaning to them (Schäfer et al. 2016a, 156). Therefore, this chapter distinguishes between three groups of agents according to their self-perception. Religious agents employ particular contents in response to particular events and circumstances. It is the relation between particular experiences and specific religious contents that makes them develop their distinct religious identities and strategies, including their different understandings of the relationship between transcendent forces and society or history and, of course, different strategies in social conflicts and competition (Schäfer et al. 2016a, 156).

What, then, are the specific meanings given to God? And more important for a praxeological analysis, is there variation among the meanings provided by the leaders? To answer these questions, this chapter is structured into three parts. The first one deals with the references to the semantic field *God's call,* which was the symbolic operator most often referenced regarding God. The second part deals with the other symbolic operators related to God, demonstrating the diversity of Pentecostal beliefs according to the social position of the interviewees. As three religious habitus formations were found, the section also presents the praxeological square of each one of them. Finally, the chapter ends with some conclusions

7.1. The Call: Articulation of a Career as a Religious Leader

In Pentecostal circles, being a missionary is not seen as an ordinary profession, but rather a particular vocation which usually requires a unique, personalized calling. Due to this understanding, the articulation of a career as a missionary seems linked to a divine call. Besides, a career as a missionary is related to a journey. In Christian circles, the primary archetype of the mobility has been the figure of Christ. According to this view, missionaries—like Christ—come into a world that is not their own, suffer rejection by those who fail to understand where they come from and which is the meaning of their lives, give themselves sacrificially for the lives of others and complete their earthly sojourn by "going home" to be with God (Swanson 1995, 17). Hence, references to a "divine call" and to a journey narrative would be intimately related to each other as the person interviewed presents himself as one who came to the United States with the vision to be a missionary.

The results of the Habitus Analyses, as shown in the previous chapter, indicate that there is a significant number of references—more concretely, 46 references—to a divine call, which were coded accordingly as "positive interpretation." All the Guatemalan independent Pentecostal leaders interviewed made references to a divine call. Additionally, most of the interviewees talked about their journey to Los Angeles. Nevertheless, these accounts turned out to be very idiosyncratic and not at all easy to be ordered into groups.

To make sense of the results, two steps were carried out. First, the literature on the "divine call" was analyzed with the aim of finding the main features of "a divine call." Second, the content of the call of the leaders in each group was analyzed: expatriate leaders by "professional consecration;" migrant leaders by "divine consecration" who see themselves as "expatriates;" and migrant leaders by "divine consecration" in intermediate leadership positions.

7.1.1. Reviewing the Literature about the "Call"

The research on the "call" in religious studies can be traced back to the work of Max Weber. In his historical studies on religious traditions, Weber (1963, 46) identified the personal call as a decisive element that distinguishes between two sociological types of religious authorities: the priest and the prophet. For Weber, the priest "lays claim to authority by his service in a sacred tradition" (1963, 47). The priest normally comes from a priestly class and dispenses spiritual resources in the power of an office for which he is remunerated. The prophet is an "individual bearer of charisma" who appears seemingly out of nowhere, proclaiming a message from the gods. His authority has nothing to do with tradition or office, but with personal revelation, that is, a unique divine call (Weber 1963, 46). As mentioned in Chapter 5, the biographical narratives of this study tend to resemble Weber's prophet rather than the priest. Most of the independent Guatemalan leaders interviewed claim that they have received a divine call. As independent leaders, they are not connected with any office or organization. Besides, some of them live by their own manual labor and some alms. Nonetheless, although certainly accurate, Weber's conceptualization of the call is somewhat abstract and provides few elements for constructing a more thorough study of the meaning of "the call."

The Call in Evangelical Circles

Consulting the literature, it is astonishing to find that there are not many sociological studies about call narratives. One notable example of a sociological study of call narratives is Jeffrey Swanson's (1995) on U.S. American Missionaries working for one agency in Ecuador. According to Swanson (1995, 20), missionaries organize their life stories around a liminal religious experience: the moment of a divine call. This experience comes to define their social and personal identities since it is understood as a personalized experience at the beginning of a religious career and leads the called person to adopt a spiritual life for which God supposedly appoints him or her. The events prior to the call are framed to prefigure it, and developments thereafter are seen as illustrations that fulfill the call, work it out, or renegotiate its terms.

Additionally, Swanson (1995, 74) examines in his study the ways employed by evangelicals to conceive the call. For him, when evangelicals want to inquire into the origins or the basis of any significant idea, they tend to look for them in the Bible. Analyzing the texts in which the words "call" and "calling" are mentioned in the Bible supports an understanding of the different meanings that evangelicals give to the call. Going from a broad sense to a more restricted meaning of words that can be translated as "the call," Swanson points out that although the call refers to the sum of God's dealings with the human race throughout the Biblical story, evangelicals tend to construe the call to mean the gospel message of the New Testament, that is, salvation in Christ. For this purpose, they employ Pauline texts such as the following one:

> [T]ake your share of suffering for the gospel in the power of God, who saved us and called us with a holy calling; not in virtue of our works but in virtue of own purpose and the grace he gave us in Christ Jesus (II Timothy 1:8-9).

For Swanson (1995, 75), evangelicals also think that the calling has to do with the spiritual division of labor, or with a person's commitment to fulfilling a particular role in the work of the church. For instance, this is what the term is taken to mean in the Apostle's opening signature in the epistle to the Romans: "Paul, a servant of Jesus Christ, called to be an apostle, set apart for the Gospel of God." In this text, a calling denotes something similar to a spiritual gift, as when Paul writes elsewhere of the specialization of the gifts in the body of Christ:

> And his gifts were that some should be apostles, some prophets, some evangelists, some pastors and teachers, for the equipment of the saints, for the work of ministry, for the building up the body of Christ (Ephesians 4:11-12)

Furthermore, the call can refer to any particular experience of divine guidance of one's life along a particular path. Evangelicals frequently report moments of crisis, often marked by the perception of miraculous phenomena such as a vision, a voice in the night, or a prophetic dream in which God told them to embark on some course of action. They usually compare such experiences to those abounding in the Old Testament: Abraham being divinely told to leave this home and go out to an unknown land; God speaking to Joseph in dreams or to Moses from a burning bush; Samuel hearing the voice of God in the night as a young boy in the house of Eli, and later (as a priest) acting as a channel through which God called David to be king of Israel; and of course, various prophets receiving their call to deliver the Word of Jehovah to a recalcitrant Hebrew people (Swanson 1995, 75).

Finally, based on the text of the New Testament, Swanson (1995, 85) presents the archetypal missionary call story for evangelicals: the story of the Apostle Paul. As stated in the Biblical text, Paul was called to preach the gospel to the Gentiles, after his dramatic conversion on the road to Damascus. Nevertheless, the personal call was first confirmed by a word from the Holy Spirit to the church at Antioch: "Set apart for me Barnabas and Saul for the work to which I have called them" (Acts 13:2). Later in the middle of his second journey, Paul received an extraordinary call to take the gospel to Macedonia: "And a vision appeared to Paul in the night: a man of Macedonia was standing beseeching him and saying, 'Come over to Macedonia and help us'" (Acts 16:9). Mentioning all of these Biblical moments, Swanson offers an enormous repertoire of images for the expressions of divine calling among evangelicals. This repertory is also, as will be shown later, employed by Pentecostals.

The Call in Pentecostal Circles

Regarding Pentecostalism, Währisch-Oblau (2012, 84) offers a convincing description of the way Pentecostals understand the call. She begins by pointing out that Pentecostals believe that God "has a plan for their lives, this means that Pentecostals consider that individual life courses have been prepared by God. Hence, one of the tasks of every Christian is to discern God's guidance particularly concerning major choices (e.g. for a career or a marriage partner)." Währisch-Oblau also argues that individual divine guidance in major life choices, though, is not the same as a "call." In Pentecostal discourse, a call is regarded as a kind of "special" vocation, often connected to a ministry, which cannot simply be filled by being able, educated, and trained. Pentecostals talk about having been called to be a pastor, an evangelist, a missionary, a teacher, but they would not usually claim to have received a call to be a scientist, a businesswoman, or a carpenter (Währisch-Oblau 2009, 84).

Besides, according to Währisch-Oblau (2009, 85), a call and a supernatural enabling are closely related to one another. As in Evangelical circles, Pentecostals frame the experience of a call appealing to biblical texts. For Pentecostals, a call is a special experience in which an individual may have had a vision, audition, or dream, may have felt an inner urge or longing, or may have understood an arbitrary encounter as "God speaking to me," with the awareness that God wanted to talk this individual into entering a ministry. A call is never just general, but always specific and personal and often these experiences are recounted in order to prove the charisma and authority of the person in charge of the ministry.

Concerning the authority to exert a position or a ministry, Währisch-Oblau (2009, 85) also notes that due to the experiential aspect or Pentecostal Christianity, which is not defined by certain dogmatic beliefs, the genre of "testimony" plays an important role in the recounting of "call experiences." By recounting a call testimony, Pentecostal leaders establish and strengthen their special position as such. In light of the independent religious character of the leaders of this study, a call narrative seems to be a crucial discursive resource to highlight the authority of their position.

7.1.2. The Call in the Cases of Guatemalan Independent Pentecostal Leaders Studied

Once the literature regarding the "divine call" was examined, it was possible to identify how biblical references inform the references to the call as the interviewees referred to hearing voices, having visions, or receiving prophetic messages from God or the Holy Spirit as the main elements that drove them to become a Pentecostal missionary. Then, some questions emerge: How and when did the Guatemalan independent Pentecostal leaders interviewed claim that they had a call? Did they consider it the beginning of their religious career? Is the call connected to their journey to Los Angeles? In the next pages, every call narrative is presented in order to answer these questions.

The Call in Expatriate Leaders by "Professional Consecration"

The first references to God's call to examine are those of the expatriate leaders by "professional consecration." In this group are Martin Carmona and Alvaro Sánchez, who move freely to a foreign country and are well-educated people who work full time in the framework of their religious organizations with more than 500 devotees. This means that they have developed a successful professional career as religious leaders, which according to their narratives has been forward-oriented.

Alvaro Sánchez: Participation in Missionary Conferences in Los Angeles

Alvaro Sánchez is the director of a Guatemalan church with congregations not only in Guatemala City but also in North Carolina, El Salvador, Costa Rica, and Mexico. He began the interview by thanking God for allowing him to participate in this study and narrated the reasons for his first trip to Los Angeles.

> En el '89 fui la primera vez a Los Ángeles, por una invitación especial de un predicador que se llama Alberto Motessi y que es argentino... Ahí fuimos... ocho días a esas conferencias misioneras, donde, pues se impulsó mucho sobre la obra misionera, y de hecho pues eso quedo pues en mi corazón: esas enseñanzas... de la obra misionera.

> [In 1989, I went to Los Angeles for the first time, by a special invitation from a preacher named Alberto Motessi, who is Argentinean ... There we went ... eight days to those missionary conferences, where missionary work

> was very much promoted, and in fact that is what remained in my heart: those teachings ... of missionary work.]

Alvaro Sanchez connected God's call to his journey to the United States, appealing to fact-terms and providing few references to his journey to Los Angeles. The call addresses the beginning of a career as a missionary and this account seems to indicate that he did not feel any need to explain or defend his decision to become a missionary. He was invited to participate in a missionary conference, learned about missionary work, and has been working as a missionary since then. From his narrative, it can be inferred that he is not in a position where his call is doubted or questioned: He feels sure about his call and he also feels unchallenged in his role as a missionary since he is the head pastor of a large independent Pentecostal church in Guatemala, with congregations made up of several hundred members and has also established numerous satellite churches in other countries.

Martin Carmona: The Call to an International Ministry in Los Angeles

Martin Carmona, who is the founder and full-time head pastor of an international church with branches in the United States, Guatemala, and Spain as well as the secretary of the *Alianza Ministerial Hispana* (Hispanic Ministerial Alliance), recounted how he started his congregation after accepting a call into full-time ministry, arguing that he experienced God's callings:

> ... allá a finales de los 90s ... Dios, Dios, nos habló. No te puedo decir cómo Dios nos habló, porque no escuche su voz audible, pero en lo profundo del corazón, yo sentía que Dios me hablaba ... y me decía que tengo que volver a mis orígenes. Y un día de estos ... le comenté a mi mamá ... Y [ella]me dice: "Quédate donde estás. No te muevas, sigue sirviendo al Señor, solo visiona que Dios va a empezar a obrar y ustedes van a ser los que van a abrir la primera iglesia en Estados Unidos ...
>
> [back in the late 90s ... God, God spoke to us. I can't tell you how God spoke to us, because I didn't hear his audible voice, but in the depths of my heart, I felt that God was speaking to me ... and he told me that I had to go back to my origins. And one of these days ... I told my mother ... And [she] says to me: "Stay where you are. Don't move, keep serving the Lord, just envision that God is going to start working and you will be the ones who are going to open the first church in the United States ...]

In Martin Carmona's biographical narrative, the call and journey to the United States are not connected in the sense of ascribing any special divine guidance to their coming to the United States. He did not define the call as the impulse that set their journey into motion; instead the call reached him in Los Angeles, marking the beginning of a career as independent pastor there, a career that has been successful since he became the founder and full-time head pastor of an international church with branches in numerous countries.

Moreover, in the biographical narrative of Martin Carmona, references to auditions not only appeared concerning the beginning of his international ministry; he also alluded to "divine auditions" whenever decisions regarding the expansion of his church had to be made. As he mentioned in the statements above, auditions have to be validated by persons whom he considers his spiritual mentors: A religious leader, whom he called "apostle," and his mother both helped him to understand what God wanted him to do. That is in part because he did not always seem sure that he appropriately understood what he heard and needed an authoritative interpretation, which is given by a mentor under whose tutelage he was working. With his kind of account, he is saying that it is God himself who made him do what he did, not his aspirations.

The Call in Migrant Leaders by "Divine Consecration" Who are Pastors of Their Own Congregations and See Themselves as "Expatriates"

This group is composed of Antonio Rodríguez, Francisca Arévalo, and Carlos Benítez. These leaders have taken some steps in the development of their professional careers as religious leaders because they are founders and head pastors of their own churches, which have social impact on their neighborhoods. Nevertheless, their paths as religious leaders have not been so successful as in the case of the expatriate leaders presented before since they have had to face personal, economic, and social obstacles in the establishment of their own churches.

Antonio Rodríguez: Miracles, Prophecies, and Visions as a Call

Antonio Rodríguez is the founder and part-time pastor of an independent Pentecostal congregation with fifty members. He provided a long call narrative located in Guatemala in which the call into ministry is intertwined with the missionary call, then continued with a number of disruptions which, although outwardly seeming to lead him away from the fulfilling of the call, actually brought him closer to its realization: being a minister in Los Angeles. He also talked about the difficulties of having a ministry and, finally, of the joys and advantages of having a small and independent congregation.

Regarding his call, Antonio Rodríguez told that he decided to be a minister after a healing miracle experience:

> ... cuando yo me case en el año 1976 ... ya íbamos muy poco a la iglesia. Yo me dediqué mucho a trabajar. Yo llegué a ser el gerente del Club Municipal, uno de los clubes mayores de liga [de fútbol] en Guatemala ... Dios me permitió llegar hasta arriba, pero hubo un momento que me dijo: "Bueno hasta aquí llegamos." Y mi hijo, el segundo, se enfermó ... En el hospital no le encontraban absolutamente nada, pero estaba grave. Y entonces, alguien se acercó con nosotros y nos dijo: "Este es un plan de Dios, Dios quiere tenerlos otra vez en la línea donde estaban, en el camino ... Ustedes tienen que hacer nuevamente un pacto con Dios." Total, de que lo hicimos, este, con lágrimas y todo hicimos el pacto ... Entonces, eh, cuando nosotros hicimos ese pacto con Dios, cuando llegamos el lunes en la mañana a verlo, él ya no tenia nada ...
>
> [... when I married in 1976 ... we were very infrequent churchgoers. I did a lot of work myself. I became the manager of the Municipal Club, one of the biggest league [football] clubs in Guatemala ... God allowed me to get to the top, but there was a moment when he said to me: "Well, we made it up to here." And my son, the second one, got sick ... In the hospital, they couldn't find anything, but it was very serious. And then, someone came up to us and said: "This is God's plan, God wants to have you in line again where you were, on the road ... You have to make a covenant with God again." So, we made the covenant ... So, uh, when we made that covenant with God, when we arrived on Monday morning to see him, he already had nothing ...]

According to this account, he was called into the ministry at a time when he was doing very well in his secular career. The call was a kind of reconversion that included repenting for not having followed God in the way that he should have done it. He interprets his secular career as a deviation from the plan that God had for his life. Then, he states that after the healing miracle, he heard constant prophetic words reminding him of a calling to be a pastor, a position that he accepted after agreeing with God:

> Entonces, un día una profecía en la iglesia, me dice: "Recuerda que un rebaño sin pastor, las ovejas se pierden" ... Total de que una vez teníamos unos servicios especiales. Y otra vez: "Recuerda que... un rebaño sin pastor, las ovejas se pierden." Y dije: "Hagamos un trato. Si en tres meses, la iglesia revienta de miembros adultos, que sobrepase los 100, yo acepto." ¿Para que hice ese pacto con Dios? En menos de 30 días teníamos hasta gente en la calle ...
>
> [Then, one day a prophecy in the church said to me: "Remember that a flock without a shepherd, the sheep are lost" ... So, once we had special services and again: "Remember that ... a flock without a pastor, the sheep are lost." And I said, "Let's make a deal. If in three months, the church bursts with adult members, more than 100, I accept." Why did I make that agreement with God? In less than 30 days we had even people on the street ...]

Presenting the events in this order, he stressed that becoming a pastor was not his idea at all, and he had doubts when he was first confronted with the call. This serves to underline the fact that what happened was really a revealed word of God, acting miraculously, and not the result of one's own desire for leadership. But his call narrative did not end with a call to ministry. Antonio Rodríguez continued relating his call to come to Los Angeles as a missionary, presenting elaborated accounts of visions:

> Y fue cuando en un viaje que yo tuve una visión ... yo salí de mi cuerpo y vine aquí a Los Ángeles, vine aquí a Los Ángeles.
>
> [And that's when on a trip I had a vision ... I left my body and came here to Los Angeles, I came here to Los Angeles.]

Antonio Rodríguez argues that he knows that this vision was about Los Angeles, because once there, he saw what he had already seen in his vision. Besides, another person validated this vision, according to his narrative. This person is a pastor working in Los Angeles, whom he met in Guatemala, but with whom he did not have a close relation.

> "Mire, hermano," me dijo, "yo tuve un sueño ... una revelación de parte de Dios, donde yo lo invitaba a venir a los Estados Unidos, y yo sé que es de Dios, hermano. Y yo he estado orando," me dijo, "yo quiero que usted escoja la aerolínea, y se venga para acá." Conociéndolo menos de una semana ...

> ["Look, brother," he said to me, "I had a dream ... a revelation from God, where I invited him to come to the United States, and I know that it is from God, my brother. And I've been praying," he said ... "I want you to choose the airline, and come here." Knowing him less than a week ...]

By saying that a stranger also had a similar dream, which inspired this person to pay Antonio Rodríguez's travel to Los Angeles, he highlighted that his trip was possible through the intervention of God. From the point of view of the interviewee, his trip to Los Angeles was a step within God's plan.

This narrative of the missionary call is also accompanied by an account about the ease of obtaining a visa to enter in the United States.

> … Total de que cuando yo fui e iba a venir para acá … me la dieron … La visa mía era una múltiple indefinida, que ... decía que podía entrar y salir desde los Estados Unidos las veces que yo quisiera … Esa fue la visa que me dieron, sin pedirme absolutamente nada. Me dice: "¿Tiene cuenta en bancos? "Si." "¿Trae el estado de cuenta?" "No." "¿Tiene cheque?" "Sí, aquí está mi chequera," le dije. "¿Y su estado de cuenta?" "No tengo," le dije, "No lo traje." "OK, no se preocupe." Así, así y ¿quien te va dar una visa así? Y así me la dieron a mí. Porque ahora piden un montón de cosas, siempre han pedido, pero ... pero no ... a mí no me pidieron nada.

> [So, when I went and was going to come here ... they gave it to me ... Mine was a multiple indefinite visa, which ... said that I could enter and leave the United States as many times as I wanted ... That was the visa they gave me, without asking me for anything at all. He says, "Do you have a bank account?" "Yes." "Do you have the statement?" "No." "Do you have a check?" "Yeah, here's my checkbook," I said. "And your statement?" "I don't have it," I said, "I didn't bring it." "OK, don't worry." Like that, like that, and who is going to give you a visa like that? And they gave it to me like that. Because now they ask many things, they have always done it, but … no no … they ask me nothing.]

By talking about the ease of obtaining a visa and traveling, the respondent set himself apart from "normal" immigrants. Based on his narrative, it is possible to see how this specificity is achieved. Antonio Rodríguez recounts that he did not present any official documents in relation to his economic situation—thus expressing that he was not like the poor Guatemalans who want to go to the United States—in sum, that he experienced totally different treatment. The fact that his story is highly implausible serves to underline the miraculous character of what happened to him. In addition, Antonio Rodríguez set himself apart from ordinary immigrants when he recounted his arrival in Los Angeles:

> Bueno nos vinimos en el año 91, en enero … Y ahí fue lo más duro, ah. Bueno, duro en el sentido de que cambiábamos totalmente de ambiente, de país, de costumbres. De todo. Éramos bendecidos porque ¿quién va a traer desde su país 5000 dólares para acá? Y yo sí los traía.
>
> [Well, we came here in 1991, in January ... And that was the hardest part, huh? Well, it was hard in the sense that we changed completely the atmosphere, the country, the customs. Everything. We were blessed because who's going to bring $5,000 here from his country? And I did bring them.]

This account serves to stress that he was not in need: he had a very good job in Guatemala, which allowed him to have an important sum of money in his pockets when he arrived in Los Angeles. Life in Guatemala was not bad at all, according to him. His trip with his family did not happen in reaction to any disaster or persecution. Nevertheless, conditions in Los Angeles were hard. Consequently, Antonio Rodríguez's narrative explains how his successful arrival in Los Angeles ended up forcing him to work as a delivery man in a pizzeria.

> nosotros pagamos el apartamento y esto y lo otro. Pero el dinero se iba acabando. Y tenía que trabajar. Señor ¿cuándo… empiezo? Total, que encontré un trabajo. Un trabajo ah ... repartiendo pizzas. Aquí empecé a repartir pizzas en el centro de Los Ángeles … pero en las noches yo me venía llorando porque como nos tocaba hacer la limpieza ... ah ... a veces nos tocaba limpiar el baño: el sanitario. Y a veces sin guantes, sin nada, sin mayor equipo. Y hay veces me venía llorando, le decía: "Señor, ¿a eso me trajiste hasta este país?"... yo era Señor Rodríguez allá, y aquí no soy nada" … fue una escuela porque yo creo que tal vez ya había subido yo muy alto y yo necesitaba bajar para volver a empezar otra vez …
>
> [we paid for the apartment and this and that. But the money was running out. And I had to work. Lord, when do I ... start? Anyway, I found a job. A job, uh ... delivering pizzas. Here I started delivering pizzas in downtown Los Angeles ... but at night I was crying because we had to do the cleaning ... ah ... sometimes we had to clean the bathroom: the toilet. And sometimes without gloves, without nothing, without bigger equipment. And there were times I would come crying, saying to Him: "Lord, is that why you brought me to this country?" ... I was Mister Rodríguez there, and here I am noth-

> ing" ... it was a important lesson because I think maybe I had climbed too high and I needed to get down in order to start again ...]

By talking again about his reproaches and deviation from the plan that God had for his life, Antonio Rodríguez presents spiritual justification for his unfavorable social position in Los Angeles. This position is immediately repaired in his narrative when he accounts that he was able to see again God's glory, which allowed him to buy his own house five years later.

According to these accounts, he received a call into the ministry and even into missionary work before he left his home country. The call developed and became clear in the course of his journey, where every step is presented as a logical consequence of the previous call. He saw himself as a missionary who went to the United States with a clear call to evangelize there. Nevertheless, he presented very elaborate accounts of his call, even with references to setbacks, disobedience and difficulties, which were used to emphasize the divine authorship of the call: He was not doing something they wanted in the first place, but something they were divinely called to achieve.

Following Steven Land's (2001, 74) arguments about the tendency in Pentecostal believers "to experience life as part of a biblical drama of participation in God's history," and Stephen Kroll-Smith's ideas (1980) about how testimonies meet the "need for identity work" with groups that operate within "a stratified belief system lacking formal passage rites," Währisch-Oblau (2012, 86) points out that call testimonies in general serve to legitimate authority and hierarchy, produce group boundaries, and enhance group coherence. By recounting a call testimony, Pentecostal leaders establish and strengthen their particular position in relation to their congregation. It is striking, however, that Antonio Rodríguez has had numerous problems regarding their authority. He cannot dedicate himself to their ministry full time and has to combine religious work with secular jobs that guarantee not only his and his family economic survival but also the maintenance of his small congregation.

Francisca Arévalo: Call into a Ministry as the Impulse to Redefine Her Life

Francisca Arévalo, who is the full-time head pastor of an independent Pentecostal congregation with approximately seventy members in Compton, also offered in her interview some accounts related to God's call. Interestingly, her call was not related to the reasons to come to the United States:

the reunification with her first husband. Her call happened some years later, after having had many problems as a single mother that forced her to abandon church participation. She mentions how after her second marriage and after actively participating in a congregation, she experienced a call:

> El Señor abrió mi corazón en términos espirituales. Entonces, yo tengo que dejar un trabajo secular para dejarme de lleno en la iglesia...
>
> [... The Lord opened my heart in spiritual terms. So, I have to give up a secular job to devote myself fully to the church ...]

That means that she defined the call into a ministry as the impulse that inspired her when she was returning to a normal life and gave a new meaning to her circumstances. In her call, there are no miracles, just a development of a specific determination during a time of exchanges and discussions with her husband. To make sure that this event is adequately understood as a call, she adds many statements such as "the Lord opened my heart." Through these statements, the option for a full-time ministry is presented as divinely led, not just merely a human idea. Besides, the change was not just a step, a further development in her biography, but a reversal of what she had experienced before.

Carlos Benítez: The Call to Conversion and Beginning in the Ministry

Carlos Benítez, a former civil engineer and full-time pastor of an independent Pentecostal congregation with approximately 100 members, did not talk about any missionary call as the reason to come to Los Angeles. Instead, he argues in his narrative that his trip to Los Angeles was the result of facing the economic and social problems caused by the war in his country of origin, as he did not find any job in his profession. In his narrative, he provides the account of his conversion in Guatemala and his first steps as a ministry there:

> … yo no acepté a Cristo en una campaña, ni en una iglesia. Yo estaba estudiando para ser ingeniero civil, y estaba en mi cuarto, donde vivía en la casa de una familia. Y llegaron dos hermanas, a visitar a la señora de la casa, que era cristiana. Y ya cuando se iban a ir dijeron: "Oremos un ratito," y antes de ponerse orar … me dijeron: "Veo que usted está estudiando, y una carrera tan importante, y usted necesita mucho de Dios, no quisiera acompañarnos a orar, para pedirle por sus estudios?" Y yo dije: "A mí no me hace daño eso" … "Arrodíllese por aquí," me dijeron. Y me

> arrodillé. Cuando empiezo yo a sentir un gran calor en mi cuerpo, y una cosa que me empezó a agarrar y a llorar, y a llorar, y a llorar, y a llorar, y yo peleando contra aquello … Cuando yo me pregunté por qué estoy llorando, sentí yo, que Dios me hablaba y me decía: "Es porque te estoy ministrando, y quiero que hoy entregues tu corazón." Y yo no pude resistir, y yo solito hice el pacto con Dios."
>
> [I did not accept Christ in a campaign, nor in a church. I was studying to be a civil engineer, and I was in my room, where I lived in a family house. And two sisters came to visit the lady of the house, who was a Christian. And when they were going to leave, they said: "Let us pray for a little while," and before they went to pray ... they told me: "We see that you are studying, and such an important career, and you need a lot from God, do you not want to accompany us to pray, to ask Him for your studies?" And I said: "That doesn't hurt me" ... "Kneel over here," they said. And I knelt down. When I begin to feel a great warmth in my body, and something that began to seize me and to cry, to cry, to cry, and cry, and I started to fight against it … When I asked myself why I was crying, I felt that God was speaking to me and saying, "It is because I am ministering to you, and I want you to deliver your heart today." And I couldn't resist, and I alone made the covenant with God."]

Carlos Benítez mentioned that he heard voices coming from God when he converted to Pentecostalism. Nevertheless, he does not return to any spectacular event to legitimize his missionary authority. Despite the size of his congregation, factual things such as being a full-time pastor able to acquire a plot of land and to build a church with an adjacent community center seem to be enough evidence of his success in his ministry.

The three last narratives analyzed show that a particular meaning is provided with a divine call narrative, particularly in the discourse within independent Latino churches. All the interviewees in this group talked about a change in their lives that gave a new meaning to their existence. This new meaning seems to be closely related to constant appeals in sermons, speeches, and leaflets that urge church members to realize that they have been "sent to the United States for a purpose," which it not related to exhausting work such as cleaning other people's toilets, but being more active in missionary endeavors.

The Call in Migrant Leaders by "Divine Consecration" in Intermediate Leadership Positions

In this group are Marcos González y Francisco Quiacaín, who presented themselves as preachers and singers in small Pentecostal churches in Los Angeles, illustrating the first steps in a professional career.

Marcos González: "Feelings Coming from God"

Marcos González, who is a part-time evangelist in an independent Latino Pentecostal church in Los Angeles and helps pastors and churches in Guatemala and Mexico, talked about having experienced "special feelings." Talking about his first trip to the United States, Marcos González provided some accounts about his missionary call. He begins his narration by mentioning that in 1980 he was in Mexico with other evangelists and they went to fast and pray in a forest in Cuernavaca, and during this retreat, he felt the presence of the God:

> Yo sentí de Dios venir aquí a Estados Unidos. Que Dios me abriera puertas.
>
> [I felt that God wanted me to come here to the US. That God would open the doors for me.]

In his accounts, there are no references to spectacular events or miracles. He just explained the development of a "feeling" coming from God, which can be understood as a theological qualifier for the call. Recurring to this qualifier, he presented his trip to the United States as divinely led, not just as his own idea.

Besides, he connects this description of his call with something that happened some weeks later when he was invited to participate in an evangelistic campaign organized by a Pentecostal church in Matamoros, Tamaulipas. In this campaign, three pastors from Brownsville, Texas were also invited:

> Estando unos días ahí, ellos escucharon la predicación que Dios me daba y ellos sintieron de parte de Dios hacerme una invitación para estar con ellos de visita en Brownsville, Texas.
>
> [While being there for some days, they heard about the message that God was giving me and they felt that God was sending me an invitation to visit them in Brownsville, Texas]

Again, he refers to a "feeling" coming from God, but this time it is experienced by other religious leaders. By stating that three strangers also had a similar felling, which made them invite him to the United States, he emphasizes that his trip was part of God's plan.

Marcos González also talked about how he entered the United States. After describing the invitation, he relates the experience with the U.S. border agent, who refused to give him the visa to spend only three days in Brownsville.

> Entonces me presenté ante el jefe de migración y él me dijo con coraje: "¿Y dónde está su pasaporte?" Y yo se lo entregué. Y me dijo: "Mira, toma el autobús y te vas a Guatemala porque yo a ti no te doy visa porque bastante problema tenemos con los guatemaltecos." Y entonces yo me paré firme, con la autoridad que Dios me ha dado, y le dije: "Esa es la voz del diablo. Porque si usted no quiere darme la visa, quiera usted o no, yo voy a estar al otro lado predicando el evangelio."
>
> [Then I went to the head of immigration and he said boldly: "And where's your passport?" And I gave it to him. And he said to me: "Look, take the bus and go to Guatemala because I won't give you a visa because we have enough trouble with the Guatemalans." And then I stood firm, with the authority that God has given me, and said to him: "That is the voice of the devil. Because if you don't want to give me the visa, whether you do or not, I will be preaching the gospel on the other side."]

In Marcos's case, the call developed and became clear in the course of their journey, where every step is presented as a logical consequence of the previous call. In the call narrative, he presented himself as a missionary who went to the United States with a clear call to evangelize there. The call marks the beginning of his journey to the United States. According to these accounts, he is in Los Angeles because God wanted him there.

Francisco Quiacaín: The Call to Serve God in a Ministry

Francisco Quiacaín, who is a musician in numerous independent Pentecostal churches, not only Latino but also Korean Pentecostal churches and has been working as a construction worker, referred explicitly to a divine call to ministry. These accounts demonstrate how he came to consider himself an independent Pentecostal leader. In his narrative, he mentions that he dedicates Sundays to serve the Lord,

> Los domingos estoy dedicado al Señor. Así, aunque haya gente que quieren que trabaje y que me paguen así al doble, pero no acepto ofertas.
>
> [On Sundays, I am dedicated to the Lord. So, even if there are people who want me to work and they would pay me twice as much, I don't accept offers.]

After this account, he explains why he does that, appealing to a God's call to ministry:

> ... yo dejé de trabajar los domingos por servir al Señor en Guatemala. Porque el negocio que yo tenia era venta de helados. El domingo es el día donde hay más venta y más ganancia ... Llegó un día en que el Espíritu Santo me habló y me di cuenta de que en mi vida era como un disco, que estaba rayado ... Iba a la iglesia ... pero nunca me propuse servir a el Señor. Pero llega un día cuando dije: "No más, hasta aquí. El domingo voy a dedicar para el Señor" ... Dios siempre cuando lo llama a uno al ministerio, siempre pone ... las cosas en el camino ... El enemigo siempre me decía que: "¿Por qué dejaste los domingos de vender? Es cuando más ganas." Pero yo siempre le pude resistir porque el Espíritu Santo me dio fuerza ...
>
> [I stopped working on Sundays to serve the Lord in Guatemala. Because the business I had was selling ice cream. Sundays were the days where I sold and made more profit ... There came a day when the Holy Spirit spoke to me and I realized that my life was like a broken record ... I was going to church ... but I never set out to serve the Lord. But a day came when I said, "No more, up to here. On Sunday, I will devote myself to the Lord" ... God always when He calls one to the ministry, He always puts ... things in the way ... The enemy always told me: "Why did you stop selling on Sundays? That's when you win the most." But I was always able to resist him because the Holy Spirit gave me strength ...]

With these accounts, Francisco Quiacaín explains how he experienced the Holy Spirit, which led him to become aware of the need to serve the Lord, even though this implies renouncing economic gain. At the same time, he also refers to the "enemy" or the devil, who confronts him with the losses he incurred in dedicating Sundays "to the Lord." In this call narrative, an inner struggle is outlined between God and his enemies, which makes it clear that the interviewee understands the world as spiritual warfare, in which only with the anointing of the Holy Spirit, is it possible to overcome the forces of the devil.

Francisco Quiacaín also talks about his tough journey to Los Angeles through Mexico. He described in detail some of the difficulties of traveling without documents, trying not to be detected by the authorities in a country dominated by corruption. Some of these difficulties were, for example, travelling hidden in a truck for more than eight hours, plagued by high temperatures and having hardly any air to breathe, or his walking journey through the desert. These descriptions are accompanied by allusions to the Lord, asking for his protection and help:

> Y aún en el desierto, cuando teníamos descanso, nos sentábamos juntos, y nos poníamos a orar, dándole gracias al Señor: "Señor, a la hora que nos vayan a levantar, que seas tú el que nos de fuerzas para salir, para llevarnos a dónde vamos."
>
> [And even in the desert, when we had rest, we sat down together and prayed, giving thanks to the Lord: "Lord, at the hour when they wake us up, let it be you who gives us strength to depart, to take us where we are going."]

Francisco Quiacaín's recollection serves to illustrate that the call gave his new meaning to their existence. In his case, there are call and journey narratives, but they are not connected. Due to the voluntary services that he carried out as a musician in different Pentecostal congregations, he did not need to return to an elaborated call narrative to assure his religious position.

God's Call Narratives: Some Final Observations

As Droogers (1998, 19) points out, Pentecostal churches rediscovered the ministry of all believers. In these churches, those who are excluded from access to the economic means of production are transformed into subjects with free access to the religious means of production since once baptized, everybody has access to the power of God through the Holy Spirit and can act from and with that authority. The cases presented above are examples of how men and women can become active in the ministry. In contrast to Catholicism, Pentecostalism allows married people without education to have active and rewarding careers in ministry. Through ministerial work in the congregation, they can see themselves as having a successful life. By recounting a call testimony, Pentecostal leaders establish and strengthen their particular position. By becoming religious specialists, they have tapped a new mechanism of empowerment.

The most exemplary case is that of the expatriate leaders by professional consecration, who thanks to their religious involvement were able to develop a successful career as religious leaders. In the case of migrant leaders by divine consecration, the religious involvement has served to give new meaning to their lives. They do not portray themselves as the victims of political or economic circumstances, but rather as agents of a divine plan, a plan that is designated for them even if they do not understand it immediately. Through a call narrative, they present themselves as people achieving the things they desire. For immigrants with broken dreams, these testimonies are made to willing listeners.

7.2. Diversity in Pentecostal Praxis

Following the examples of the symbolic operator "God's call," in the next pages other symbolic operators related to God will be presented. As mentioned in Chapter 6, the Guatemalan Pentecostal independent leaders interviewed saw God as a material goods provider connected to their economic success. They also consider God as the Almighty, a facilitator, and a door opener, who makes things happen at the right time for the benefit of his believers. They commented that God's blessings allowed them to travel frequently to other countries to preach. They recounted that such trips to Los Angeles or other places happened because these are God's will. Some leaders also referred to God as a healer, while others indicate that God gives them the wisdom to conduct their life. Although it is notable that the discursive reference to God is abundant and connected with several social experiences, there is one element in common: These accounts show that the interviewees see God as an answer to their existential and physical concerns, providing tangible material results in their lives.

After a close analysis of accounts regarding transcendent entities, it was found that there is not only one kind of Pentecostalism among Guatemalan religious leaders in Los Angeles, but at least three paradigms or religious habitus formations, which are distinguished according to practices. In the next pages, I will present the symbolic operators of each paradigm by category: expatriate leaders by "professional consecration," migrant leaders by "divine consecration" who are pastors of their own congregations and see themselves as "expatriates," and migrant leaders by "divine consecration" in intermediate leadership positions. The symbolic operators included in each paradigm should not be read as being exclusive to the group described; it would be more accurate to say that they are more prevalent in that group.

7.2.1. God-as-Restorer Paradigm

The first paradigm is found among the expatriate leaders "by professional consecration" group, which includes Martin Carmona and Alvaro Sánchez. They were believers in Pentecostalism since their early childhood and youth. In Guatemala, they became Pentecostal leaders in middle positions before reaching the age of 18. Since then, they have worked in religious organizations until they became head pastors of independent congregations, which have always had an international character. This fact allowed them to travel with a visa as religious workers to the United States. Besides, they travel regularly between the United States and Guatemala as well as to other countries where their churches have established branches. Both claim to have university degrees in religious studies as well as children who were able to complete their university studies.

These two leaders understand that God is a good father who cares for the welfare of his children and is always willing to restore them if they fall into sin. For them, eternal life does not just mean a future in a spiritual realm; it means a physical life lived in fullness, with "wealth, fame, any success" even today. These words hint at influences from the neo-Pentecostal Faith Movement,[12] although there are no explicit references to this movement in the interviews.

12 The Word of Faith movement was originated as an outgrowth of U.S. Pentecostalism during the second half of the twentieth century. Its main leaders were Kenneth Hagin and Kenneth Copeland. The movement claims that health, financial well-being, and success are the "covenant rights" of any believer and can be possessed by "faith and proclamation," that is, that any believer can create a positive reality by believing in it and "confessing" it. If ill, for instance, one is supposed to constantly repeat the words "I am already healed" rather than reflecting on and speaking about the illness. The spoken word stands against the visible reality and will eventually affect and change it.

Alvaro Sánchez, the Guatemalan Pentecostal pastor and missionary who frequently travels to Los Angeles highlighted the importance of a personal relationship with God, remarking that with God all is possible.

> lo que necesita el migrante es que el pastor dé el mensaje de autoestima … De decirle que puede, que en el Señor las cosas son diferente ... Animarlos a que vivan la vida en Dios, yo creo que las personas se levantan y hacen la obra.
>
> [What the migrant needs is that the pastor gives him the message of self-esteem ... To tell him that he can, that in the Lord things are different ... To encourage them to live life with God, I believe that people rise and do the work.]

According to him, many Latino migrants feel intensely lonely because they are far from their family, far from their countries. Under these circumstances, they distance themselves from God as they face problems such as infidelity or a life devoted to materialism or alcoholism, and it is precisely in those moments when a friend is needed. He mentioned that as a Pentecostal pastor in Los Angeles he presented himself as a friend with whom immigrants could talk about their problems:

> … Eso sí nace del corazón, cuando yo le pedí al Señor que yo quería estar con los muchachos … platicar con ellos, hablar de la palabra, aconsejarlos, y hacerme amigo de ellos para ayudarlos, para saber cuál es su verdadera necesidad y de hecho … Dios me concedió de ir allá y estar allá con ellos … porque ellos … realmente sí necesitan más que todo … una ayuda pastoral …
>
> [… That is born from the heart when I asked the Lord that I wanted to be with the young men ... to talk with them, to talk about the Gospel, to advise them, and to befriend them in order to help them, to know what their real need is and in fact ... God allowed me to go there and be there with them... because they ... really do need more than anything pastoral help ...]

Alvaro Sánchez's Pentecostal understanding is, therefore, directed towards people facing problems that distance them from God. He rejects any moral condemnation of the people to whom he preaches. For him, infidelity, materialization, or alcoholism are not wrong ethical choices, but slightly blind, desperate, and therefore failed attempts to avoid loneliness and attain happiness. Stressing the importance of the restoration of the relationship with God, pastor Alvaro Sánchez presents a message in which the support that has eluded immigrants can be obtained.

Martin Carmona, the founder of an international church with branches in the United States, Guatemala, and Spain, refers to his ministry in Los Angeles mentioning God's will to restore his people. Describing his ministry, he emphasizes that it is a ministry of restoration:

> porque nuestro ministerio se llama Ministerio Internacional de Restauración … hay personas que habían sido como dejadas a un lado, no había un ministerio que restaure a las personas. No había un ministerio que crea que, si alguien falló, puede ser perdonado y puede ser restaurado. Y Dios nos dio a nosotros esa visión: De restaurar, no de condenar. Juan 3:17 dice: "Porque Dios no envío a su hijo al mundo para condenar al mundo, sino para que el mundo sea salvo por él." Entonces que extraordinario tener eso en la mente y en el corazón.

> [our ministry is called the International Ministry of Restoration because ... some people had been set aside, there was no ministry that restored people. There was no ministry that believed that if someone failed, he or she could be forgiven and restored. So, God gave us that vision: To restore, not to condemn. John 3:17 says, "Because God did not send his son into the world to condemn the world, but that the world might be saved by him." How extraordinary, then, to have that in mind and heart.]

Like Alvaro Sánchez, Martin Carmona also refuses any moral condemnation of the people to whom he preaches. Issues such as infidelity are not wrong ethical choices, but rather the result of being alone without spiritual support. Appealing to this ministry of restoration, Martin Carmona argues that thanks to it, he has had the opportunity to meet numerous pastors over the years and gained some recognition, eventually becoming the secretary of the *Alianza Ministerial Hispana* (Hispanic Ministerial Alliance). Concerning this position, he also presents himself as a social and political activist:

> … la mayoría de las iglesias, con las que nosotros convivimos son latinas. Entonces hay, puedo decirte, que hay de repente, un 70% de migrantes ilegales … Yo no quiero ... no quiero auto-nombrarme un activista, pero lo soy. Porque de alguna manera ... eh ... elaborado propuestas. He salido a la vanguardia, a dar la cara por la comunidad, no solo latina, sino por la comunidad que no tiene documentos. Por ejemplo, yo he salido en Univisión, televisión a nivel mundial, hablando acerca de la migración. Lo

> importante que es eso, que los pastores entendamos, tenemos que entender, que nosotros, no solo somos pastores de una iglesia, sino de la ciudad. Entonces, si los que están soportando tu congregación se van, ¿Quién te va a ayudar en tu congregación? ...
>
> [... most of the churches we live with are Latino. Then suddenly there are, I can tell you, 70% are illegal immigrants ... I don't want to ... I don't want to call myself an activist, but I am. Because somehow ... uh ... elaborate proposals. I have gone out in the vanguard, to stand up for the community, not only for the Latinos but the whole undocumented community. For example, I have been on Univision, worldwide television, talking about migration. The important thing is that, we, the pastors, understand, we have to understand, that we are not only pastors of a church, but of the city. So, if those who are supporting your congregation leave, who will help you in your congregation? …]

From this social and political activism a criticism also emerges both of Latino immigrants and Latino Pentecostal leaders. Regarding the Latino immigrants, he argues that they do not want to study and have a fear of leadership. Concerning the Latino Pentecostal leaders, he argues that not all of them feel a responsibility for the illegal immigrants, although they are the ones who support the churches. He argues that Latinos should change this mentality. They do not have to live that way; God wants to provide for them:

> si tan solo los pastores nos diéramos cuenta que importante es que entendamos que este es nuestro tiempo, que entendamos que esta nación americana ha sido como la herencia que Dios les dio a los latinos, a los latinoamericanos … Tenemos que ministrarlos ... a la gente, haciéndole ver que ha venido acá, y sus hijos son de acá, que no piense en Colombia, no piense en Guatemala, que no piense en México, porque han venido acá, y sus hijos son de acá … Tienen que seguir acá, porque de alguna manera Dios los trajo acá, como Dios llevo a su pueblo a la tierra prometida. Sí, lo que pasa es que les entregaron una tierra, pero había que echar fuera a los gigantes. Había que conquistar la tierra … Pero Dios quiere que nos levantemos, porque este es el tiempo, yo sé que Dios nos trajo acá, así como un día llevo a los europeos y norteamericanos a Latinoamérica para evangelizar, ahora Dios nos ha traído acá, para la evangelización de esta nación ...
>
> [if only the pastors would realize how important it is for us to understand that this is our time, that we understand that this American nation has been

> like the inheritance that God has given to Latinos, to Latin Americans ... We have to minister them ... to people, making them see that they have come here, and their children are from here, that they don't think of Colombia, don't think of Guatemala, that they don't think of Mexico, because they are here, and their children are from here … They have to remain here, because in a way God brought them here, the same way that God led His people to the promised land. Yes, they were given land, but the giants had to be thrown out. We had to conquer the earth ... But God wants us to rise because this is the time, I know that God brought us here, as one day He brought Europeans and North Americans to Latin America to evangelize, now God has brought us here for the evangelization of this nation.]

For him, the diagnosis is clear: The United States was a Christian country, and not in the very distant past, but faith has diminished, and the country needs a revival. Pentecostals from Latin America have to go to the United States to bring about this revival. They are workers of God, developing their religious work in the United States. Therefore, they do not have to accept ideologies that make them victims. With God, they will accomplish all their objectives.

The Praxeological Square: God-as-Restorer Paradigm

To understand the logic of this paradigm, it is best to begin considering the negative experiences. In this case, the interviewees refer to *lack of aspiration and fear of leadership in the Latino population.* They counter these experiences with a specific promise of salvation, their most important religious belief, which corresponds to the category "positive interpretation," that is, *God as a father willing to restore his believers*, who provides success in material and spiritual issues. From this promise, they derive their self-description or identity, presenting themselves as *committed leaders proclaiming their faith in God.* Through their faith, they achieved a life lived in fullness with leadership and success today. These three steps combine to form the basic transformation, modeling the generation of identity.

The second transformation models the "generation of strategy." From their positive experiences, the leaders also express articulated grievances and, most importantly, they ascribe reasons and causes for those grievances, something which is articulated in the category "negative interpretation:" *life without faith.* Knowing the reasons for these grievances, the religious agents can design the appropriate strategies to fight those grievances. Therefore, they follow a ministry of restoration based on coaching.

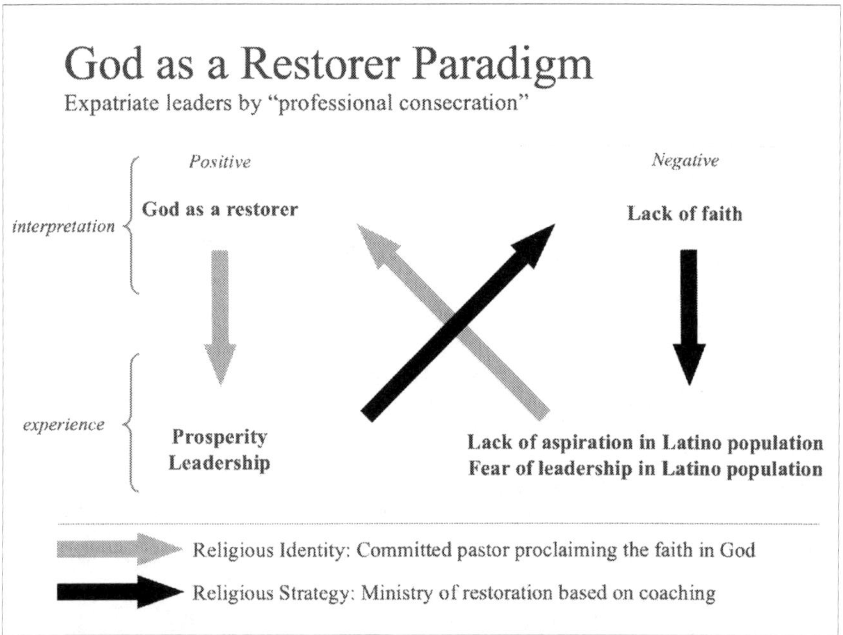

According to this logic, people facing difficult social structures like Guatemalans in Los Angeles, for whom political action offers little hope of ending the cycles of poverty, undereducation, and political marginalization, can only rely on a message based on God's promises of restoration as the unique solution to their problems: They do not have to accept ideologies that make them victims. They have the power, through faith and coaching, to obtain things that have eluded them through secular means.

Leaders in the God-as-restorer paradigm seem to have been generating habitual dispositions in which success is the primary goal. Through their ministerial work and evangelism, they have acquired certain kind of competencies such as leadership skills, generation of self-confidence, and rhetoric, among others, strengthened in a revaluation of the individual and a collective self, through the small group. For them, success is directed to the work for God, the missionary work, the church, the Christian family, a life without vices, etc. Hence, the religious life of these leaders is often combined with relatively analytical methodologies to achieve prosperity goals, directly imported from the repertoire of secular-business positive thinking (Ehrenreich 2009). Therefore, it is not surprising that the interviews of expatriate leaders "by professional consecration" reflect the principles of positive thinking, invoking coaching, and the leaders consider them the best option to achieve their objectives.

7.2.2. God's Love Paradigm

Migrant leaders by "divine consecration" who are pastors of their congregations and see themselves as "expatriates" constantly refer to the importance of God's love. Francisca Arévalo, Carlos Benítez, and Antonio Rodríguez illustrate this paradigm very well, which is found among migrants from urban areas, particularly Guatemala City, who had the opportunity to go to the university, came from families with a rural background, were "self-employed" workers, or housewives working in small businesses. Two of them were born into a Pentecostal family and the other converted in his early youth. They migrated because of the devastating economic and security consequences of the confrontation between the military government and the guerrilla groups, although none of them personally experienced political violence. Because of the time they immigrated, they were able to legalize their residence in the United States; all three were United States citizens at the time of the interview. In the United States, two of them, Francisca Arévalo and Carlos Benítez, worked full-time as religious leaders. Only Antonio Rodríguez worked part-time in his congregation since he had a job in the service sector. In addition, their children were able to complete their university studies, achieving a better economic and social position in Los Angeles than that of their parents.

These interviewees conceive of God as a loving father who promises material and spiritual goods to everyone who has enough faith to reach the promises. They emphasize the physical manifestations of salvation, highlighting God's desire for his people to prosper and be in good health. The underlying paradigm here is a paradigm of a life lived in fullness based on John 10:10, reflecting also some influences from the neo-Pentecostal Faith Movement. Nevertheless, as it was in the case of "God as a restorer" paradigm, there were no explicit references to this movement in the interviews.

Francisca Arévalo, the female pastor who suffered mistreatment and made her negative experiences as a single mother the articulating motivation for her religious work, recounted several moments when she saw God's mediation in health concerns. These moments took place when she suffered from cancer and received a surgical treatment, which almost led to her death:

> Y dijo el ginecólogo: "Ella está grave ... está grave, no sabemos cuándo abramos. Puede ser que haya cáncer adentro." Entonces el doctor habló conmigo: "Mira estás grave, estás grave … no sé ... no sé qué decirte." Yo le dije: "Yo tengo un Dios grande y poderoso" … Y que, si vuelvo de la anestesia, yo pegaba unos grandes gritos y yo sentía la muerte …Y entonces, ahí, mi mamá clamó a Dios. Yo sentí que se disipo mi dolor.
>
> [And the gynecologist said: "She's seriously ill ... we don't know when we open [conduct surgery]. There may be cancer inside." Then the doctor spoke to me: "Look, you're serious ill ... I don't know ... I don't know what to tell you." I said to him: "I have a great and powerful God" ... And that, when I came back from the anesthetic, I was screaming a lot and I felt death… And then, at that moment, my mom cried out to God. I felt my pain dissipate.]

She also mentions God as a provider of money, when she recounts how she got the money for her daughter's university tuition fees:

> "Mamita, esta universidad está cara." "No importa, Dios va a proveer el dinero." Y empezamos a orar…, a pedirle a Dios: "Dios, el mundo tú lo hiciste, y la plata. La plata es tuya, Señor." Y empezamos ahí, y no más llegando a la casa porque le hacían falta a ella como trece mil dólares, ella había pedido un préstamo, y entonces, cuando llegamos a la casa, como a las 4 de la tarde, entró una llamada, que ya estaba resulto, la admitían al colegio.
>
> ["Mommy, this college is expensive." "It doesn't matter, God is going to provide the money." And we began to pray ... to ask God: "God, you made the world, and the money. The money is yours, Lord." And we started there, no longer going home, because she needed about thirteen thousand dollars, she had asked for a loan, and then, when we arrived home, at about 4:00 p.m., a phone call came in, that it was already solved, she was admitted to the school.]

These accounts serve to show that she conceived of God within a "pragmatic" paradigm, stressing that God provides solutions to concrete problems in everyday life. This practical idea of God also influences her missionary message. As she has had to face recurrent family problems during her life, the topic "family" plays an important role in her narrative. One of the most important tasks she performs as a religious leader is family counseling, which she not only offered to members of her congregation but also to a wider public through conferences and participation in radio programs. She uses her own "salvation" from family abuse as a paradigmatic narrative to invite others to follow her example. Because she was freed, others can "come out" too. Additionally, her missionary message is more experiential: It is not phrased in terms of a certain truth or information that needs to be related to people, but rather as a personal encounter with God, which has fundamentally transformed her life. Regarding drug abuse, she is also in favor of rehabilitation promoted through a personal relationship with God and participation in the church. For Francisca Arévalo, God heals and frees from drug addiction, and He enriches human lives.

Antonio Rodríguez, the founder and part-time pastor of a small, independent Pentecostal congregation also talked about God, emphasizing God's blessings as material manifestations to solve physical concerns. First, as it was presented regarding his call, he argued that he decided to pursue the ministry after experiencing a healing miracle that saved his son, stressing the intervention of God in health concerns:

> Entonces, eh, cuando nosotros hicimos ese pacto con Dios, cuando llegamos el lunes en la mañana a verlo, él ya no tenía nada. Ya le habían desconectado y esto y lo otro. Y cuando hablamos con los doctores, dicen: "¿Saben qué? El niño ayer en la noche empezó a reaccionar. El niño ayer en la noche empezó a respirar por su cuenta, ya no le dio fiebre …"
>
> [So, uh, when we made that covenant with God, when we arrived on Monday morning to see him, he had nothing [no longer needed medical intervention]. He'd already been disconnected and this and that. And when we talk to the doctors, they say, "You know what? The boy last night started to react. The boy last night started breathing on his own, he no longer has a fever ..."]

Second, he talked about God as a provider of material goods as he recounted how he acquired his house in Los Angeles:

> Y ... pude ver la gloria de Dios, que a los cinco años de estar en este país, yo compre mi casa. Y nadie de los inmigrantes aquí en cinco años fue a comprar una casa. Que trabaje, pues, honradamente. Está bien difícil. Ahí vi la mano del Señor. Y digo yo: "Señor, gracias."

> [And ... I could see the glory of God, that after ... five years of being in this country, I bought my house. And none of the immigrants here in the past five years were able to buy a house ... working honestly, then. It's very difficult. I saw the Lord's hand there. And I say, "Lord, thank you."]

Concerning his understanding of his mission in the United States, Antonio Rodríguez highlights in his narrative that the gospel is for everyone, arguing that in his preaching he puts more emphasis on God's love than on God's authority. Antonio Rodríguez avoids any moral condemnation of the people to whom he preaches. For him, it is God who changes people and shows them what they have to do:

> … Cuando tú tienes más amor que autoridad, entonces, vas a ver cosas muy diferentes … Yo no te voy a decir: "Necesitas cambiar. No, deja que el espíritu de Dios te cambie." Y … entonces ya tienes que pedir a Dios que te cambie …
>
> [... When you have more love than authority, then you will see very different things ... I'm not going to tell you, "You need to change. No, let the spirit of God change you. And ... then you have to ask God to change you ...]

Based on these accounts, it is possible to assume that Antonio Rodríguez understands that a personal relationship with God transforms the life of the believer, even in physical and material concerns. A personal relationship with God provides solutions for concrete problems in everyday life.

Carlos Benítez, the founder and head pastor of a congregation with 100 members, also talks about the importance of God as a direct provider of material goods, particularly regarding his church. He begins by arguing that he is not a conformist leader, and thanks to his faith in an almighty God he can picture great things for his church:

> Para el número que somos, no nos metiéramos en grandes compromisos, pero como hemos creído en un Dios grande, entonces hemos comprado propiedades…para ir pagando mensualmente ... ahí donde estamos compramos por un millón de dólares …
>
> [For the number that we are, we will not get into significant compromises, but as we have believed in a great God, then we have bought properties… so to speak, we pay monthly for it ... in our location we buy for a million dollars …]

These references show that for Carlos Benítez human beings can control their destiny through their faith in God and positive visualizations, fulfilling the physical, material, and spiritual promises that God has already given to them.

The Praxeological Square: God's Love Paradigm

The narratives examined above are different, but they present a similar structure. Narrators talked about a personal relationship with God, which is manifested through God's intervention in the physical, material, and spiritual realms. Based on the accounts presented before, the next praxeological square has been developed:

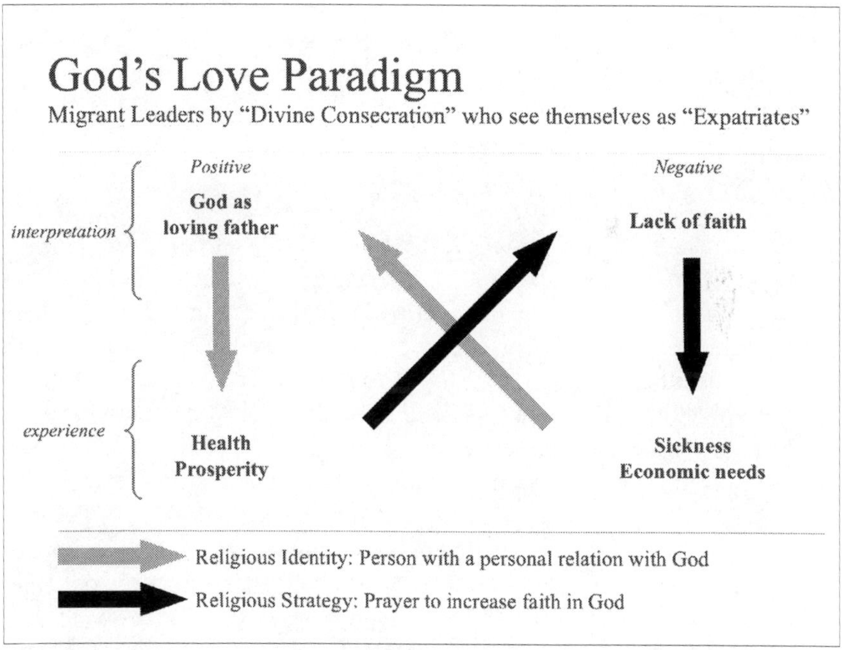

Regarding negative experiences, in God's love paradigm, the leaders referred to existential and physical concerns: *sickness* and *economic needs.* They confront these experiences with a specific promise of salvation, their most important religious belief, which corresponds to the category "positive interpretation," that is, *God as a loving father*, who provides material and spiritual good. Hence, God is seen as an answer to existential and physical concerns. From this promise, they derive their self-description or identity, presenting themselves as a *person with a personal relationship with God.* Through their faith, they achieve a life lived in fullness with health and wealth. These three steps combine to model the generation of identity.

The second transformation models the "generation of strategy." From their positive experiences, the leaders face articulated grievances and, most importantly, they ascribe reasons and causes for those grievances, something which it is articulated in the category "negative interpretation": *life without faith.* Knowing the reasons for the grievances, the religious agents can design the appropriate strategies to fight those grievances. Therefore, they follow a *ministry based on prayer to increase faith.* According to this logic, people facing difficult social structures like Guatemalans in Los Angeles can achieve good things like health and propriety if they are willing to increase their true faith in God.

7.2.3. Spiritual Warfare Paradigm

The third paradigm emerges from the biographical narratives of migrant leaders by "divine consecration" in intermediate leadership positions. In this group, leaders have an indigenous and rural background. None of them ever became a pastor of their congregation, but were rather leaders with mid-level positions. Before their travel to the United States, they had already migrated from the countryside to Guatemala City on a temporary basis. In their migratory experiences in Los Angeles, impediments to the attainment of prosperity play a much more critical role than in previous paradigms; above all, they are often presented as insurmountable. In the face of this experience, the religious practice can only be effective if the impediments are interpreted in religious terms: They are caused by demonic forces that are at constant war with the believer.

Marcos González and Francisco Quiacaín are the two interlocutors in this study who referred to an antagonistic relationship between God and the devil. This confrontation is the principal element of the *Spiritual warfare* paradigm. This paradigm is built from Biblical passages, usually the letters of Paul to the Ephesians. The "spiritual warfare" discourse emphasizes that human life is fragile and precarious since it is lived under constant threat from evil powers. According to it, manifest and unseen realities are connected: Unseen spirits cause problems in the manifest world. Problems such as illness, poverty, misfortune, infertility, and many others are seen as the consequence of the deeds of Satan, demons, evil spirits, or witchcraft, which are still active in this realm. Hence, demonic possession or oppression is suspected when problems of any kind persist. To combat evil powers, Christians need to be commissioned or "anointed by the Holy Spirit." The anointing by the Holy Spirit means that the believer is connected with the divine power, enabling him or her to evangelize, preach, teach, heal, and work miracles. "Anointing" means that the Holy Spirit is "upon" a person, working in and through this person's life and acts. Only the power of the Holy Spirit enables an evangelist to speak, to heal, and to free people from demonic powers.

Marcos González, the part-time evangelist of this study, recounted his role as an evangelist, presenting some ideas regarding his missionary message. He said, for instance, that:

> Un predicador tiene que ponerse en las manos de Dios, y así … es cuando vienen las invitaciones. … Cuando viene una invitación, ya yo me preparo espiritualmente. Ya me pongo a orar, me pongo a ayunar … Y a veces hago mis bosquejos así, pero ya en el púlpito, como que el Señor me lo hace a un lado y predico a través de la Biblia. ¿Por qué? Porque así es la voluntad de Dios, que te quiere usar a través del Espíritu Santo.
>
> [A preacher has to put himself in the hands of God, and so ... that's when the invitations come. …When an invitation comes, I prepare myself spiritually. I start praying, fasting ... And sometimes I make my sketches, but already in the pulpit, the Lord sets them aside for me, and I preach through the Bible. And why? Because that is God's will, that is how He wants to use you through the Holy Spirit.]

According to this statement, evangelism is seen as a spiritual undertaking that needs spiritual preparation. He presents evangelism as an endeavor that is not easy to undertake. He emphasizes that it is only possible if the person is invested with spiritual power. Therefore, an evangelist needs to be purified, to be free from sin, evil thoughts, and deeds. To be prepared, one must pray and fast. Besides, he points out that the particular situation of evangelizing is not something accomplished only by the intellect but instead directly through God's intervention. It is this intervention that allows the evangelist to see the situation as it is, which means according to its "spiritual basis."

Consequently, evangelism is seen as a difficult task. One should not merely be engaged in it but should be adequately prepared. Evangelism can only be effective if it is connected with the "divine gift" provided by the Holy Spirit. Based on Marcos González's accounts, divine endowment seems more important than training in communication. Besides, his work is described in spiritual terms, and therefore in need of being nurtured and nourished by spiritual means. Prayer and fasting are described as tools that equip the evangelist with spiritual armor and weapons for the spiritual battle.

He also argues that each Christian can experience the anointing:

> el Espíritu Santo es el que lo guía a uno a toda verdad y a toda justicia. Usted quiere hacer algo malo, teniendo el Espíritu Santo, el mismo Espíritu le va redargüir su corazón, su alma, su mente y le va a decir: "No lo haga" … Cuando la persona no tiene la unción del Espíritu Santo … la persona fracasa en su vida espiritual.
>
> [the Holy Spirit is the one who leads you to all truth and all righteousness. You want to do something bad, having the Holy Spirit, the Spirit Himself will reprove your heart, your soul, your mind, and will say to you: "Don't do it" ... When the person doesn't have the anointing of the Holy Spirit … the person fails in his spiritual life.]

He also describes a world that was ruled by demons and devils. He saw himself and the congregation where he preaches under attack by demons and devils and states that in these battles only the spiritual strength could help to win the battle. For this reason, he argues that his work consists of promoting the search for the anointing of the Holy Spirit in those who are present at his preaching.

All these accounts presented by Marcos González serve to show that his missionary message is framed within a paradigm of "spiritual warfare" that, as mentioned above, considers that life is lived under a constant threat from evil powers. According to it, manifest and unseen realities are connected, and unseen spirits cause problems in the manifest world. Problems such as illness, poverty, misfortune, infertility and many others are seen as the effects of the presence of Satan, demons, evil spirits, or witchcraft, which are still active in the world.

The other leader who referred to "spiritual warfare" was Francisco Quiacaín, the Pentecostal leader with a Mayan background, who arrived in Los Angeles in the 2000s. In his narrative, he made numerous accounts regarding his religious work in Los Angeles. For instance, he noted that the positive side of being in Los Angeles is that he is still "serving the Lord" in the different churches, supporting numerous ministries without claiming personal or economic gain. This comment is supported in his narration by some descriptions of his parallel religious involvement as a musician in numerous congregations. These congregations not only have a Latin American background but also a Korean one:

> en a South Beach, me congregué en una iglesia bautista por 4 años. Y de ahí estuve tocando, en la iglesia. Y el día domingo cantamos con los niños, hay un grupo de niños, cantando con ellos … fui a una iglesia en la calle Vermont, porque el hermano, también de Guatemala … no tenía músico y estaba levantando la obra y me cambié allí para apoyarlo … Y estoy colaborando con una iglesia coreana …
>
> [in South Beach, I congregated in a Baptist church for four years. And that's where I was playing, in the church. And on Sunday we sang with the children, there is a group of children, singing with them ... I went to a church on Vermont Street, because the brother, also from Guatemala ... he didn't have a musician and I moved there to support him ... And I am collaborating with a Korean church ...]

According to his narration, cooperation with leaders from other Pentecostal organizations is a very significant part of understanding his religious labor in Los Angeles. For him, his mission is based on supporting the ministry of the music in congregations with different cultures and backgrounds. Moreover, the importance of music is also reflected in Francisco Quiacaín's understanding of his missionary message. For him, music plays a vital role in connecting religious teachings with one's own life. For him, Pentecostal appropriate music and worship styles do not rely on hymns or creeds that were written hundreds of years ago, but instead, they can be devised by the believers themselves, who are inspired by God:

> Porque la mera verdad a través del servicio al Señor, Dios me ha dado unos cantos bíblicos, que los estamos cantando en la iglesia… en el servicio con los hermanos coreanos... cuando comienzan a leer el pastor los versículos… comienzo a buscar y encuentro versículos. Y me concentro y me salen cantos. Si, entonces, y tengo varios cantos, versículos bíblicos
>
> [Because the mere truth through the service to the Lord, God has given me some biblical songs, which we are singing in church ... in the service with

> the Korean brothers ... when they begin to read the pastor's verses ... I begin to look for them, and I find verses. And I concentrate, and I sing. Yeah, so, and I have several songs, Bible verses]

Although Francisco Quiacaín's way of composing religious music seems entirely different from the way in which the professionally orchestrated music that one can hear in large Pentecostal churches has been composed, his way seems effective in communicating a message coming from God. Whatever the style of the music, in his view the ultimate goal is to enable the worshipper to experience God directly.

Whereas evangelism is still a concern for him, in Francisco Quiacaín's narrative, the focal point rests in the spiritual action, which is personal and interior, aimed at improving the individual situation (prayer, discipline, and a change of lifestyle) as is prescribed in the "positive thinking" literature. Concerning the circumstances surrounding his life as an immigrant without any legal permit to reside and work in Los Angeles, Francisco Quiacaín refers to his study of the Bible and the anointing of the Holy Spirit as the key to experiencing happiness in life:

> Y eso es lo que me ha hecho fortalecer en la palabra del Señor. El Espíritu Santo me ha ayudado. Porque como ser humano, como de carne y hueso, hay momentos de angustia y aflicción, y momentos que el enemigo nos derriba … siempre Dios nos levanta y a seguir adelante y así vamos, vamos haciendo la vida, feliz cada día.
>
> [And that is what has strengthened me in the word of the Lord. The Holy Spirit has helped me. Because as a human being, as one of flesh and blood, there are moments of anguish and affliction, and moments that the enemy knocks us down ... God always raises us up and moves us forward and so we go, we go on making life, happy every day.]

With this account, the spiritual warfare paradigm is revealed as the articulating axis of his understanding of the Pentecostal message. For him, the Gospel and the anointing of the Holy Spirit help him to overcome the negative experiences of an unfavorable context:

> el tiempo que estuve allá, estuve solo ... Fuera una persona amargada, estresada, y así es muy duro para mí. Pero bendito sea Dios, que el Espíritu Santo me ha fortalecido y me ha hecho no quedarme solo. No sentirme solo.

> [the time I was there, I was alone ... I was a bitter, stressed person, and so it was very hard for me. But blessed be God, the Holy Spirit has strengthened me and allowed me not to be alone. I don't feel alone.]

In the Gospel and the anointing of the Holy Spirit, he finds crucial weapons to defeat the Devil. Therefore, he does not see himself as powerless and marginalized, even though he lives in the United States without a secure visa, but rather as a person who through his spiritual life gains access to a power that is stronger than any other social or political power, and that allows him to live happily.

Praxeological Square: Spiritual Warfare Paradigm

The narratives examined in the spiritual warfare paradigm have a similar pattern: they reflect a dual worldview. Straightforwardly, the world is divided into two parts: that of God and his believers and that of the Devil and his followers. As Pentecostal believers, the interviewees are on God's side and, as a consequence, they feel saved. In both the social and the personal sense, they take sides in the war that they say is being waged between these two parts of the world. Looking back at the evil world from whose sinfulness believers are fleeing away, they are comforted by having made the right decision. Once this fundamental choice has been made, the convert's life becomes both transparent and comprehensible. Also, as God's warriors, they have access to a spiritual power that is stronger than any social or political power: the power of the Holy Spirit. Following the accounts mentioned above, a praxeological square was developed.

In this paradigm, the grievances, uncertainty, or threats are related to *solitude/sadness, economic needs* and *alcohol problems*. These negative experiences are confronted with the specific promise of salvation, *the authority of God*. To be "under the authority of God," the person *requires the anointing of the Holy Spirit*, experiencing *companionship, health, wealth and happiness* in opposition to the impediments this group faces. These three steps combine to form the basic transformation, which models the generation of identity. The second transformation models the generation of strategy. From their positive experiences, the religious agents face articulated grievances, assigning reasons and causes to them, which are articulated through "negative interpretations": *the intervention of the Devil, the Enemy*. By recognizing the reasons for the grievances, the leaders can design the appropriate strategies to fight them: As religious leaders, they carry out personal actions to improve the individual's situation, consisting primarily of *spiritual work based on discipline* and *prayer.*

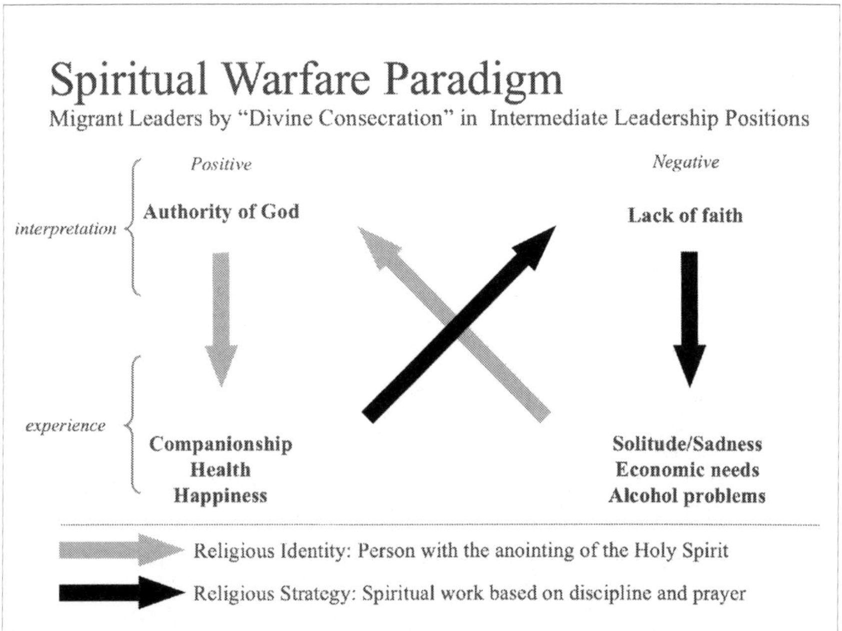

Hence, Guatemalan religious leaders in this group do not present themselves as powerless and marginalized even though they live in the United States without a secure visa or a secure job, but rather as people, who, through their spiritual lives, gain access to a superior power, allowing them to live a fulfilled life. In doing so, they attempt to bring order and security to their lives in Los Angeles.

The spiritual warfare morals seem very effective in the migratory context of Los Angeles for those who have been Pentecostal believers since their youth and are facing legal and/or economic disadvantages. From being in a marginal position, they become heroes of faith, having the gifts of the spirit. Thus, differences in social positions influence the preaching message of the religious leaders. Leaders who can be placed among the most marginalized and powerless groups in Los Angeles tend to perceive themselves as powerful in the spiritual world, expecting to make positive changes on the social and material level. Nevertheless, the strategy fostered by this paradigm—*spiritual work based on internal discipline* and *prayer*—seems not to be very attractive in the Latino migratory context of Los Angeles. This lack of interest in discipline was precisely pointed out for leaders "by divine consecration" as they referred to the existence of a "modern" Pentecostalism that allows any kind of behavior (see Chapter 6).

7.3 Pentecostal Praxis and the Habitus Oriented Towards Professionalization as a Religious Agent: Some Final Observations

After presenting these three Pentecostal paradigms, one can see that Guatemalan independent Pentecostal leaders in Los Angeles are firm in their conviction that it was God's guidance that brought them to the United States. Consequently, everything that happened and continues to happen to them must be part of God's plan. Having such an interpretation, the narrators show themselves as empowered: They are not marginal actors, but essential instruments of a divine plan manifested through a divine call. Therefore, those without much economic success and who have to face discrimination and inequality as in the case of Guatemalan migrants in Los Angeles become precious individuals: Their lives matter, they are special, chosen, the bearers of a divine commission direct from God himself. By stressing special election and achievement, they can experience self-worth, ultimate meaning, purpose, and a way to make sense of a harsh world. This new personal meaning is particularly significant for the development of a profession and integration into the labor market.

In megacities like Los Angeles, the deregulated flexible labor markets of the post-industrial, service-based economy prevail. Guatemalan immigrants, and Latinos in general living there, are not typically part of a manufacturing "proletariat" but workers in the service sector, frequently in the informal economy, within a high-tech, information-based global capitalism (see Chapter 4). In such a structural context, the ability to be punctual, disciplined, and obedient, so crucial in the Fordist system, is less relevant than the capacity to be self-motivating, to control the work process without direct supervision, to be reflective and self-monitoring, and to manage interpersonal encounters skillfully. These skills are as vital for janitors, waiters, and busboys in new restaurants, street salesman, gardeners, or domestic servants (the ubiquitous nanny-housekeeper working unsupervised in the home of her employers) as they are for the software engineer, the media professional, or the manager. This new labor market not only calls for deference and hierarchy but also for independence, initiative, high-octane energy, a willingness to work following the compass of the twenty-four-hour economy and above all, a refusal to accept failure.

Latino Pentecostalism supplies just these personal qualities. The self-confidence that comes from the certainty that God is on your side is a powerful resource to face such a structural context. The framework of moral controls set by the strict rules of the believing congregation and the need to render individual accounts to God enable the believer to internalize self-control and make the best of what God provides them. The majority of Guatemala Pentecostal leaders are in economic disadvantageous positions, nevertheless, as the analyzed interviews showed, their virtues enable them to make the best of what little they have. Yet even in the most unpromising economic circumstances, there are striking instances of economic initiative conceived in the spirit of doing the Lord's work. This includes the street traders, the self-employed, and all the myriad creators of their own work in the informal economy who combine work and evangelism and seize every entrepreneurial chance that comes their way.

Hence, Guatemalan and Latino independent Pentecostal churches offer leadership opportunities to all believers. Pentecostal theology emphasizes the priesthood of all believers and the gifts of the Holy Spirit, which allow people with limited educational opportunities, but with natural leadership abilities, to succeed. In addition, organizational forms like cell systems require little financial resources in order to start and keep a church. In independent churches, those excluded from the material means of production are transformed into subjects with free access to the religious means of production. The people assured of an urgent, divine call are willing to serve God by taking a leadership position in the church or to start a new church with very few resources, resting on "God-given power" to do so against all the odds (material, social, or educational).

The preaching, teaching, worship, prayer and Bible study continually reinforce their belief that God has a plan for them, which often includes becoming a religious leader. In the case of expatriate leaders by "professional consecration," the opportunity to develop a career as a religious leader came at a young age when they attained a leadership position. They took advantage of it by maintaining an active commitment to the "expansion of Pentecostalism" beyond their country of origin. Moreover, they also used all the resources around them such as participation in training seminars up to university studies. Therefore, it is not surprising that their understanding of "God" and the message they convey as leaders is that of God as a father willing to restore his believers, who provides success in material and spiritual ways.

Migrant leaders by "divine consecration" who see themselves as expatriates followed another path. Although they were able to reach a leadership position at an early age, political, economic, and social problems derived from the war in Guatemala caused their migration to Los Angeles and their distancing from active Pentecostal praxis. After a few years, the religious dispositions fostered by Pentecostal praxis allowed them to face the disadvantages of the social context of Los Angeles and they became religious leaders. Hence, they see "God" as an answer to existential and physical concerns and the message they communicate as leaders is that of *God as a loving father*, who provides material and spiritual good.

Finally, in the case of migrant leaders by "divine consecration" who are in intermediate leadership positions, economic and social issues linked to ethnicity and family background did not offer the opportunity to reach a successful leadership position at an early age. Since they come from indigenous families with a rural origin, economic and social opportunities have been limited, and they have had to face a context marked by the struggle for survival. Migration to the United States was presented as an opportunity to overcome that context. The religious beliefs of Pentecostalism have served them to prosper economically, thanks to their hard work. The position as leader is understood as a way to serve "God," who has given them so much.

It should not be inferred from the preceding considerations that the beliefs and practices of Guatemalan independent Pentecostal leaders studied represent a response to the social and economic conditions prevailing in Los Angeles. They are not primarily or intentionally an answer to economic or social problems. Following Bourdieu's praxeological approach, the habitual dispositions or schemes of thought and action of an agent are prone to adapt to the dominant social conditions, generating subjective and objective dispositions and developing social strategies. Hence, in response to the requirements of the social space, the religious habitus tends to adapt itself, conceiving social compulsions as a precondition for the confirmation and verification of faith in God. The grace of God and the strength that He gives influences the believer to be the successful maker of his fortune. In this sense, the religious dispositions not only adapt to the challenges, but they adapt in a creative way, generating particularly religious identities and thus specifically religious strategies to build up self-confidence to make a living in the foreign megacity.

Also, religious convictions and practices maintain their dynamics, differentiating them from the ones of the economic field. It is precisely this relatively autonomous relationship between conditions of economic production and religious convictions that makes Pentecostalism's offers useful and attractive in the face of the compulsions of the labor market. As Schäfer, Tovar Simoncic, and Reu (2013, 19) argue, the spiritual dispositions generated by religious movements in the early twenty-first century offer more than just general strategies. They offer something that has the power to create success, precisely because it is not primarily directed to economic success but to the work of God, the church (worship/mass, home cell, ministry, evangelization, prayer), a life of morality without vices, Christian education, the Christian family, etc. For instance, the fostering of the family as a viable moral, cultural, and economic household through the reformation of the male represents a powerful mechanism that contrasts sharply with the traditional license afforded to men. Invoking a sense of a unique worth and spiritually driven empowerment, men are individualized in a cultural way that promotes a life without alcohol, deals in bars, or the weekend male spree. From this can follow all the other forms of betterment—in health (many spiritual/physical healings arise on account of the excesses of a licentious life), in work, in giving priority to feeding, clothing, disciplining, and educating the children and oneself, in discovering a potential for leadership and initiative within the life of the church. It is in such a way, Pentecostal beliefs infuse particular effectiveness to the individual strategies of labor integration in a "habitual way," that is, without conscious intention and explicit calculation.

This effectiveness without resorting to explicit calculation takes place because religious convictions are independent enough so that the religious agent adopts them. At the same time, these religious dispositions have so much objective similarity with the conditions of production that socioreligious strategies (the good, self-employed Christian) can become effective without specific calculation (Schäfer, Tovar Simoncic, and Reu 2013, 19).

7.4. Conclusion

This chapter analyzed what are, concretely, the ideas of divine beings or a "transcendent entity" that Guatemalan independent Pentecostal leaders working in Los Angeles have. This transcendent entity is God and, in some other cases, the Holy Spirit.

The reference to God which had the most entries was God's call. In Pentecostal circles, being a missionary or a religious leader is not seen as an ordinary profession, but rather a particular vocation which usually requires a unique, personalized calling. Therefore, all the Guatemalan independent Pentecostal leaders interviewed made references to a divine call. Nevertheless, these accounts turned out to be very idiosyncratic and not at all easy to be ordered into groups.

Two steps were carried out in order to make sense of these accounts. First, the literature on the "divine call" was analyzed with the aim of finding the main features of "a divine call." Second, the content of the call of the leaders in each group was analyzed— expatriate leaders by "professional consecration"; migrant leaders by "divine consecration" who see themselves as "expatriates"; and migrant leaders by "divine consecration" in intermediate leadership positions. Finally, the interview addressed how and when the interviewees claimed to have received a call and if the call was connected to their journey to Los Angeles.

The results of the analysis of the narratives regarding a divine call showed that the call was not always linked to the trip to Los Angeles but to the beginning of service in a ministry. Through missionary work, Guatemalan Pentecostal leaders can see themselves as having a successful life. By recounting a call testimony, the leaders establish and strengthen their particular position. By becoming religious specialists, they have tapped a new mechanism of empowerment since they see themselves as agents following a "divine plan," a plan that is accomplished for them even if they do not understand it immediately.

Once the symbolic operator "God's call" was analyzed, the other symbolic operators related to God were considered. After a close analysis of accounts regarding transcendent entities, it was found that there is not only one kind of Pentecostalism among Guatemalan religious leaders in Los Angeles, but at least three paradigms or religious habitus formations, which are distinguished according to practices. Each of these paradigms reflect the position in the religious field and in the social space of the interviewees.

The first paradigm "God as restorer" was found among expatriate leaders by "professional consecration," who understand that God is a good father who cares for the welfare of his children and is always willing to restore them if they fall into sin. As successful leaders working in Los Angeles, they talk about "God" as a provider of success in material and spiritual issues.

Migrant leaders by "divine consecration" who are pastors of their congregations and see themselves as "expatriates" refer to the importance of "God's love." As migrants who have suffered economic and health problems and have faced difficulties for the establishment of their small churches, they convey a message based on God's desire for his people to prosper and be in good health, arguing that with God all is possible.

The third paradigm is "spiritual warfare," which emerged from the biographical narratives of migrant leaders by "divine consecration" in intermediate leadership positions. As migrants who see migration as an opportunity to overcome a context marked by economic and social inequalities, struggling for survival, they understand that God is at war with his enemy, the devil, and they are God's warriors. This religious belief has allowed them to prosper economically thanks to their hard work.

Within the context of deepening economic globalization, "the rise of technocratic policy-making, the decline of trade unions, the growing disillusionment with political parties and elections, and the dismantling of the welfare state" (Peterson, Vásquez, and Williams 2001, 12) have led to a growing gap between government and citizens in both Latin America and the United States. Under these conditions of an extremely "de-regularized" labor market and individualized economic competition caused by the neoliberal policies in Los Angeles, inequality is perceived as a problem of the individual.

The "flexibilization" of labor relations and the extended absence of collective representation for migrant employees generate the phenomenon of precarious work. Its objective effects are disastrous for Guatemalan and Latino immigrants. A precarious working position threatens instability, possible or probable failure, and social decline, regardless of the original social position of the individual and their family.

Pentecostal beliefs presented by Guatemalan independent Pentecostal leaders offer a striking way to see this situation. God and the Holy Spirit accept the person unconditionally, assure him of heaven and provides him with precepts to lead a life with competence and thus achieve success. The strategic goal of dispositions is no longer so much heaven, but earthly blessings in the form of economic prosperity and a stable life as the result of successful socioeconomic integration including, as a critical experiential factor, the stability of the family nucleus. Prosperity is not understood as the attainment of disproportionate fortunes, but as a code for economic integration at the level of the family promoted by the mass media.

If the believer fails with the program for their life, the person is fired, loses the house, etc., the blame remains on them because they did not have sufficient faith in God or did not have the anointing of the Holy Spirit to fight against the attacks of the enemy. In this sense, the three Pentecostal habitus formations found among Guatemalan independent Pentecostal leaders are clear examples regarding the "work of imagination," to quote Appadurai (1996), among Guatemalan independent Pentecostal leaders working in Los Angeles. These particular forms of praxis delineated above allow immigrants to imagine their displacements to other counties and their stay there. Through these three Pentecostal habitus formations, people challenged by the migration processes can regenerate and re-center their selves, producing new habitus, introducing new forms of individual and collective identity, developing new strategies to have success in life. Although these processes are "imagined," they are not inconsequential; they have tangible effects on the self, the body, and the social space. Being a Pentecostal missionary in Los Angeles at the beginning of the twenty-first century serves to reproduce the patterns of domination that have been central in the marginalization of Latina/os in the Americas. Pentecostal messages communicated by the interviewees promise to true believers that they can harness God's power without the mediation of any hierarchy or external authority as long as they have faith or the anointing of the Holy Spirit. Nevertheless, these messages avoid mentioning material and societal explanations and solutions for the marginalized status of Latina/os in favor of spiritual explanations such as individual faith to release God's blessings, or in the exorcism of many evils. In this respect, these messages are not conducive to taking seriously the social and political causes of oppression, poverty, illness, and other, very real types of suffering.

8. Conclusions

This study aimed to understand the religious praxis of Pentecostal missionaries who came from the South to evangelize the North, following the case of Guatemalan independent Pentecostal leaders in Los Angeles. The research focused on the study of their Pentecostal beliefs and practices and on the interaction between their religious praxis and the context of social conflict, change, and inequality that Guatemalans have to face in Los Angeles.

In general, Pentecostal missionary flows coming from the South to the North—in this case from Guatemala to the United States—have been studied within the framework of the relationship between religious organizations and migration. In this literature, as it was highlighted in Chapter 2, it is possible to distinguish between two approaches: One is the "incorporation approach" and the other is the "religion on the move approach."

Under the "incorporation approach," Pentecostal leaders from the South are understood as "migrants" and their religious organizations are presented as sources of spiritual, social, and economic support in settlement of immigrant groups (León 1998; Vasquez 1999; Lorentzen and Mira 2005; Maduro 2007).

In contrast, the "religion on the move approach" argues that in the contemporary world, religious praxis is more than just a vehicle for incorporation and identity reaffirmation. As the sociologist Peggy Levitt (2001; 2007; and 2013) has pointed out, religion also enables people to stay intimately connected to their homeland and to be members of a shared culture, tradition, and faith. In this approach, Pentecostal leaders are conceptualized as "expatriates," and these studies (Menjivar 1999; Vasquez and Marquardt 2003; Martínez 2013; Danielson 2015) argue that migration and the development of transnational relations have facilitated the spread and cross-fertilizations of Pentecostal missionary efforts across political boundaries through the emergence of transnational Latino Pentecostal organizations.

While both approaches offer interesting points for contextualizing the religious experience of moving individuals within religious organizations, neither of them focuses on the specific contents of that religious praxis. Authors in both approaches have mainly paid attention external factors rather than on Pentecostalism itself. They are mainly interested in what religious praxis does, not in what religious praxis is. In addition, they have been focused on organizations and have primarily left aside the study of individual participants, for instance, religious leaders. While immigration and Pentecostal organizations are at the heart of the studies on Latino Pentecostalism in the United States, none of these studies have analyzed the agency of Pentecostal leaders, how they see themselves and the world, and the way they understand their missionary work.

These are, therefore, the gaps that this dissertation has addressed: the analysis of the religious praxis itself in transnational spaces and the role as religious leaders that individual agents play in the spreading of Pentecostalism from South to North America. The research has followed a praxeological approach, the Habitus Analysis (Schäfer 2005; 2009; 2015), which is based on several conceptualizations developed by P. Bourdieu. This approach allowed, on the one hand, the incorporation of the influence of external factors into the analysis and, on the other hand, the integration of the specific contents of Pentecostal beliefs and practices, by analyzing the relation among the social positions of Guatemalan Pentecostal agents, their religious identities, and their strategies.

The dissertation has examined the biographical narratives of seven Guatemalan independent Pentecostal leaders, placing them within their social space, and showing the different practical logics in which they live. To systematically analyze the biographical narratives, the research relied on the *praxeological square* methodology, which was also developed by Heinrich Schäfer (2005; 2009; 2015) within the Habitus Analysis approach.

8.1. Being a Pentecostal Missionary

Guatemalans and Guatemalan independent Pentecostal leaders have been arriving in Los Angeles since 1970. In Chapter 4, the complexity of the Guatemalan migratory experiences was explored, presenting the changing structural conditions both in the context of origin and in the context of arrival. Since then, Guatemalans have migrated to Los Angeles, leaving a country hit by successive economic, political, and military crises. They have crossed the borders of Mexico and the United States, facing hardships and dangers, and ending in often difficult and sometimes unwelcoming environments in Los Angeles, in which they encountered the pressures of finding a job, working long hours, and coping with the harmful effects of antimigratory policies. These are the structural conditions of the transnational space articulated between Guatemala and Los Angeles.

At the same time, Chapter 4 was concerned with Guatemalan Pentecostal leaders' trajectories, delineating the social position of the agents in the social space articulated between Guatemala and Los Angeles. It has shown that the social and ethic background of each leader and opportunities for a legalized stay in Los Angeles led to the achievement of more significant economic, social, and educational resources after many years in Los Angeles, generating opportunities to launch tenacious and perdurable religious initiatives.

These religious initiatives are part of the most striking development in religious terms in Los Angeles, which is the steady growth of Latino Protestantism in Los Angeles, particularly Latino Pentecostalism. To trace the impact of Latino Pentecostalism in Los Angeles, this dissertation also reconstructed Los Angeles's religious field in 2014 according to the dimensions of "achievement of eminence" and "authenticity." These dimensions were pointed out by Pierre Bourdieu regarding the field of cultural production and were adjusted by Schäfer, Seibert, Tovar Simoncic, and Köhrsen (2016a, 190) for the study of the religious field. The first dimension, achievement of eminence, refers to the relation between the performers and the audience of a religious organization and the level of religious complexity. The second, authenticity, refers to the credibility of a religious organization, to its presence, autonomy, and resilience.

According to these dimensions, even though the Catholic Church still has the most substantial impact on the religious field, combining organizational complexity and credibility, there are essential competitors in the religious field. The U.S. Pentecostal denominations with Latino churches in Los Angeles have quite a high score for credibility, competing with the Catholic Church. They compete not so much through their religious organizational power as through compromise and religious credibility.

Finally, the small, independent Latino Pentecostals, like the Guatemalan leaders analyzed in this dissertation, occupy a weak position in the field concerning their financial capital and their organizational complexity. However, they generate significant changes in the religious field since they offer a very personal and practical experience of God in spaces where Latinos can express their faith in their way and lead their congregation—in short, they enjoy a good deal of credibility among Latin migrants.

This reconstruction of Los Angeles's religious field also allowed a distinction between Latino Pentecostal leaders who are in marginal positions: those who are in a definitely marginal position and those who are positioned a bit higher. Those in the more marginal position understand their activities as a result of "divine consecration." They are pastors and leaders that work in the frame of religious organizations with 50 to 100 devotees, carry out transnational religious work through their personal network, and do not have social involvement beyond the boundaries of their near neighborhood. Those agents who are in the higher position are leaders who came with a missionary project to the United States and deem their activities as a result of "professional consecration." This group includes full-time pastors in religious organizations with more than 500 devotees. They tend to have social and even political involvement as well as carry out transnational religious work through the official network of their organizations; they also have satellite congregations in other countries.

After establishing this distinction between leaders by "divine consecration" and leaders by "professional consecration," the biographical narratives of seven Guatemalan independent Pentecostal leaders were analyzed using Habitus Analysis. The question that emerges is: How do independent Guatemalan Pentecostal leaders working in Los Angeles present themselves?

Considering the dominant North Atlantic discourse, which is also reflected in the approaches that have been dealing with the relation between migration and the expansion of Pentecostalism delineated previously, it was pointed out that two terms are used to denominate people involved in movement and settlement. One is "migrant/ immigrant"; the other is "expatriate." As I have explained in this dissertation following the ideas of Währisch-Oblau (2012, 137), the term migrant/immigrant is applied to people who move out because of need. They are refugees, asylum seekers, or economic migrants fleeing war, poverty, and deprivation. In this account, migrants come from the South to the North; they are usually dark-skinned, tend to work in low-skilled jobs, have a low financial status, and as highlighted by the authors of the above-mentioned "incorporation approach" they are expected to adapt and integrate.

In turn, the term "expatriate" (Währisch-Oblau 2012, 137) alludes to the displacement from one country to another as an act of personal agency. As the "religion on the move approach" remarks, expatriates, similar to objects, technology, and ideas, travel at different rates and rhythms, across various levels and scopes of the social fields in which they are embedded. Expatriates move to a foreign country (commonly from the North to other parts of the world) with a sense of purpose, to do a specific job or to fulfill an ideal. They move freely and can go back home (or to yet another country) if they chose to do so.

Based on the results presented in Chapter 6, the narratives provided by Guatemalan Pentecostal independent leaders showed that it is not easy to place these agents concerning only one term, being a "migrant" or an "expatriate." These two terms should not be understood as opposite poles but as clarifying elements to capture the rich experience and interpretation presented by people involved in spatial movements. In the case of "leaders by divine consecration," some of the negative experiences enumerated seem to fit better into the "migrant" type. For instance, most of the "leaders by divine consecration" did not get a visa to come to the United States and had to go through Mexico under dangerous conditions.

Situations such as paying the *coyotes*, the fear of being caught by migration authorities, encounters with migration agents and the severe consequences appeared in their narrations. They also recalled negative experiences during their first years living in Los Angeles including difficulties due to working conditions, mobility problems, and language barriers. Finally, two of them mentioned economic reasons to settle in Los Angeles since both have problems getting a well-paid job in Guatemala.

Nevertheless, a close consideration of narratives provided by "Guatemalan Pentecostal leaders by divine consecration" shows that they do not follow the structure of migrant/immigrant type. Most of the narratives analyzed are not about a search for a better life or a struggle for integration. Most quotations coded as positive experiences referred to their missionary work, mainly to preaching in missionary campaigns, presenting themselves as active religious agents who go from one place to another. Similarly, as the positive interpretations showed, their narratives carry a sense of "God's calling" to the country to which they have moved. That means that they see themselves as "missionaries," something that seems much more related to the expatriate type.

Looking at these biographical narratives, particularly at what leaders by "divine consecration" say about their evangelistic calling, it is evident that these Pentecostal leaders see themselves as living in the United States due to a divine calling and guidance and not because the U.S. authorities have allowed them to stay. Making these remarks, interviewees implicitly negate the right of the U.S. government to decide who can come to the United States and who cannot, or even the right of the U.S. population to allow immigration or not. For them, their right to stay is a divine one that overrides any human policy or interest. They see the U.S. as theirs, a place that God has given to them. The same God who gave that land to the missionaries coming from Europe now gives the same land to the missionaries coming from Latin America. This interpretation of their missionary experience is easily on a collision course with the strong anti-migration sentiment in the United States.

References to missionary work allow leaders by "divine consecration" to give meaning to their displacement to Los Angeles. It also serves to articulate a narrative in which their stay there finds a religious reason, arguing that they have a divine order to spread the Gospel and a congregation to serve. Invoking such an understanding of their situation in Los Angeles, they transform the meaning of space. Missionary work thus emerges in the biographies as a symbolic operator for space where the experiences of crossing borders are creatively resignified by appealing to religious metaphors based on biblical texts. By invoking evangelism and missionary work, Guatemalan Pentecostal leaders by "divine consecration" can establish and strengthen a particular position, tapping a mechanism of empowerment. Their missionary work is proof of their infinite personal value, not in the eye of the law, but in the eye of the author of all law, the Lord.

Regarding Guatemalan Pentecostal leaders "by professional consecration," it is clearer that they see themselves as "expatriates." As the thematic areas of their positive experiences such as "Facilities to enter or reside in the United States" and "Missionary work" have shown, facts such as having a visa to travel to the United States and their continued work in established religious organizations there reflect that their move to the United States was for professional reasons as it usually is for expatriates.

In their case, the abundant references to missionary work not only allow a transformation in the meaning of the space, as noted in relation to Guatemalan Pentecostal leaders by "divine consecration," but also demonstrate that missionary work can be combined with the hope for political change and thus transform into political action (e.g., through civic participation in political parties). Leaders "by professional consecration" refer to their involvement in the defense of the right of migrants, articulated through protest in front of official buildings in Los Angeles and their support in the creation of other organizations to gather Latino American pastors and leaders.

The analysis of the biographical narratives shows how through a concrete religious practice, Pentecostalism, migrants with a Guatemalan background in Los Angeles manage to positively resignify their experience of living and working there. Presenting themselves as Pentecostal missionaries committed to the spread of the gospel worldwide, Guatemalan Pentecostal leaders give a religious meaning to their displacement and settlement in Los Angeles. Through this highly creative process of resignification, Guatemalan independent Pentecostal leaders manage to develop a high degree of personal worth and confidence, which translates into a formidable way to confront the problems of living in a context marked structurally by inequality in both material resources and social opportunities along with growing racism.

In addition, from Guatemalan independent Pentecostal leaders' religious beliefs emerge certain habitual dispositions, according to which a habitus is articulated. With the formation of this habitus, there is a change in the identity of believers. Their self-conception, which is articulated around their faith, allows them to develop a way of seeing the world oriented towards professionalization in religious life, even before they become professionals.

Following the reconstruction of the religious field for Los Angeles, a distinction has been made between leaders by divine consecration and leaders by professional consecration. This distinction refers to an objective position in a given field and social space. The consideration of the elements linked to the terms "migrant" and "expatriate" in the formation of the practical sense of the interviewees allows for a better understanding of how the interviewees perceive themselves and where they situate themselves according to their habitual dispositions, particularly those with a religious content or idea; the idea of divine beings or a "transcendent entity."

Thus, the interviewees can be clustered in a new way:

- Preachers and singers who function as migrant leaders by divine consecration, illustrating the first step in a professional career.
- Pastors of their own congregations who can also be categorized as migrant leaders by divine consecration and see themselves as "expatriates." These leaders have taken further steps in their professional careers as religious leaders because they are founders and head pastors of their own churches, having certain social impact in their neighborhoods.
- Pastors and missionaries who perform as expatriate leaders by professional consecration, move freely to a foreign country, and are

well-educated people who work full time in the frame of religious organizations with more than 500 devotees.

This differentiation makes sense in the reconstruction of religious habitus formations in which the statements connected to the idea of divine beings or a "transcendent entity" are analyzed in depth.

8.2. Diversity in Pentecostal Praxis

The results of the Habitus Analysis also showed that the religious praxis of Guatemalan Pentecostal independent leaders exhibits diversity. The distinction between migrant leaders by "divine consecration" in intermediate leadership positions; migrant leaders by "divine consecration" who see themselves as "expatriates;" and expatriate leaders by "professional consecration" illustrates how an understanding of God that at first glance seems quite similar actually varies considerably when the social position of the interviewees is considered. The close analysis of accounts regarding transcendent entities presented in Chapter 7 shows that according to beliefs and practices, there is not only one kind of Pentecostalism among Guatemalan religious leaders in Los Angeles, but at least three.

Throughout this study, I have highlighted the importance of socioeconomic differences among Guatemalan Pentecostal independent leaders. The two expatriate leaders "by professional consecration," who came with a missionary project to the United States and were the founders and main pastors of churches with more than 500 members and branches in several countries, understood that God is a "restorer" since He is a good father who cares for the welfare of his children and is always willing to restore them if they fall into sin. For them, as successful leaders working in Los Angeles, they talk about "God" as a provider of success in material and spiritual issues as well as a ministry based on counseling is the best strategy to increase the faith and overcome any difficulties.

In the cases of migrant leaders by "divine consecration," three leaders, who were migrants presenting themselves as expatriates, were able to secure higher-paying jobs in the service sector, while the other two ended up in low-paying jobs in the same sector. In all cases, the socioeconomic background before arriving in the United States played a significant role. Leaders who are pastors of their own congregations and see themselves as "expatriates" with a middle-class background and high school or university studies could achieve higher social positions in Los Angeles. Their narratives reflect a religious paradigm that explains migration, the suffering derived from low-prestige jobs, and lifestyles that they were forced to accept as immigrants, and justifies the favorable social position that they obtained after living many years in the receiving country. It alludes to a loving God who gives health, wealth, and success to their faithful and committed believers. Invoking this paradigm, these leaders present themselves as faithful leaders having a personal relationship with God and turn their negative experiences of suffering into a personal faith commitment with a mission in response to God's call. For them, the strategy to overcome difficulties is through faith and prayer.

Narratives of the Guatemalan leaders coming from rural and lower social classes who are preachers and singers, in contrast, refer to the spiritual warfare paradigm in which they are spiritual warriors fighting against the Devil. In comparison to their situation in Guatemala, these leaders have obtained more economic and social resources in Los Angeles. Even though they live in the United States without a secure visa or a stable job, this group of Guatemalan religious leaders do not see themselves as powerless and marginalized, rather as persons, who, through their spiritual lives, gain access to a power that is stronger than any other power, allowing them to live a life in fullness. For them, spiritual work concentrated in discipline and prayer is the best strategy to defeat the Devil and overcome their problems.

Although the three theodicies are different, they show how Pentecostal praxis regenerates and recenters identities challenged by the migration processes, producing new "habitus" and introducing new forms of individual and collective identity and action. Nevertheless, these new forms of identity and action need to be related to the structural conditions in Los Angeles.

8.3. Bringing Together Guatemalan Pentecostal Independent Leaders' Identities and the Structural Conditions in Los Angeles

Finally, on the basis of these discoveries, the dissertation could delineate numerous reasons for the growing expansion of Pentecostalism among the Latino population in Los Angeles, which serves as an example to explain its expansion in the United States. To arrive at these reasons, in Chapter 7 the dissertation connected the structural conditions of Los Angeles, which derive from the tendencies of globalization and liberation of economic relations with the religious dispositions or ways of seeing reality generated by Pentecostalism. Thus, the chapter was able to show that there is a surprising homology.

The economic structural conditions of Los Angeles since the end of the 1970s can be summarized in a few trends: Los Angeles County is nowadays the third largest metropolitan economy in the world, with very good established technological industries. In spite of this, it also has the highest poverty rate in California and the United States, primarily concentrated among the Latino and African American population.

This economic inequality is the product of the dramatic economic changes due to global deindustrialization and reindustrialization consecutively. These changes were complemented with a restructuration of the labor market in which the growth in the number of firms in the electronics and aerospace industries linked to new technological developments was connected with a substantive increase in the low-paid jobs in the service sector. Moreover, rising concern over what many perceived to be an uncontrolled wave of immigration, particularly of undocumented migrants, has emerged since the 1990s. This trend culminated in the enactment of several laws that called for the denial of services, including education and healthcare to undocumented immigrants and their children, and increased the resources for immigration enforcement measures and significantly curtailed immigrant rights.

Under the conditions of an extremely "deregularized" labor market, individualized economic competition and anti-migratory discourses caused by the neoliberal policies in Los Angeles, inequality is perceived as a problem that exclusively pertains to the individual. Within the framework of these processes, "promises of salvation" offered by religious specialists are largely translated into promises of success, where the individual and the family are the base. The idea of family represents the nucleus formed by a heterosexual couple with children within a union blessed by God and the male progenitor as economic pillar of that nucleus.

The three Pentecostal paradigms referred to by Guatemalan independent Pentecostal leaders showed that they are firm in their conviction that everything happens because it is part of God's plan. Having such an interpretation, the Guatemalan leaders present themselves as empowered: They are not marginal actors but essential instruments of a divine plan manifested through a divine call. Therefore, those without much economic success and who have to face discrimination and inequality, as is the case for Guatemalan migrants in Los Angeles, become distinguished individuals: their lives matter, they are special, chosen, the bearers of a divine commission direct from God himself. These new personal meaning is particularly significant for the development of a profession and integration into the labor market.

In Los Angeles, the deregulated, flexible labor markets of the post-industrial, service-based economy prevail. Guatemalan immigrants, and Latinos in general living there, are workers in the service sector, frequently in the informal economy, within a high-tech, information-based global capitalism. This new labor market calls for independence, initiative, energy, a willingness to work following the compass of the twenty-four-hour economy. In this context, not only software engineers, the media professionals, or the managers need the ability to be self-motivating, to control the work process without direct supervision, to be reflective and self-monitoring, and to manage interpersonal encounters skillfully play a crucial role. These skills are also very important for janitors, waiters and busboys in restaurants, street salesman, gardeners or domestic servants.

Through the Guatemalan Pentecostal praxis analyzed in this study, believers acquire precisely habitual dispositions that reinforce these personal qualities. The self-confidence which comes from the certainty that God is on your side is a powerful resource to face such a structural context. The framework of moral controls set by the need to render individual accounts to God enable the believer to internalize self-control and make the best of what God provides them. The majority of Guatemala Pentecostal leaders are in economically disadvantageous positions, nevertheless, as their analyzed interviews showed, Pentecostal habitual dispositions fostered by their faith enable them to make the best of what little they have. Yet even in the most unpromising economic circumstances, there are striking instances of economic and religious initiatives conceived in the spirit of doing the Lord's work. This includes the street traders, self-employed and all the myriad creators of their own work in the informal economy who combine work and evangelism and seize every chance that comes their way.

Following Bourdieu's praxeological approach, it seems that the believer's habitual dispositions or schemes of thought and action are prone to adapt to Los Angeles' social conditions, generating subjective and objective convictions that allow religious agents to develop religious and social strategies consistent with those convictions. Hence, in response to the requirements of the social space, the religious habitus tends to adapt itself, conceiving social compulsions as a precondition for the confirmation and verification of the faith in God. Thanks to God's grace and the strength that He provides, the believer can succeed.

Under these conditions, religious convictions and practices maintain their own dynamics, differentiating them from those of the economic field. It is precisely this relatively autonomous relationship between economic conditions and religious convictions that makes Pentecostalism's offers of spiritual management useful and attractive in the face of the compulsions of the labor market and consumer capitalism. As Schäfer, Tovar Simoncic, and Reu (2013, 19) argue, the dispositions generated by Pentecostalism in the early twenty-first century offer more than just rational economic strategies. They offer something that has the power to produce success precisely because it does not refer directly to economic success but to work concerning God, the church, and a moral life without vices.

The efficacy of religious convictions without resorting to explicit calculation takes place because they are independent enough that the religious agent adopts them regardless of his or her socioeconomic position. At the same time, they have so much objective similarity with the conditions of production that socio-religious strategies can become effective even without this explicit intention (Schäfer et al. 2013, 19).

And this is much more evident in the case of Latino independent Pentecostal church founders and leaders. Pentecostal theology emphasizes the priesthood of all believers, allowing people with limited educational opportunities, but with natural leadership abilities, to be successful. In churches with simple organizational forms, those excluded from the material means of production are transformed into subjects with free access to the religious means of production since, once baptized, they have access to the power of God and the Holy Spirit and can act from and with that authority.

Following this logic, God and the Holy Spirit accept the individual unconditionally, assuring them of heaven and providing them with precepts to lead a life oriented to the achievement of health, prosperity, and success. If the believer fails to fulfill their life program, if he/she is ill, fired, loses the house, or experiences any other kind of failure, the blame is on them because of their lack of faith in God, or not having the anointing of the Holy Spirit to fight against the attacks of the enemy.

In any case, objective reasons such as business policies, social exclusion, precarious working conditions, anti-migratory policies and such are presented as causes for failure. The blame for not achieving success is on the individual and his insufficient religious involvement. In consequence, what I have consistently shown in this dissertation is that being a Pentecostal missionary from the South in North America is a paradoxical endeavor.

At one level, it provides resources that help make sense to a life in movement, retaining at the same time a strong sense of agency: They are not victims, but people whom God called to achieve his aim of worldwide evangelism. Being a missionary provides morally sanctioned territories, mitigating the most damaging effects of multiple transnational marginalities.

At another level, however, being a Pentecostal missionary in Los Angeles in neoliberal times serves to reproduce the patterns of domination over the self and the body that have been central to the marginalization of Latinos in the Americas. Pentecostal messages communicated by the interviewees promise to their flock that they can harness God's power without the mediation of any hierarchy or external authority as long as they have faith or the anointing of the Holy Spirit. Nevertheless, these messages avoid merely material and societal explanations and solutions for the marginalized status of Latinos in favor of spiritual explanations such as the individual's sowing of seeds of faith to release God's blessings or the exorcism of many evils. In this respect, these messages are not conducive to taking seriously the social and political causes of oppression, poverty, illness, or any other types of suffering.

8.4. Contribution to the Sociological Study of the Relationship Between Religious Life and Migration

I would not like to finish this study without reference to its contribution to the sociological study of the relationship between religious life and migration.

Whereas for much of the 20th century, the development of the social sciences, in particular the sociology of religion, was marked by the claim that religious manifestations are immersed in a progressive and irreversible decline due to the impact of modernity, in recent decades an opposite development has taken place: Far from corroborating the continuous loss of plausibility of religious belief systems, since the end of the twentieth century, new expressions of religiosity have emerged with enormous vitality in diverse aspects of individual and collective life.

In fact, events such as the terrorist attacks of September 11, 2001 and the constant references by both the politicians and the mass media to religious systems as critical variables for the explanation of such attacks, or the increasing religious heterogeneity of global cities, which fuels controversies about the legitimacy of ritual practices in both the public and private spheres, have made religious beliefs and practices once again the focus of the social, political and cultural debates at the dawn of the twenty-first century.

In this context, the markedly heterogeneous expressions of religiosity are now examined by sociologists using new lenses. How are religious systems produced and reproduced under the impact of globalization processes? What place do expressions of faith occupy among increasingly mobile populations? At the heart of these reflections, migrant believers appear as a paradigmatic case for the analysis of new expressions of contemporary religiosity.

Indeed, the individual who moves with his beliefs and reproduces, with greater or lesser impact, a specific religious system, constitutes a significant analytical challenge since it requires the construction of new conceptual tools to think about individual and collective identities, strategies, discourses, and practices.

But it is also an exceptional opportunity for reflection as the analysis of migrant believers' daily activities allows seeing the implementation of different strategies for the production and reproduction of religious beliefs and practices. Migrants and their religious beliefs and practices enable social scientists to observe the new forms that the relationship between individual and religious life acquires in a context of marked mobility. The fascinating creativity in the ways in which those who move live their religious beliefs and practices is a clear expression of new ways to deal with difficult contexts.

Consequently, aware of the relevance of the expressions of religiosity within migratory contexts for understanding the new forms that religiosity acquires in contemporary societies, this dissertation aimed to analyze the particular religious beliefs and practices emerging from the structural factors that condition the available religious options, examining the case of Guatemalan Pentecostal independents leaders evangelizing in Los Angeles.

While these cases are small within the considerable diversity that characterizes Latino Pentecostalism in Los Angeles, and the study of other migrant groups with different ethnic and social backgrounds warrant further exploration, this group is an excellent sample to examine how beliefs (especially religious ones) and their associated practices turn out to be critical cultural tools to give meaning to the new realities and scenarios of otherness generated by displacement processes.

The first contribution of this dissertation to the study of the relation between religious life and migration is that any religious phenomenon constitutes a religious praxis. That means that any study connecting spiritual life to the migratory context should account for both the subjective and objective conditions of production of practices and discourses. Religious life cannot be separated from the material circumstances in which specific instances of religious behavior and imagination arise and to which they respond. It is needed to relate the worldview of agents—especially their religious beliefs—to the social structures and processes in which the agents are involved, that is, the social space.

Using the Habitus Analysis approach for the analysis of practical religious operators, this dissertation has captured specific contents of discourses and practices, as well as placing the agency of migrant believers within the objective social structures that articulate the social space in which they are involved. This analytical process allowed the discovery of three paradigms among Guatemalan Pentecostal independent leaders, which are God-as-a-restorer paradigm, God's love paradigm, and spiritual warfare paradigm, overcoming the limitations of the studies dealing with the relation between migration and religious praxis.

Guatemalan Pentecostal independent leaders accentuate their agency through their specific contents of belief and practice. They also creatively develop strategies invoking spiritual entities to face the structural conditions of Los Angeles. They have also chosen between the available religious options, generating religious identities and strategies.

Under these conditions of an extremely "de-regularized" labor market, individualized economic competition and anti-migratory discourses caused by the neoliberal policies in Los Angeles, Guatemalan Pentecostal religious paradigms offer "promises of salvation" presented as promises of health, prosperity, and success. Nevertheless, the religious identities and strategies derived from each paradigm have not always had positive effects. As the narratives presented in this study have shown, immigrant believers can attain greater self-esteem and autonomy thanks to their religious beliefs and practices, while not necessarily eradicating the conditions of subordination and marginalization.

In order to identify the opportunities and risks that each religious style generates, only a detailed study of the particular contents of religious beliefs should be performed. If the religious diversification of global cities has made religious beliefs and practices once again the focus of the social, political, and cultural debates at the beginning of the twenty-first century, only a detailed study of the particular contents of religious beliefs and the identities, strategies, discourses, and practices derived from them in response to the structural condition can allow the identification of the opportunities and risks that each religious style generates, either for the articulation of empowerment or social integration.

9. Works Cited

Anderson, Allan. 2004. *An Introduction to Pentecostalism. Global Charismatic Christianity*. Cambridge: Cambridge University Press.

_____. 2007. *Spreading Fires: The Missionary Nature of Early Pentecostalism*. London: SCM.

Anderson, Robert M. 1979. *Vision of the Disinherited: The Making of American Pentecostalism*. Peabody: Hendrickson Publ.

Anderson, Susan. 1996. "A City Called Heaven: Black Enchantment and Despair in Los Angeles." In *The City: Los Angeles and Urban Theory at the End of the Twentieth Century*, ed. Allen J. Scott and Edward W. Soja, 336–364. Berkeley/Los Angeles: University of California Press.

Appadurai, Arjun. 1996. *Modernity at Large: Cultural Dimensions of Globalization*. Minneapolis: University of Minnesota Press.

Bastian, Jean-Pierre. 1993. "The Metamorphosis of Latin American Protestant Groups: A Sociohistoric Perspective." *Latin American Research Review* 28, no. 2: 33–61.

BEA (U.S. Bureau of Economic Analysis). 2011. *Economic growth widespread across metropolitan areas in 2010: Advance statistics of GDP by metropolitan area*. September 13. Accessed May 15, 2017. https://www.bea.gov/newsreleases/regional/gdp_metro/2011b/pdf/gdp_metro0211b.pdf.

Bergunder, Michael. 2007. "Constructing Pentecostalism: On Issues of Methodology and Representation." *Journal of the European Pentecostal Theological Association* 27, no. 1: 52–71.

Bohn, Sarah, Caroline Danielson, Matt Levin, Marybeth Mattingly, and Christopher Wimer. 2013. *The California Poverty Measure: A New Look at the Social Safety Net*. Public Policy Institute of California. Accessed May 15, 2017. http://ppic.org/content/pubs/report/R_1013SBR.pdf.

Bourdieu, Pierre. 1977. *Outline of a Theory of Practice*. Cambridge: Cambridge University Press.

_____. 1980. *Le sens pratique*. Paris: Minuit.

_____. 1983. "The field of cultural production or the economic world reversed." *Poetics* 12, no. 4: 311–356.

_____. 1985. "The social space and the genesis of groups." *Theory and Society* 14, no.6: 723-744.

_____. 1987. "Legitimation and Structured Interests in Weber's Sociology of Religion." In *Max Weber, Rationality and Modernity*, ed. Scott Lash and Sam Whimster, 119–136. London: Allen & Unwin.

_____. 1990a. "Die biographische Illusion." *BIOS* (Zeitschrift für Biographieforschung und Oral History), no. 3: 75–81.

_____. 1990b. *The Logic of Practice*. Cambridge: Polity Press.

_____. 1991. "Genesis and structure of the religious field." Edited by Craig Calhoun. *Comparative Social Research* 13: 1–44.

_____. 1998. *Practical Reason. On the Theory of Action*. Stanford: Stanford University Press.

_____. 2010. *Distinction: A Social Critique of the Judgement of Taste*. London: Routledge.

Bourdieu, Pierre, and Loïc J.D. Wacquant. 1992. *An Invitation to Reflexive Sociology*. Cambridge: Polity Press.

Brusco, Elizabeth. 1995. *The Reformation of Machismo: Evangelical Conversion and Gender in Colombia*. Austin: University of Texas Press.

Comaroff, Jean, and John Comaroff. 2001. "Millennial Capitalism: First Thoughts on a Second Coming." In *Millennial Capitalism and the Culture of Neoliberalism*, ed. Jean Comaroff and John Comaroff, 1–56. Durham: Duke University Press.

Cornejo, Marcela, Francisca Mendoza, and Rodrigo Rojas. 2008. "La Investigación con Relatos de Vida: Pistas y Opciones del Diseño Metodológico." *Psykhe* 17, no. 1: 29–39.

Corten, André. 1999. *Pentecostalism in Brazil. Emotion of the Poor and Theological Romanticism*. Basingstoke: Macmillan.

Corten, André, and Ruth Marshall-Fratani, eds. 2001. *Between Babel and Pentecost: Transnational Pentecostalism in Africa and Latin America*. Bloomington: Indiana University Press.

Crittenden, Ann. 1988. *Sanctuary: A Story of American Conscience and the Law in Collision*. London: Weidenfeld & Nicolson.

Csordas, Thomas. 2009. "Introduction: Modalities of Transnational Transcendence." In *Transnational Transcendence: Essays on Religion and Globalization*, ed. Thomas Csordas, 1–29. Berkeley: University of California Press.

Danielson, Robert A. 2015. "Transnationalism and the Pentecostal Salvadoran church. A case of study of Misión Cristiana Elim." In *Pentecostals and*

Charismatics in Latin America and Latino communities, ed. Nestor Medina and Sammy Alfaro, 111–124. New York: Palgrave MacMillan.

Davidson, Miriam. 1988. *Convictions of the Heart: Jim Corbett and the Sanctuary Movement*. Tucson: University of Arizona Press.

Dayton, Donald. 2004. *Theological Roots of Pentecostalism*. Peabody: Hendrickson Publ.

Dear, Michael. 1996. "In the City, Time Becomes Visible: Intentionality and Urbanism in Los Angeles, 1781-1991." In *The City: Los Angeles and Urban Theory at the End of the Twentieth Century*, ed. Allen J. Scott and Edward W. Soja, 76–105. Berkeley/Los Angeles: University of California Press.

Dosse, François. 2007. *La apuesta biográfica: Escribir una vida*. Valencia: Universidad de Valencia.

Droogers, André. 1998. "Paradoxical Views on a Paradoxical Religion: Models for the Explanation of Pentecostal Expansion in Brazil and Chile." In *More than Opium: An Anthropological Approach to Latin American and Caribbean Pentecostal Praxis*, ed. Barbara Boudewijnse, André Droogers, and Frans Kamsteeg, 1–34. Lanham/London: Scarecrow Press.

_____. 2001. "Globalisation and Pentecostal Success." In *Between Babel and Pentecost. Transnational Pentecostalism in Africa and Latin America*, ed. André Corten and Ruth Marshall-Fratani, 41–61. Bloomington: Indiana University Press.

_____. 2012. "The Popular Use of Popular Religion: Power and Meaning in Three Brazilian Popular Religions." In *Play and Power in Religion: Collected Essays*, 92–103. Berlin/Boston: De Gruyter.

Durkheim, Émile. 1968. *Suicide: A Study in Sociology*. London: Routledge & Kegan Paul.

Ehrenreich, Barbara. 2009. *Smile or Die: How Positive Thinking Fooled America & the World.* London: Granta Publications.

Espinosa, Gaston. 2004. "Hispanic Pentecostal Women." In *The Encyclopedia of Women and Religion in North America*, ed. Rosemary Skinner Keller and Rosemary Radford, vol. 1, 492–497. Bloomington: Indiana University Press.

_____. 2014. *Latino Pentecostals in America: Faith and Politics in Action.* Cambridge/London: Harvard University Press.

Falla, Ricardo. 1984. "We Charge Genocide." In *Guatemala: Tyranny on Trial: Testimony of the Permanent People's Tribunal*, ed. Susanne Jonas, Ed McCaughan, and Elizabeth Sutherland Martínez, 112–119. San Francisco: Synthesis Publications.

Fenggang, Yang, and Helen Rose Ebaugh. 2001. "Transformations in New Immigrant Religions and Their Global Implications." *American Sociological Review* 66, no. 2: 269–288.

Flick, Uwe. 1998. *Qualitative Forschung. Theorie, Methoden Anwendung in Psychologie und Sozialwissenschaften.* Reinbek: Rowohlt.

_____. 2007. *Design qualitative research.* Los Angeles/London/New Delhi/Singapore: SAGE Publications.

Flory, Richard. 2012. "Making Sense of Religion in Southern California." Center for Religion and Civic Culture, University of Southern California. December 21. Accessed June 1, 2018. https://crcc.usc.edu/making-sense-of-religion-in-southerncalifornia/.

Garrard-Burnett, Virginia. 1998. *Protestantism in Guatemala. Living in the New Jerusalem.* Austin: University of Texas Press.

Glaser, Barney G. and Anselm L. Strauss, 2006. *The Discovery of Grounded Theory: Strategies for Qualitative Research.* New Brunswick: Aldine Transactions.

Greimas, Algirdas Julien, and François Rastier. 1971. "The Interaction of Semiotic Constraints." In *Game, Play, Literature*, ed. Jacques Ehrmann, 86–105. Boston: Beacon Press.

Gupta, Akhil, and James Ferguson, eds. 1997. *Anthropological Locations. Boundaries and Grounds of a Field Science.* Berkeley: University of California Press.

Gzesh, Susan. 2006. *Central Americans and Asylum Policy in the Reagan Era.* Migration Policy Institute. Accessed May 22, 2018. https://www.migrationpolicy.org/article/central-americans-and-asylum-policy-reagan-era.

Hagan, Jacqueline Maria. 2008. *Migration Miracle: Faith, Hope, and Meaning on the Undocumented Journey.* Cambridge: Harvard University Press.

Hamilton, Nora, and Norma Stoltz Chinchilla. 2001. *Seeking Community in a Global City: Guatemalans and Salvadorans in Los Angeles.* Philadelphia: Temple University Press.

Handlin, Oscar. 2002. *The Uprooted: The Epic Story of the Great Migrations that Made the American People*. Philadelphia: University of Pennsylvania Press.

Herberg, Will. 1955. *Protestant – Catholic – Jew: An Essay in American Religious Sociology*. Garden City: Doubleday/Company.

Hollenweger, Walter J. 1997. *Pentecostalism*. Peabody: Hendrickson Publ.

Homeland Security (DHS), U.S. Department of. 2004. *2003 Yearbook of Immigration Statistics*. Washington, D.C.: U.S. Department of Homeland Security (DHS).

Hoskin, Marie, and Jo-Anne Stolz. 2005. "Fear of Offending: Disclosing Researcher Discomfort When Engaging in Analysis." *Qualitative Research* 5, no. 1: 95–111.

Husserl, Edmund. 2014. *Ideas Pertaining to a Pure Phenomenology and to a Phenomenological Philosophy. First Book: General Introduction to a Pure Phenomenology*. Indianapolis/Cambridge: Hackett Publishing Company.

Hüwelmeier, Gertrud, and Kristine Krause. 2010. "Introduction." In *Traveling Spirits: Migrants, Markets and Mobilities*, ed. Gertrud Hüwelmeier and Kristine Krause, 1–16. New York: Routledge.

Jenkins, Philip. 2002. *The Next Christendom. The Coming of Global Christianity*. Oxford: Oxford University Press.

Johnson, Hans, and Laura Hill. 2011. "Illegal immigration." *At Issue: Critical Facts on Critical Issues*. Public Policy Institute of California. Accessed May 22, 2018. http://www.ppic.org/content/pubs/atissue/AI_711HJAI.pdf.

Jonas, Susanne. 1991. *The Battle for Guatemala: Rebels, Death Squads, and U.S. Power*. Boulder: Westview Press.

Jonas, Susanne, and Nestor Rodríguez. 2014. *Guatemala-US Migration: Transforming Regions*. Austin: University of Texas Press.

Kroll-Smith, Stephen. 1980. "The Testimony as Performance: The Relationship of an Expressive Event to the Belief System of Holiness Sect." *Journal for the Scientific Study of Religion* 19, no.1: 16–25.

Lalive d'Epinay, Christian. 1969. *Haven of the Masses. A Study of the Pentecostal Movement in Chile*. London: Lutterworth.

Land, Steven. 2001. *Pentecostal Spirituality: A Passion for the Kingdom*. Cleveland: CPT Press.

León, Luís. 1998. "Born Again in East LA: The Congregation as Border Space." In *Gatherings in Diaspora: Religious Communities and the New Immigration*, ed. R. Stephen Warner and Judith Wittner, 163–196. Philadelphia: Temple University Press.

Lévi-Strauss, Claude. 1963. *Structural Anthropology*. New York: Basic Books.

Levitt, Peggy. 2001. "Between God, Ethnicity, and Country: An Approach to the Study of Transnational Religion." Paper presented at workshop on Transnational Migration: Comparative Perspectives, Princeton University, Princeton, NJ, June 30-July 1.

_____. 2004. "Redefining the Boundaries of Belonging: The Institutional Character of Transnational Religious Life." *Sociology of Religion* 65, no. 6: 1–18.

_____. 2007. *God Needs No Passports: Immigrants and the Changing American Religious Landscape*. New York: The New Press.

_____. 2013. "Religion on the Move: Mapping Global Cultural Production and Consumption." In *Religion on the Edge: De-centering and Re-centering the Sociology of Religion*, ed. Courtney Bender, Wendy Cage, Peggy Levitt, and David Smilde, 159–176. New York: Oxford University Press.

Lorentzen, Lois Ann, and Rosalina Mira. 2005. "El milagro está en casa: Gender and Private/Public Empowerment in a Migrant Pentecostal Church." *Latin American Perspectives* 32, no. 1: 57–71.

Loucky, James. 1996. "Maya Americans: The Emergence of a Transnational Community." In *Central Americans in California: Transnational Communities, Economies and Cultures*, ed. Nora Hamilton and Norma Chinchilla, 30–34. Los Angeles: Center for Multiethnic/Transnational Studies.

Maduro, Otto. 1996. "Notes Toward a Sociology of Latina/o Religious Empowerment." In *Hispanic/Latino Theology: Challenge and Promise*, ed. Ada Maria Isasi-Díaz and Fernando F. Segovia, 151–166. Minneapolis: Fortress Press.

_____. 2007. "¡Sálvese quien pueda! Usos y funciones del pentecostalismo entre migrantes latinoamericanos." In *Más allá del espíritu: Actores, acciones y prácticas en iglesias pentecostales*, ed. Carolina Rivera Farfán and Elizabeth Juárez, 91–115. Mexico D.F.: Centro de Investigaciones y Estudios Superiores en Antropología Social (CIESAS).

_____. 2012. "Becoming *Pastora*: Latina Pentecostal Women's Stories from Newark, New Jersey." In *Global Pentecostal Movements: Migration, Mis-*

sion, and Public Religion, ed. Michael Wilkinson, 195–210. Leiden/Boston: Brill.

Maguid, Alicia. 1999. “Los esfuerzos de las poblaciones. las migraciones en centroamérica.” In *I Informe estado de la región en desarrollo humano sostenible*, edited by Estado de la Región, 359–384. San José: Editorama.

Mahler, Sarah, and Katrina Hansing. 2005. “Toward a Transnationalism of the Middle: How Transnational Religious Practices Help to Bridge the Divides between Cuba and Miami.” *Latin American Perspectives* 32, no. 1: 121–146.

Malinowski, Bronisław. 2014. *Argonauts of the Western Pacific: An Account of Native Enterprise and Adventure in the Archipelagoes of Melanesian New Guinea*. Oxford: Benediction Classics.

Marcus, George E. 1995. “Ethnography in/of the World System: The Emergence of Multi-sited Ethnography.” *Annual Review of Anthropology* 24: 95–117.

Martin, David. 1990. *Tongues of Fire. The Explosion of Protestantism in Latin America*. Oxford: Blackwell.

Martínez, Juan Francisco. 2011. *Los Protestantes: An Introduction to Latino Protestantism in the United States*. Santa Barbara: ABC.

_____. 2012. “The Latino Church Next: The Religious Scene in Latino Los Angeles.” USC Center for Religion and Civic Culture Studies. Accessed May 22, 2018. https://crcc.usc.edu/files/2015/02/LatinoNext-2012.pdf.

_____. 2013. “Remittances and Mission: Transnational Latino Pentecostal Ministry in Los Angeles.” In *Spirit and Power: The Growth and Global Impact of Pentecostalism*, ed. Donald Miller, Kimon Sargeant, and Richard Flory, 204–221. New York: Oxford University Press.

Menjívar, Cecilia. 1999. “Religious Institutions and Transnationalism: A Case Study of Catholic and Evangelical Salvadoran Immigrants.” *International Journal of Politics, Culture, and Society* 12, no. 4: 589–561.

Merleau-Ponty, Maurice. 1962. *Phenomenology of Perception*. Atlantic Highlands: Humanities Press.

Miles, Matthew, and Michael Huberman. 1994. *Qualitative Data Analysis: An Expanded Sourcebook*. Thousand Oaks/London/New Delhi: SAGE Publications.

Miller, Donald. 2013. “Introduction: Pentecostalism as a Global Phenomenon.” In *Spirit and Power: The Growth and Global Impact of Pentecostalism*, ed.

Donald Miller, Kimon Sargeant, and Richard Flory, 1–19. New York: Oxford University Press.

Myers, Dowell, Ray Calnan, Anna Jacobsen, and Josh Wheeler. 2012. *California Roller Coaster: Income and Housing in Boom and Bust*, 1990-2010. http://popdynamics.usc.edu/pdf/2012-Update_Myers-etal_California-Roller-Coaster.pdf.

O'Neill, Kevin Lewis. 2010. *City of God: Christian Citizenship in Postwar Guatemala*. Berkeley: University of California Press.

Ong, Paul, and Evelyn Blumenberg. 1996. "Income and Racial Inequality in Los Angeles." In *The City: Los Angeles and Urban Theory at the End of the Twentieth Century*, ed. Allen J. Scott and Edward W. Soja, 331–364. Berkeley/Los Angeles: University of California Press.

Orsi, Robert. 1997. "Everyday Miracles: The Study of Lived Religion." In *Lived Religion in America: Toward a History of Practice*, ed. David D. Hall, 3–21. Princeton: Princeton University Press.

Paerregaard, Karsten. 2008. *Peruvians Dispersed: A Global Ethnography of Migration*. Lanham: Lexington Books.

Pereira Fernández, Alexander. 2011. "Notas para jugar con la ilusión biográfica y no perderse en el intento." *Revista Científica Guillermo de Ockham* 9, no. 1: 105–122.

Pérez Sainz, Juan Pablo. 2001. "Exclusión y mercado laboral en Guatemala." *Cuadernos de Desarrollo Humano* 2. Guatemala: Sistema de Naciones Unidas.

Peterson, Anna, Manuel Vásquez, and Philip Williams. 2001. "Christianity and Social Change in the Shadow of Globalization." In *Christianity, Social Change, and Globalization in the Americas*, ed. Anna Peterson, Manuel Vásquez, and Philip Williams, 1–22. New Brunswick: Rutgers University Press.

Pew Research Center. 2014. *Religion in Latin America: Widespread Change in a Historically Catholic Region*. Pew Research Center, November 13. Accessed May 22, 2018. https://www.pewforum.org/2014/11/13/religion-in-latin-america/.

_____. 2014b. *The Shifting Religious Identity of Latinos in the United States: Nearly One-in-Four Latinos are Former Catholics*. Pew Research Center, May 7. Accessed May 22, 2018. http://www.pewforum.org/2014/05/07/the-shifting-religious-identity-of-latinos-in-the-united-states/.

Pierce Bomann, Rebecca. 2011. "The Salve of Divine Healing: Essential Rituals for Survival Among Working-Class Pentecostals in Bogotá, Colombia." In *Global Pentecostal and Charismatic Healing*, ed. Candy Gunther Brown, 185–205. Oxford/New York: Oxford University Press.

Popkin, Eric. 1996. "Guatemalan Hometown Associations in Los Angeles." In *Central Americans in California: Transnational Communities, Economies and Cultures*, ed. Nora Hamilton and Norma Stoltz Chinchilla, 35–39. Los Angeles: Center for Multiethnic/Transnational Studies, University of Southern California.

_____. 2005. "The Emergence of Pan-Mayan Ethnicity in the Guatemalan Transnational Community Linking Santa Eulalia and Los Angeles." *Current Sociology* 53, no. 4: 675–706, doi: 10.1177/0011392105052721.

Portes, Alejandro, Luis Guarnizo, and Patricia Landolt. 1999. "The Study of Transnationalism: Pitfalls and Promise of an Emergent Research Field." *Ethnic and Racial Studies* 22, no. 2: 217–237, doi: 10.1080/01419879 9329468.

Pries, Ludger. 2010. *Transnationalisierung. Theorie und Empirie grenzüberschreitender Vergesellschaftung*. Wiesbaden: VS Verlag.

Ramírez, Daniel. 2015. *Migrating Faith. Pentecostalism in the United States and Mexico in the Twentieth Century*. Chapel Hill: University of North Carolina Press.

Ribando Seelke, Clare. 2014. *Gangs in Central America*. CRS Report RL34112. August 29. Congressional Research Service, Washington, DC.

Robbins, Joel. 2004. "The Globalization of Pentecostal and Charismatic Christianity." *Annual Review of Anthropology* 33: 117–143.

_____. 2009. "Is the *Trans-* in *Transnational* the *Trans-* in *Transcendent*? On Alterity and the Sacred in the Age of Globalization." In *Transnational Transcendence: Essays on Religion and Globalization*, ed. Thomas Csordas, 56–70. Berkeley/Los Angeles: University of California Press.

Rocco, Raymond. 1996. "Latino Los Angeles: Reframing Boundaries/Borders." In *The City: Los Angeles and Urban Theory at the End of the Twentieth Century*, ed. Allen J. Scott and Edward W. Soja, 365–389. Berkeley/Los Angeles: University of California Press.

Rodríguez, Nestor. 2007. "Comparing Mexicans and Central Americans in the Present Wave of U.S. Immigration." In *The Other Latinos: Central and*

South Americans in the United States, ed. José Luis Falconi and José Antonio Mazzoti, 81–100. Cambridge: Harvard University Press.

Rosenthal, Gabriele. 2004. "Biographical research." In *Qualitative Research Practice*, ed. Clive Seale, Giampietro Gobo, Jaber F. Gabrium, and David Silverman, 48–64. London: SAGE.

_____. 2006. "The Narrated Life Story: On the Interrelation between Experience, Memory and Narration." In *Narrative, Memory and Knowledge: Representations, Aesthetics and Contexts*, edited by Kate Miles, Christiane Horrocks, Nancy Kelly, Brian Roberts, and David Robinson, 1–16. Huddersfield: University of Huddersfield Press.

Rudolph, Susanne H., and James Piscatori, eds. 1997. *Transnational Religion and Fading States*. Boulder: Westview Press.

Sartre, Jean-Paul. 1956. *Being and Nothingness: An Essay on Phenomenological Ontology*. New York: Philosophical Library.

Saussure, Ferdinand de. 1966. *Course in General Linguistics*. New York: McGraw-Hill.

Schäfer, Heinrich Wilhelm. 1992. "Líbranos del mal! Estructuras simbólicas y funciones políticas en el protestantismo centroamericano." In *Protestantismo y crisissocial en América Central*, ed. Heinrich Wilhelm Schäfer, 189–214. San José: Departamento Ecuménico de Investigaciones.

_____. 2005. "Identität als Netzwerk. Ein Theorieentwurf am Beispiel religiöser Bewegungen im Bürgerkrieg Guatemalas." *Berliner Journal für Soziologie* 15, no. 2: 259–282.

_____. 2009. "The Praxeological Square as a Method for the Intercultural Study of Religious Movements." In *Cultures in Process: Encounter and Experience*, ed. Stephen Gramley and Ralf Schneider, 5–19. Bielefeld: Aisthesis.

_____. 2015. *HabitusAnalysis 1: Epistemology and Language*. Wiesbaden: Springer VS.

Schäfer, Heinrich Wilhelm, Adrián Tovar Simoncic, and Tobias Reu. 2013. "Cambios en el campo religioso de guatemala y nicaragua: de 1985 a 2013." *Revistas Sendas. Instituto de Investigaciones del Hecho Religioso* 1, no. 1: 11–31.

Schäfer, Heinrich Wilhelm, Leif Hagen Seibert, Adrián Tovar Simoncic, and Jens Köhrsen. 2016a. "Towards a Praxeology of Religious Life: Modes of Observation." In *Making Religion: Theory and Practice in the Discursive*

Study of Religion, ed. Frans Wijsen and Kocku von Stuckrad, 147–171. Leiden: Brill.

_____. 2016b. "Towards a Praxeology of Religious Life: Tools of Observation." In *Making Religion: Theory and Practice in the Discursive Study of Religion*, ed. Frans Wijsen and Kocku von Stuckrad, 175–202. Leiden: Brill.

Schütze, Fritz. 1976. "Zur Hervorlockung und Analyse von Erzählungen thematisch relevanter Geschichten im Rahmen soziologischer Feldforschung: dargestellt an einem Projekt zur Erforschung von kommunalen Machtstrukturen." In *Kommunikative Sozialforschung: Alltagswissen und Alltagshandeln, Gemeindemachtforschung, Polizei, politische Erwachsenenbildung*, ed. Ansgar Weymann, 159–260. Munich: Fink.

Seibert, Leif. 2010. "Glaubwürdigkeit als religiöses Vermögen. Grundlagen eines Feldmodells nach Bourdieu am Beispiel Bosnien-Herzegowinas." *Berliner Journal für Soziologie* 20, no. 1: 89–117.

_____. 2018. *Religious Credibility under Fire: Determinants of Religious Legitimacy in Postwar Bosnia and Herzegovina.* Wiesbaden: Springer VS.

Soja, Edward W. 1989. *Postmodern Geographies: The Reassertion of Space in Critical Social Theory*. London: Verso.

Soja, Edward W., and Allen J. Scott. 1996. "Introduction to Los Angeles: City and Region." In *The City: Los Angeles and Urban Theory at the End of the Twentieth Century*, ed. Allen J. Scott and Edward W. Soja, 1–21. Berkeley/Los Angeles: University of California Press.

Sotomayor, Frank. 1991. "State Shows 69.2% Rise in Latino Population." *Los Angeles Times* online edition, March 28.

Spiegel, Anna. 2010. *Contested Public Spheres: Female Activism and Identity Politics in Malaysia.* Wiesbaden: VS Verlag für Sozialwissenschaften.

Stepick, Alex. 2006. "God is Apparently Not Dead: The Obvious, the Emergent, and the Still Unknown in Immigration and Religion." In *Immigrant Faiths Transforming Religious Life in America*, ed. Karen I. Leonard, Alex Stepick, Manuel Vásquez, and Jennifer Holdaway, 11–37. New York: Altamira Press.

Stoll, David. 1990. *Is Latin America Turning Protestant? The Politics of Evangelical Growth*. Berkeley: University of California Press.

Stoll, David, and Virginia Garrard-Burnett, eds. 1993. *Rethinking Protestantism in Latin America*. Philadelphia: Temple University Press.

Swanson, Jeffrey. 1995. *Echoes of the Call: Identity and Ideology Among American Missionaries in Ecuador*. New York: Oxford University Press.

Vásquez, Manuel. 1999. "Pentecostalism, Collective Identity and Transnationalism among Salvadorans and Peruvians in the US." *Journal of the American Academy of Religion* 67, no. 3: 617–636.

Vásquez, Manuel, and Marie Friedmann Marquardt. 2003. *Globalizing the Sacred: Religion across the Americas*. New Brunswick: Rutgers University Press.

Währisch-Oblau, Claudia. 2012. *The Missionary Self-perception of Pentecostal/Charismatic Church Leaders from the Global South in Europa*. Leiden/Boston: Brill.

Weber, Max. 1963. *The Sociology of Religion*. Boston: Beacon Press.

Wittgenstein, Ludwig. 2001. *Philosophical Investigations: The German Text, with a Revised English Translation*. Malden: Blackwell.

Yinger, J. Milton. 1970. *The Scientific Study of Religion*. New York: Macmillan.

Inter-American Studies
Cultures – Societies – History

Estudios Interamericanos
Culturas – Sociedades – Historia

This interdisciplinary series examines national and transnational issues in the cultures, societies, and histories of the Americas. It creates a forum for a critical academic dialogue between North and South, promoting an inter-American paradigm that shifts the scholarly focus from methodological nationalism to the wider context of the Western Hemisphere.

Vol. 1
Raab, Josef, Sebastian Thies, and Daniela Noll-Opitz, eds. *Screening the Americas: Narration of Nation in Documentary Film / Proyectando las Américas: Narración de la nación en el cine documental.* 2011. 470 pp.

WVT Wissenschaftlicher Verlag Trier	ISBN 978-3-86821-331-7	€ 29,50
Bilingual Press / Editorial Bilingüe	ISBN 978-1-931010-83-2	$ 29.50

Vol. 2
Raussert, Wilfried, and Michelle Habell-Pallán, eds. *Cornbread and Cuchifritos: Ethnic Identity Politics, Transnationalization, and Transculturation in American Urban Popular Music.* 2011. 292 pp.

WVT Wissenschaftlicher Verlag Trier	ISBN 978-3-86821-265-5	€ 29,50
Bilingual Press / Editorial Bilingüe	ISBN 978- 1-931010-80-1	$ 29.50

Vol. 3
Butler, Martin, Jens Martin Gurr, and Olaf Kaltmeier, eds. *EthniCities: Metropolitan Cultures and Ethnic Identities in the Americas.* 2011. 268 pp.

WVT Wissenschaftlicher Verlag Trier	ISBN 978-3-86821-310-2	€ 29,50
Bilingual Press / Editorial Bilingüe	ISBN 978-1-931010-81-8	$ 29.50

Vol. 4
Gurr, Jens Martin, and Wilfried Raussert, eds. *Cityscapes in the Americas and Beyond: Representations of Urban Complexity in Literature and Film.* 2011. 300 pp.

WVT Wissenschaftlicher Verlag Trier	ISBN 978-3-86821-324-9	€ 29,50
Bilingual Press / Editorial Bilingüe	ISBN 978-1-931010-82-5	$ 29.50

Vol. 5

Kirschner, Luz Angélica, ed. *Expanding* Latinidad*: An Inter-American Perspective.* 2012. 292 pp.

WVT Wissenschaftlicher Verlag Trier	ISBN 978-3-86821-309-6	€ 29,50
Bilingual Press / Editorial Bilingüe	ISBN 978-1-931010-84-9	$ 29.50

Vol. 6

Raussert, Wilfried, and Graciela Martínez-Zalce, eds. *(Re)Discovering 'America': Road Movies and Other Travel Narratives in North America / (Re)Descubriendo 'América': Road movie y otras narrativas de viaje en América del Norte.* 2012. 252 pp.

WVT Wissenschaftlicher Verlag Trier	ISBN 978-3-86821-384-3	€ 29,50
Bilingual Press / Editorial Bilingüe	ISBN 978-1-931010-91-7	$ 29.50

Vol. 7

Kaltmeier, Olaf, ed. *Transnational Americas: Envisioning Inter-American Area Studies in Globalization Processes.* 2013. 278 pp.

WVT Wissenschaftlicher Verlag Trier	ISBN 978-3-86821-415-4	€ 29,50
Bilingual Press / Editorial Bilingüe	ISBN 978-1-931010-92-4	$ 29.50

Vol. 8

Raab, Josef, and Alexander Greiffenstern, eds. *Interculturalism in North America: Canada, the United States, Mexico, and Beyond.* 2013. 312 pp.

WVT Wissenschaftlicher Verlag Trier	ISBN 978-3-86821-460-4	€ 29,50
Bilingual Press / Editorial Bilingüe	ISBN 978-1-931010-99-3	$ 29.50

Vol. 9

Raab, Josef, ed. *New World Colors: Ethnicity, Belonging, and Difference in the Americas.* 2014. 418 pp.

WVT Wissenschaftlicher Verlag Trier	ISBN 978-3-86821-461-1	€ 29,50
Bilingual Press / Editorial Bilingüe	ISBN 978-1-939743-00-8	$ 39.50

Vol. 10

Roth, Julia. *Occidental Readings, Decolonial Practices: A Selection on Gender, Genre, and Coloniality in the Americas.* 2014. 284 pp.

WVT Wissenschaftlicher Verlag Trier	ISBN 978-3-86821-446-8	€ 26,50
Bilingual Press / Editorial Bilingüe	ISBN 978-1-939743-07-7	$ 32.50

Vol. 11

Thies, Sebastian, Gabriele Pisarz-Ramirez, and Luzelena Gutiérrez de Velasco, eds. *Of Fatherlands and Motherlands: Gender and Nation in the Americas / De Patrias y Matrias: Género y nación en las Américas.* 2015. 344 pp.

WVT Wissenschaftlicher Verlag Trier	ISBN 978-3-86821-528-1	€ 29,50
Bilingual Press / Editorial Bilingüe	ISBN 978-1-939743-08-4	$ 39.50

Vol. 12
Fuchs, Rebecca. *Caribbeanness as a Global Phenomenon: Junot Díaz, Edwidge Danticat, and Cristina García*. 2014. 298 pp.
WVT Wissenschaftlicher Verlag Trier ISBN 978-3-86821-533-5 € 26,50
Bilingual Press / Editorial Bilingüe ISBN 978-1-939743-09-1 $ 32.50

Vol. 13
Andres, Julia. *¡Cuéntame algo! – Chicana Narrative Beyond the Borderlands*. 2015. 202 pp.
WVT Wissenschaftlicher Verlag Trier ISBN 978-3-86821-569-4 € 25,00
Bilingual Press / Editorial Bilingüe ISBN 978-1-939743-11-4 $ 28.50

Vol. 14
Hertlein, Saskia. *Tales of Transformation: Emerging Adulthood, Migration, and Ethnicity in Contemporary American Literature*. 2014. 228 pp.
WVT Wissenschaftlicher Verlag Trier ISBN 978-3-86821-570-0 € 25,00
Bilingual Press / Editorial Bilingüe ISBN 978-1-939743-10-7 $ 31.50

Vol. 15
Raab, Josef, and Saskia Hertlein, eds. *Spaces – Communities – Discourses: Charting Identity and Belonging in the Americas*. 2016. 382 pp.
WVT Wissenschaftlicher Verlag Trier ISBN 978-3-86821-590-8 € 29,50
Bilingual Press / Editorial Bilingüe ISBN 978-1-939743-13-8 $ 39.50

Vol. 16
Mehring, Frank, ed. *The Mexico Diary: Winold Reiss between Vogue Mexico and Harlem Renaissance. An Illustrated Trilingual Edition with Commentary and Musical Interpretation* (includes color plates and audio CD). 2016. 244 pp.
WVT Wissenschaftlicher Verlag Trier ISBN 978-3-86821-594-6 € 29,50
Bilingual Press / Editorial Bilingüe ISBN 978-1-939743-14-5 $ 39.50

Vol. 17
Raussert, Wilfried, Brian Rozema, Yolanda Campos, and Marius Littschwager, eds. *Key Tropes in Inter-American Studies: Perspectives from the* forum for inter-american research (fiar). 2015. 374 pp.
WVT Wissenschaftlicher Verlag Trier ISBN 978-3-86821-627-1 € 29,50
Bilingual Press / Editorial Bilingüe ISBN 978-1-939743-16-9 $ 39.50

Vol. 19
Rehm, Lukas, Jochen Kemner, and Olaf Kaltmeier, eds. *Politics of Entanglement in the Americas: Connecting Transnational Flows and Local Perspectives*. 2017. 226 pp.
WVT Wissenschaftlicher Verlag Trier ISBN 978-3-86821-675-2 € 27,50
Bilingual Press / Editorial Bilingüe ISBN 978-1-939743-17-6 $ 32.50

Vol. 20
Britt Arredondo, Christopher. *Imperial Idiocy: A Reflection on Forced Displacement in the Americas*. 2017. 194 pp.

WVT Wissenschaftlicher Verlag Trier	ISBN 978-3-86821-706-3	€ 26,50
Bilingual Press / Editorial Bilingüe	ISBN 978-1-939743-20-6	$ 30.00

Vol. 21
Schemien, Alexia. *Of Virgins, Curanderas, and Wrestler Saints: Un/Doing Religion in Contemporary Mexican American Literature*. 2018. 218 pp.

WVT Wissenschaftlicher Verlag Trier	ISBN 978-3-86821-724-7	€ 27,50
Bilingual Press / Editorial Bilingüe	ISBN 978-1-939743-22-0	$ 32.50

Vol. 22
Fulger, Maria Diana. *The Cuban Post-Socialist Exotic: Contemporary U.S. American Travel Narratives about Cuba.* 2020. 266 pp.

WVT Wissenschaftlicher Verlag Trier	ISBN 978-3-86821-769-8	€ 32,50
Bilingual Press / Editorial Bilingüe	ISBN 978-1-939743-27-5	$ 36.00

Vol. 24
Kaltmeier, Olaf, Mirko Petersen, Wilfried Raussert, and Julia Roth, eds. *Cherishing the Past, Envisioning the Future. Entangled Practises of Heritage and Utopia in the Americas.* 2021. 176 pp.

WVT Wissenschaftlicher Verlag Trier	ISBN 978-3-86821-804-6	€ 23,50
UNO University of New Orleans Press	ISBN 978-1-60801-206-0	$ 27.50

Vol. 26
Raussert, Wilfried. *'What's Going On': How Music Shapes the Social.* 2021. 224 pp.

WVT Wissenschaftlicher Verlag Trier	ISBN 978-3-86821-811-4	€ 28,50
UNO University of New Orleans Press	ISBN 978-1-60801-199-5	$ 34.00

Vol. 27
Frank-Job, Barbara. *Immigration as a Process: Temporality Concepts in Blogs of Latin American Immigrants to Québec.* 2021. 138 pp.

WVT Wissenschaftlicher Verlag Trier	ISBN 978-3-86821-820-6	€ 20,00
UNO University of New Orleans Press	ISBN 978-1-60801-215-2	$ 24.00

Vol. 28
Roth, Julia. *Can Feminism Trump Populism? Right-Wing Trends and Intersectional Contestations in the Americas.* 2021. 166 pp.

WVT Wissenschaftlicher Verlag Trier	ISBN 978-3-86821-821-3	€ 23,00
UNO University of New Orleans Press	ISBN 978-1-60801-205-3	$ 26.00

Vol. 30

Buitrago Valencia, Clara. *Missionaries: Migrants or Expatriates? Guatemalan Pentecostal Leaders in Los Angeles.* 2021. 236 pp.

WVT Wissenschaftlicher Verlag Trier	ISBN 978-3-86821-818-3	€ 28,50
UNO University of New Orleans Press	ISBN 978-1-60801-210-7	$ 34.50

Vol. 31

Schwabe, Nicole. *De-Centering History Education: Creating Knowledge of Global Entanglements.* 2021. 92 pp.

WVT Wissenschaftlicher Verlag Trier	ISBN 978-3-86821-828-2	€ 18,00
UNO University of New Orleans Press	ISBN 978-1-60801-214-5	$ 21.00

Vol. 32

Manke, Albert. *Coping with Discrimination and Exclusion. Experiences of Free Chinese Migrants in the Americas in a Transregional and Diachronic Perspective.* 2021. 162 pp.

WVT Wissenschaftlicher Verlag Trier	ISBN 978-3-86821-829-9	€ 23,00
UNO University of New Orleans Press	ISBN 978-1-60801-207-7	$ 27.00

Vol. 33

Rohland, Eleonora. *Entangled Histories and the Environment? Socio-Environmental Transformations in the Caribbean, 1492-1800.* 2021. 92 pp.

WVT Wissenschaftlicher Verlag Trier	ISBN 978-3-86821-833-6	€ 18,00
UNO University of New Orleans Press	ISBN 978-1-60801-208-4	$ 21.00

Vol. 34

Kaltmeier, Olaf. *National Parks from North to South. An Entangled History of Conservation and Colonization in Argentina.* 2021. 210 pp.

WVT Wissenschaftlicher Verlag Trier	ISBN 978-3-86821-834-3	€ 27,50
UNO University of New Orleans Press	ISBN 978-1-60801-204-6	$ 32.50

Vol. 35

Raussert, Wilfried. *Off the Grid. Art Practices and Public Space.* 2021. 232 pp.

WVT Wissenschaftlicher Verlag Trier	ISBN 978-3-86821-835-0	€ 29,50
UNO University of New Orleans Press	ISBN 978-1-60801-213-8	$ 34.50

Vol. 36

Ravasio, Paola. *This Train Is Not Bound to Glory. A Study of Literary Trainscapes.* 2021. 114 pp.

WVT Wissenschaftlicher Verlag Trier	ISBN 978-3-86821-836-7	€ 18,00
UNO University of New Orleans Press	ISBN 978-1-60801-216-9	$ 21.00

Vol. 37

Schäfer, Heinrich Wilhelm. *Protestant 'Sects' and the Spirit of (Anti-)Imperialism. Religious Entanglements in the Americas.* 2021. 242 pp.

WVT Wissenschaftlicher Verlag Trier ISBN 978-3-86821-855-9 € 29,50

UNO University of New Orleans Press ISBN 978-1-60801-209-1 $ 34.50